TRAUMA and SURVIVAL

TRAUMA and SURVIVAL

POST-TRAUMATIC AND DISSOCIATIVE DISORDERS IN WOMEN

Elizabeth A. Waites

W. W. NORTON & COMPANY, INC. · NEW YORK · LONDON

The text of this book was composed in Elante. Composition by Bytheway Typesetting Services, Inc. Manufacturing by Haddon Craftsmen, Inc.

Library of Congress Cataloging-in-Publication Data
Waites, Elizabeth A.
    Trauma and survival : post-traumatic and dissociative disorders in women / Elizabeth A. Waites.
        p. cm.
    "A Norton professional book"—P. preceding t.p.
    Includes bibliographical references and index.
    ISBN 0-393-70150-6
    1. Post-traumatic stress disorder.   2. Abused women—Mental health.   3. Dissociative disorders.   I. Title.
    [DNLM: 1. Dissociative Disorders—therapy.   2. Psychotherapy.
3. Stress Disorders, Post-Traumatic—therapy.   4. Women—psychology.
WM 170 W145t]
RC552.P67W35   1993
616.85′21′0082—dc20
DNLM/DLC
for Library of Congress   92-49027 CIP

W. W. Norton & Company, Inc., 500 Fifth Avenue, New York, N.Y. 10110
W. W. Norton & Company, Ltd., 10 Coptic Street, London WC1A 1PU

1 2 3 4 5 6 7 8 9 0

To my mother, Willie Phillips Waites,
and the memory of my father, Oscar Louis Waites

Contents

Acknowledgments

IN MANY RESPECTS, what I have written here is a knitting together of many diverse strands of my life. I am especially grateful to Gerald Blum, who encouraged me as a graduate student to explore the phenomenon of state-related learning, and to Frederick Wyatt, who encouraged me to become a psychotherapist.

Special thanks to Sonya Kennedy. Throughout the planning and writing of the book, I have relied on her unfailing assistance as a technical consultant, computer trouble shooter, friend in need, and personal cheerleader. Others who have been generous with time and energy include Valerie Clarke, whose perspectives on feminist issues as well as practical help have been invaluable, and Kenneth Hannon who helped with tedious chores like moving my office. Thanks, too, to Nicholas and Emily Ehrlich for putting up with all the hassles while their mother was engrossed in this seemingly endless project.

I will always be grateful to Susan Barrows Munro, who believed in the book and was patiently supportive while I struggled with it, and to Margaret Farley, whose skillful editing helped turn it into a reality.

In retrospect, I realize how fortunate I was to begin working as a therapist during the era when the women's movement was becoming influential in American culture. Many of the insights that have changed my life personally as well as professionally came from interactions with women in consciousness-raising sessions, workshops, and political caucuses. I want to thank many who cannot be named here because their voices have outlived their names in my memory or because they were never named at all. Over the years their ideas, passion, and wit have sustained me, and the contributions they have made to my therapeutic work are immeasurable.

Finally, I thank my clients. This book is an attempt to give back some of the good things they have given me.

TRAUMA and
SURVIVAL

Introduction: An Overview of Female Victimization

THE EPIDEMIOLOGY OF sexual abuse and violence against females is a modern phenomenon, having been systematically studied only during the last 20 years or so. Studies correlating specific types of abuse with specific psychological sequelae are even more recent. Questions concerning the relationship between abuse and physical health have scarcely been addressed at all, in spite of the frequency of chronic pain, physical scarring, disabling physical impairments, and psychosomatic symptomatology with which clinicians who treat victims are familiar.

Even so, available figures are a convincing indication of the magnitude of the problem. Physical battering, which is frequently accompanied by sexual assault, has been found in some studies (Kurz & Stark, 1987; Stark, 1984) to be the most common cause of female injury brought to medical attention. Nineteen percent of injured females presenting for treatment in one study were battered women, and of these, one half were reported to be beaten several times a week. Walker (1979) estimated that as many as one half of all women will be physically assaulted at some point in their lives.

Domestic violence is a growing concern among physicians (AMA Council on Scientific Affairs, 1992) and adverse effects on pregnant women are a special concern (Randall, 1992).

Statistics on sexual assault are equally compelling. Russell's (1984) random sample revealed 41% of women surveyed reported at least one experience that met common legal definitions of rape. Koss (1985), who surveyed a national sample of male and female college students, found that 15.4% of college women reported having experienced and 4.4% of college men reported perpetrating an act that met the legal definition of rape.

Child molestation, including incest, is perhaps the form of female abuse that has received the most public attention in recent years. Reporting laws enacted in many states have sensitized professionals to the problem, and media accounts have brought it to the attention of the general public. The resulting statistics are in sharp contrast to earlier data. Incest, in particular, was long considered to be a rare occurrence. When Kinsey and his associates (1953) surveyed female respondents in one of the earliest efforts at systematic documentation, 25% reported a childhood sexual encounter with an adult male and 1% reported an incestuous relation with a father or stepfather. In 1984, Finkelhor estimated that between 10% and 30% of American female children are likely to be sexually abused. But Russell (1984), who studied the problem through extensive in-depth interviews, found a much higher incidence. Thirty-eight percent of her sample reported childhood sexual contact with an adult, and 4.6% reported father-daughter incest.

Many investigators believe such reported figures to be conservative estimates, although some have suggested that the numbers reveal an increased willingness to report rather than actual changes in the incidence of abuse. In fact, the sources of most relevant statistics can be criticized on methodological grounds. Surveys rely not only on the respondent's cooperation and willingness to disclose information, but on the reliability of the respondent's memory, a reliability that may itself be affected by post-traumatic symptomatology. Hospital records usually omit much relevant information, although current reporting laws have prompted professionals to document more signs of childhood abuse and neglect. Police records and crime statistics are likely to underestimate the incidence of any behavior that victims themselves are reluctant to report.

Nevertheless, the increasing number of victims who do report and the records of those who seek professional help indicate that physical and sexual abuse has become a major public health problem. The cost in human suffering and in social and economic resources is immeasurable. Formerly, it was generally believed that abuse was a problem of the lower socioeconomic classes. But the considerable research that is accumulating (Blackman, 1989; Russell, 1984; Walker, 1979) indicates that no segment of the population is exempt. Every class, race, and ethnic group is represented as well as individuals at every level of educational and professional standing. It is scarcely deniable, however, that socioeconomic and class status do affect access to treatment and the type of treatment received. The poorest and most frequently victimized women may be those most likely to be institutionalized in public facilities or to swell the ranks of America's homeless.

Most available statistics do not allow us to distinguish in any reliable way how often victimization occurs as a single isolated life event and how often it is part of a pattern of repetitive abuse that results in cumulative trauma. Victims in psychotherapy frequently report a history of abuse that began in childhood and continues into adult life, often complicated by such revictimizing factors as iatrogenic disorders and sexual abuse in the guise of treatment (Bates & Brodsky, 1989; Burgess & Hartman, 1986; Chesler, 1972). It is also generally acknowledged that abuse in one generation tends to be associated with abuse in the next, though not in any simplistic fashion (Gelles & Cornell, 1990). Women who have been assaulted often marry assaultive partners. Previously abused parents cannot be predicted to abuse their own children, but parents who do abuse their children often have a history of being themselves abused.

The patriarchal family has received considerable attention as the milieu in which female victimization, particularly repetitive victimization, occurs. But females are also at risk in other institutional contexts, such as educational and religious institutions and health care settings. Day care facilities have received considerable notoriety following several well-publicized trials (Crewdson, 1988). Americans are also troubled by what seems to be an increase in random social violence, including impulsive acts of assault by youthful gangs. At the other end of the spectrum of group behavior, well organized cults inflict ritual abuse, including assault, as an aspect of indoctrination and programming (Galanter, 1989).

HISTORICAL CONTEXTS

Although victimization is obviously not exclusively a female problem, females have been targeted as a special class of vulnerable and dependent individuals throughout recorded history. The development of patriarchal social structures both sanctioned the legal subordination of women, which left them at risk for abuse, and specified the protection of females as the actual property of males (Lerner, 1986). As a result of the codification of patriarchal law, females were thus somewhat protected within the culture but left vulnerable within the family. Until recent times, even in Western culture, the right of the male patriarch to control the females in his household was almost absolute and included the right to unlimited sexual access to his wife and physical control of her by beating (Lerner, 1986).

The symbolic significance that accrued to females as male property made rape an expression not only of aggression and power, as some modern investigators have concluded (Groth, 1979), but of possession. Men used rape not only to control women, but to assert their dominance over other men; in wartime, rape even became an expression of the triumph of one nation over another (Brownmiller, 1975). Bizarre fantasies of being "possessed," which sometimes appear symptomatically in severely traumatized individuals, can be understood in this context. Throughout history, females have been literally possessed, and the fantasies about possession that are part of some of the notorious chapters in the history of female victimization, such as the witch trials that arose in both Europe and America, express a symbolic response to a harsh social reality.

Insofar as female victimization became socially sanctioned and institutionalized, it became, like many habitual aspects of daily life, invisible to those who accepted it as part of the natural scheme of things. Social denial, like denial as an individual defense, functions constantly to enable people to avoid the most troublesome features of their lives, particularly those features that run counter to cherished traditions and myths. Religious and social ideals often forbid victimization and urge human beings to live up to the best and most compassionate aspects of themselves. Even in periods in which wife beating or the rape of occupied populations was widely accepted, such acts were still often deplored as unfortunate aberrations contrary to the ideals of civilized conduct. Incest, especially, was likely to be denied as an act completely contrary to human nature.

Given the widespread denial of victimization, the possibility of studying the individual and social consequences of victimization was long foreclosed. The expansion of scientific research after the Enlightenment revolutionized modern life; but it was slow to include the scientific study of either victims or women. Biological as well as psychological research on women continued to be constrained by myths and unexamined beliefs rather than by unbiased investigation. As a result, the significance of trauma as an etiological factor in pathology was eclipsed well into the twentieth century.

Traditionally, in the absence of empirical studies of women's health, one medical concept was evoked to explain a wide and changing array of symptoms. Hysteria is a diagnostic category dating from antiquity; the word itself is derived from the Greek word for womb, and the disease, as conceptualized for generations, was believed to be a disorder to which the female sex is biologically as well as psychologically prone.

The oldest surviving Egyptian papyri on medicine deals specifically with hysteria (Veith, 1965). Hippocrates carefully differentiated between hysteria and organic diseases, such as epilepsy. Etiologically, hysteria was believed to be associated with sexual abstinence; marriage, which sanctioned sexual intercourse, was one prescribed treatment. In antiquity, however, although the sexual behavior of women was carefully regulated, sex was considered a natural function and was not intrinsically associated with social stigma.

The ascendence of Christianity, in contrast, led to explicit attempts to inhibit, rather than merely regulate, all expressions of sexuality. Female sexuality was particularly devalued; woman was viewed as the agent by means of which sin came into the world. When women displayed psychological symptoms, these were still traced to their sexuality, as in antiquity, but now sexuality was a shameful and socially stigmatized female attribute. The devaluation of sexuality in general and female sexuality in particular was simultaneously associated with an obsession with sexuality that, during the Inquisition, led to widespread persecution.

For hundreds of years, medicine, like science generally, existed in the shadow of religious authority. When medical models replaced religious ones, hysteria as a diagnostic concept again came to the forefront of scientific attention. By the nineteenth century, a particular constellation of symptoms and behavior labeled "hysteria" was seemingly epidemic in Europe. Ellenberger (1970) has given an extensive historical account of this period, which saw the rise of the dynamic psychiatry that prevailed during the following century. Female hysteria was the disease classification that led to many of the most significant developments in dynamic psychiatry, including the development of psychoanalysis.

Hysteria has been called "the elusive neurosis" (Krohn, 1978) because of the changing and diverse symptom patterns that have been associated with it during different historical epochs. As a diagnostic category, it became such a catch-all diagnosis for women's symptoms, that "hysterical" became almost synonymous with "feminine" in clinical contexts. And although the specific diagnostic classification has been deleted from modern guidelines like *DSM-III-R* (APA, 1987), it has by no means been deleted from popular ways of thinking about women's problems.

As described by 19th-century physicians like Janet and Charcot, however, hysteria was a severe disorder with debilitating physical and psychological symptoms, including such serious disturbances as deafness, blindness, and loss of tactile sensitivity. The symptoms often mimicked those of organic disease, but occurred in the absence of observable disease processes or could be readily distinguished from the effects of known neurological lesions. Hysteria was also accompanied by such psychological symptoms as oscillations in affect or emotional storms, radical variations in self presentation, and altered states of consciousness, including somnambulism and fugue states. Such symptoms, some of which were later classified as conversions because a psychological problem had seemingly been converted into a physical one, could often be greatly ameliorated through hypnosis, and many hysterics were highly hypnotizable. Dramatic spontaneous recoveries were also common, as were equally dramatic relapses.

Pierre Janet concluded from extensive studies of hysterical patients that traumatic life events frequently precipitated the disorder. He developed a psychological theory in which dissociation, a disconnection of normally associated ideas, was a prominent concept. It was Sigmund Freud, however, who first consistently connected two factors—trauma and sexuality—in a theory of hysteria. Freud (1896) frankly postulated that hysterical patients were suffering from the aftereffects of being sexually abused as children.

Freud's subsequent repudiation of this so-called seduction hypothesis has received much critical attention in recent years. Critics have claimed that Freud denied the existence of sexual abuse in childhood (Masson, 1984). This was not quite the case; what Freud denied was the etiological significance of sexual abuse in the development of neurosis. His repudiation of the seduction hypothesis did, however, lead to the development of a psychological theory, psychoanalysis, in which real events, including actual sexual abuse, are deemphasized in favor of a focus on infantile fantasy, particularly the fantasies supposedly associated with the Oedipus Complex. Following Freud, psychoanalysis became one of the most influential intellectual currents in the twentieth century. It was idealized, vilified, and popularized. Since Freud, numerous theories labeled "psychoanalytic" or "psychodynamic" have continued to proliferate; many currently influential ones, such as self psychology and object relations theories, differ radically from the psychology Freud originally invented. Even so, the role of trauma in psychological development and psychopathology has remained in the background of psychoanalytic theory and treatment.

Another important consequence of Freud's views on hysteria bears mentioning because of the important implications it had for subsequent research on dissociation. Josef Breuer, with whom Freud collaborated in *Studies on Hysteria* (1893–1895), postulated that an etiological factor in hysteria was the development of an altered state of consciousness he termed a "hypnoid state." Freud specifically opposed this concept, emphasizing instead his own concept of "repression." This shift in emphasis shaped the subsequent approach of psychoanalysts to the dynamics of forgetting and had the effect of obscuring some of the most perplexing symptoms of hysterical patients. The concept of repression explains how ideas associated with conflict are excluded from consciousness. It does not account for phenomena associated with altered states of consciousness, particularly the oscillations in cognitive and perceptual experience and self-awareness characteristic of the dissociative disorders. Modern research on dissociation has only recently enabled researchers to rediscover this psychoanalytically repudiated "missing link," the hypnoid state, and reconnect it with biological as well as psychological responses to trauma (Hilgard, 1986; Rossi, 1986).

Freud's psychoanalytic theory as it was appropriated, used, and misused during the twentieth century had two other important consequences for women that should be noted: the tendency to blame mothers and ignore the role of fathers in psychopathology, and the tendency to dismiss abused women as "masochistic." Both of these consequences have especially affected the study of female victimization and the kinds of services offered to victims of incest, rape, and battering.

As psychoanalysis was refined and elaborated, it became a prominent orientation in the study of child development. Resulting research and theory increasingly emphasized the effects of mother-child interaction during the earliest periods of life. Ironically, many of these theories, particularly those that stressed the importance of object relations, did allow for the significance of trauma in psychopathology. But they focused most insistently on the role of the mother. Severe forms of psychopathology, such as schizophrenia and borderline personality organization, were traced to distortions in the early mother-infant relationship (Mahler, 1968) or to processes of "splitting" supposedly originating in infancy (Kernberg, 1975). The traumatogenic impact of disturbed or abusive fathering was generally left out of the picture.

Modern studies of the role of family dynamics, such as those by Lidz and Fleck (1985), have corrected some of the inadequacies of such psycho-dynamic approaches. But much of the literature on development, whether psychoanalytic or not, simply remains unintegrated with modern clinical studies of the effects of trauma. We are only beginning to learn about the differential effects of trauma on particular developmental stages, an area which, as van der Kolk has pointed out (1987), is one of the most poten-tially significant in future research.

The concept of female masochism, as developed in a number of psycho-analytic theories, has also had a great impact on clinical approaches to female victimization (Caplan, 1985; Waites, 1977-78). According to histori-cally influential psychoanalytic views of female sexuality, sexual gratifica-tion is biologically as well as psychologically associated with pain in women (Bonaparte, 1951; Deutsch, 1930). Fantasies about being beaten derive from masturbation conflicts (Freud, 1919). It follows that rape is not neces-sarily traumatic and women stay with violent partners because beating excites them. Even though these views are outdated, they have not disap-peared from either professional approaches to women or popular mythol-ogy; they continue to be used to rationalize the existence of sexual and physical abuse rather than to solve the problem.

TRAUMA AND DISORDERS OF
HIGH PREVALENCE IN WOMEN:
AN OVERVIEW

As a result of the theories about female development and female pathol-ogy that prevailed historically, the contribution of trauma to the disorders prevalently diagnosed in women has often remained obscure. Health pro-fessionals are confronted with a paradox: Morbidity data suggest that fe-males have a biological advantage over males at every stage of life, yet women are more likely to report medical illnesses and to receive treatment (Gove & Hughes, 1979; Strickland, 1988). According to Russo and Olmedo (1983), females account for more than 60% of admissions to outpatient mental health facilities. Females exceed males in the use of prescription drugs generally (Verbrugge & Steiner, 1985), and two thirds of the prescrip-tions for psychotropic medications such as Valium and Librium are for women (Moore, 1980).

A number of explanations have been proposed for such observed differences in male and female utilization of health care options. One is that women simply complain more. Myth reminds us of stereotypes about female bitchiness; social scientists point to such learned female behaviors as helplessness (Seligman, 1975) and dependency (Fodor, 1974). Some researchers have also concluded that, for women, illness has often been the only way of gaining support or escaping the burdens of the traditional female role. The "female complaint," a vague constellation of symptoms that sometimes incapacitated 19th-century women, can be seen in this light (Ehrenreich & English, 1973). When female sickness was romanticized, it even became a positively valued sign of femininity and a means of gaining male attention by appeals for rescue and protection. A landmark finding by Broverman et al. (1970) reported that the characteristics of healthy human beings are considered the characteristics of healthy males, but not of healthy, that is, well-adjusted, females.

The assumption that physical symptoms in women often had psychological motives (although the role of real life trauma was usually overlooked) contributed to physicians' reliance on diagnostic assessments like "hysteria," which in turn sometimes resulted in the failure to diagnose physical disease or to an indiscriminate dispensing of painkillers and tranquilizers that led to addiction but left underlying problems untouched. The implications of the overzealous use of diagnostic terms like hysteria has received considerable attention from feminists (Chesler, 1972; Kaplan, 1983; Millett, 1969) who have also raised criticisms about the gender biases inherent in psychiatric classifications generally.

But whatever their limitations, widely used classifications of mental disorders, such as the diagnostic and statistical manuals prepared and periodically revised by the American Psychiatric Association, reflect a broad consensus of professional thinking about particular types of problems. Because such manuals as *DSM-III* and *DSM-III-R* are in general use, they are also accepted as standard in research on the incidence and prevalence of particular psychiatric problems. Thus, whatever the deficiencies of the classifications, they offer us an opportunity to examine how females are perceived, diagnosed, and treated in the mental health system and to review the correlates between diagnosed disorders and other aspects of female experience. They also offer the opportunity to explore certain clinical hypotheses about how women cope not only with their internal conflicts but with the external difficulties they face.

A common perception among clinicians, for example, is that women tend to internalize their problems while men are more given to behavioral acting out. Kaplan (1983) found gender differences in diagnosed disorders that has some bearing on this belief. When organic problems were excluded, women were found to be more often classified as depressed, phobic, suffering from "psychogenic" physical symptoms, or characterized by

sexual inhibitions. Men were diagnosed with problems that reflected unacceptable social behavior, such as substance abuse problems, atypical patterns of sexual behavior, or disorders of impulse control. Differences in
the diagnosis of severe personality disorders were also noted: Females were
more often classified as histrionic, borderline, or dependent, while males
were diagnosed as paranoid, antisocial, or compulsive. Kaplan remarks on
the relation between these incidences of diagnosed disorder and sex-role
stereotypes. Certain personality disorders, such as the dependent personality and the histrionic personality, as well as certain phobic disorders can
be understood as representing caricatures of the traditional female role.

Franks and Rothblum (1983) argue persuasively, however, that sex differences in diagnosed illnesses are no mere artifact of clinicians' stereotypes but reflect the real and debilitating consequences of sex-role stereotyping in the larger society. The debilitating consequences of violence
against women are also beginning to emerge in studies of psychiatric populations. Carmen, Rieker, and Mills (1984), in a retrospective study of psychiatric inpatients, found that almost half of their sample had histories of
physical or sexual abuse or both. Female patients were much more likely
than males to be victims, and there were sex differences in patterns of
abuse. Males were abused in childhood or adolescence, but females were
abused from childhood through adulthood. The most significant distinction between the behavior of males and females was that abused males
reacted by becoming more aggressive, while abused females became more
passive or directed their aggression toward themselves by becoming self-
destructive — self-mutilating, or suicidal.

Depression

Research findings are pertinent to both observed sex differences in the
incidence of depression and to theories that link depression to anger
turned against the self. According to *DSM-III-R* (APA, 1987), both major
depressive disorders and dysthymia, or depressive neurosis, occur more
frequently in women than in men. In a review of the epidemiology of
depression reported by Weissman and Klerman (1977) covering a span of
over 40 years and including about 30 Western countries, the authors found
that depression is more common among women than men and that the
rates for women are relatively high. Weissman (1980) concludes that there
are biological as well as psychosocial reasons for these sex differences, but
she confines her biological considerations to the effects of genetic factors
and to such endogenous factors as hormonal fluctuations associated with
menstruation or childbearing. That environmental risks such as violence
against women affect female biology is not considered. Even so, she discusses some data relating depression to women's social role that may have

an indirect bearing on the problem of family violence. Paykel et al. (1969), for instance, found marital difficulty to be the problem most frequently presented by depressed women.

Weissman also relates female depression to an experience of loss, noting that women commonly outlive their spouses. Certain depressions are clearly related to grief and to complications in grieving. As early as 1917, Freud hypothesized that excessive ambivalence is a factor in melancholia. Female victims may be especially prone to ambivalence, particularly when the abuser is a family member. Victims are often unable to leave an abusive relationship because of practical difficulties or threats, but it is the love-hate characteristic of the relationship that sometimes leads the victim to cling to it in spite of ongoing abuse. Although the victim experiences many losses — loss of trust, loss of a good parent or spouse who has now turned destructive, loss of illusions about the safety and dependability of significant relationships — occasional indications of love or even the memory of loving behavior may enable the victim to avoid confronting the clear evidence that love has been lost.

Self-esteem inevitably suffers in such a context and is one of the losses the victim faces. Self-esteem is also eroded by the tendency of human beings to reflect the views of themselves held by others. The victim sees herself treated as an object of abuse and contempt; she may then view herself that way. Her abuser may also seem, paradoxically, to value her highly. Ordinarily being valued might raise her self-esteem, but since she is only valued as a possession, or only valued as long as she continues to submit to abuse, she may be unable to extricate herself from the victimizing relationship and seek other sources of self-esteem.

All these factors provide explanations for the empirical observation that depression is more prevalently diagnosed in women. There is another factor, however, that needs to be considered in the context of diagnostic criteria per se. Depression is frequently diagnosed on the basis of reports of persistent dysphoria or signs of emotional sadness — weeping, expressions of inner pain, etc. But depression is also sometimes clinically inferred from signs of inhibited emotional expression and complaints of inability to feel anything. Some of these symptoms are a response to the emotional numbing that is a psychobiological response to trauma (van der Kolk, 1988). Numbing should be distinguished from sadness; numbing typically blocks both the memory of trauma and the affect appropriate to trauma. In the course of treatment, it is usually necessary to regain access to the memories lost through dissociation and the affect lost through numbing. Depression — sadness as a response to loss and the anger that has been turned inward — needs to be experienced in order for healing to take place. But, although getting in touch with depressive affect can be therapeutic, it can also be one of the most dangerous points in therapy, particularly if the client becomes suicidal.

Anxiety and Phobic Disorders

The relation of trauma to anxiety can be understood as part of our biological heritage. Anxiety is a powerful internal warning signal that leads to avoidance behavior in both animals and people. It is readily conditioned to symbolic as well as concrete stimuli and plays an important role in learning and memory. Clinicians have emphasized the connection between anxiety and infantile helplessness that helps shape our earliest interpersonal relations. Obviously, anxiety has a positive role to play in survival generally, as well as in social organization.

Anxiety disorders illustrate what happens when such a fundamental survival response goes haywire. Avoidance behavior then becomes associated with seemingly innocuous stimuli. When confronted by such stimuli, the phobic individual experiences increased arousal and subjective feelings of distress, which may reach levels of panic. Physiological symptoms such as shortness of breath, palpitations, trembling, choking sensations, and nausea can become so uncomfortable that the afflicted person becomes almost as terrified of the symptoms themselves as of the original precipitating stimulus.

Anxiety is a major symptom of post-traumatic stress disorder (PTSD) as described in *DSM-III-R* (APA, 1987). It is typically associated with such psychobiological symptoms as hypervigilance and difficulty in falling asleep, is often accompanied by depression, and frequently complicated by dependence on psychoactive substances.

Traditionally, anxiety symptoms in women were often diagnosed as expressions of female hysteria. Anxiety is stereotypically associated with female weakness, timidity, and emotionality. Phobic excitement in the presence of certain kinds of stimuli, such as mice or snakes, is an aspect of the female stereotype commonly exploited in jokes or cartoons. The idea that females are simply more prone to anxiety than males also leads people to dismiss and devalue women's concerns.

One anxiety disorder frequently diagnosed in women has especially interested researchers. Agoraphobia, a fear of being in situations from which escape might be difficult or embarrassing, is a syndrome in which the ratio of females to males is particularly high (*DSM-III-R*, APA, 1987). Agoraphobia can be a disabling symptom. Traveling restrictions or a refusal to leave the home at all may constrict a woman's whole life.

According to Chambless and Goldstein (1980), more than a million American women suffer agoraphobic symptoms. These authors emphasize the relation between such phobic responses and hysteria, noting that the problem is often compounded by social tolerance for the sick or fearful female role. Brehony (1983) contends that women are socially conditioned to behaviors that may predispose them to agoraphobia and offers empirical data indicating that women are more likely to be reinforced for home-bound activities. She also stresses the developmental literature that indicates that adults encourage independence in male children and reinforce dependence and helplessness in females.

While arguments emphasizing the relationship between sex-role socialization and agoraphobia make important points, they need to be supplemented by an awareness of the literature on female victimization. Fears of going out alone or of going into certain places outside the home are constantly reinforced in females by actual reports of rape and assault. One stereotyped response to the raped woman, in fact, has been that "she should not have been there," that is, walking on the street or jogging in the park. From childhood, females are not merely taught to avoid risks; they are warned by countless cautionary tales about how adventurous activities may be dangerous to them, how they are especially vulnerable just because they are female. Crime statistics give credence to such tales.

Another aspect of female victimization relevant to phobic avoidance has been stressed in the literature on both battering and incest. Victims are typically instructed in secrecy. The reputation of both victim and perpetrator must be protected, along with an idealized image of the family. Abusers threaten dire consequences or actual punishment if their assaultive behavior becomes publicly known. In some cases, assaultive males are also extremely possessive and forbid normal social behavior in a wife or daughter because of pathological jealousy. Being a victim produces motivations for secrecy, too. Guilt, however irrational, leads to fear of discovery; shame leads to hiding. Sometimes staying in the house is the only way to maintain secrecy; battered women often have obvious signs of injury. It is difficult to conceal a black eye or a neck brace, or a prominent bruise on the face, and simply avoiding social contact may be easier and safer than trying to invent an explanation.

Even if the need for hiding victimization is not a basic cause of agoraphobia, responses to violence or potential violence can greatly reinforce the effects of sex-role socialization. Behavioral constriction, such as fear of leaving the house, is also a common temporary symptom in PTSD. Some women diagnosed as agoraphobic may be suffering from chronic manifestations of PTSD, but may have neither memory of nor insight into the original causes of the symptoms.

Several other kinds of symptom pictures often observed in women can be better understood in terms of anxiety although anxiety per se is not the presenting problem. Sexual disorders frequently have a phobic component. Confusion and inhibition concerning sexuality, for example, is one aftereffect of rape trauma (Burgess & Holmstrom, 1974) or of incest (Courtois, 1988). In battered women, rage and associated anxiety, either suppressed or experienced, may inhibit sexual desire. Difficulties in experiencing orgasm can be related either to a fear of sexual excitement generally or a fear of losing physical and emotional control. Such inhibitions and anxieties are complicated by the guilt and shame associated with sexual assault. Women who fear having somehow caused their own victimization may try especially hard to escape the accusation that "You really enjoyed it!"

Eating disorders in women are often a special way of coping with anxiety. The literature on anorexia, bulimia, and obesity does not typically stress the role of trauma in such disorders. Nevertheless, theories that describe the relationship between food intake and a sense of control indirectly suggest possible links with responses to trauma. The individual with an eating disorder handles her anxieties about many problems through an obsessive focus on food and compulsive patterns of using food (Boskind-Lodahl, 1976; Wooley & Wooley, 1980). These obsessive and compulsive symptoms can absorb a woman's attention for most of her waking hours. They thus enable her to avoid thinking about and coping with troubling aspects of life, including interpersonal and sexual conflicts or memories of trauma. Anorexia and bulimia contribute to an illusion of total control, but this illusion is constantly threatened and must be bolstered by repetitive behavior that never really reassures. Such patterns sometimes resemble addictive behavior and may result in psychobiological states that trigger self-perpetuating cycles as the body vainly attempts to regulate itself.

Defensive responses to anxiety, whether they involve phobic avoidance or a compulsive focus on some circumscribed area of activity, such as eating, are usually highly resistant to change. When anxiety is a response to trauma, defenses also usually involve escaping specific memories. Psychotherapy, which encourages clients to confront unpleasant thoughts and memories, then becomes a threat in itself. Even so, most clients recognize that their avoidant symptoms do not really contain their anxiety but merely compound their problems. Therapy, even though it may temporarily heighten anxiety, can bring very welcome relief.

Dissociative Disorders

The prevalence of dissociative disorders in women is a subject of considerable ongoing debate. According to the *DSM-III-R* (APA, 1987), the most severe example, multiple personality disorder, is diagnosed from three to nine times more frequently in females than in males. For other dissociative disorders, such as psychogenic fugue and depersonalization disorder, information on sex ratios is not available.

The significance of dissociation as a female problem can be evaluated in the light of familiar controversies concerning hysteria. One simple fact worth noting is that the current classification has replaced an older category, hysterical neuroses, dissociative type. All forms of hysteria were formerly more commonly diagnosed in women, and it is not unreasonable to assume that such historical tendencies may be carried over into modern diagnostic trends.

There is reason to believe, however, that the observed sex ratios result from the relation between dissociation and trauma, a finding consistent with data on female victimization. The evidence linking severe dissociative disorders like MPD with sexual abuse in childhood is proliferating (Putnam, 1989). Some researchers, noting the contribution of stress response syndromes to dissociative disorders, conceptualize these disorders as closely related to PTSD (van der Kolk, 1988). It is reasonable to predict that future studies of abused women will uncover many specific symptoms of dissociation that might have been previously lumped together under the vague diagnostic rubric of "female hysteria."

Dissociation, like other symptomatic behavior, can often be understood as a defense against unbearable anxiety. Traumatic experience typically produces an overwhelming need to escape what is, in reality, inescapable. Dissociation is a psychobiological mechanism that allows the mind, in effect, to flee what the body is experiencing, thus maintaining a selective conscious awareness that has survival value. The shock of trauma produces states that are so different from ordinary waking life that they are not easily integrated with more normal experience. As a result of this discontinuity, the traumatic state may be lost to memory or remembered as a dream is sometimes remembered, as something vague and unreal.

The sense of unreality, which results from physiological as well as psychological responses to trauma, is compounded by the wish that a terrible event were not really occurring or had never happened. This wish, in conjunction with unusual sensations and perceptions, can lead to the conviction that "This is not happening to me; I am merely observing it." In such circumstances, a victim may perceive her physical body as an alien entity from which her mind is detached. Having experienced such a dissociation, she may elaborate on it when subsequently confronted by painful memories or by a repetition of trauma. She may even create an organized identity that is untouched by the trauma, or an identity that remembers the trauma but is disconnected from her usual identity. In extreme cases, like MPD, a series of identity configurations are organized by particular sets of memories but remain isolated from one another.

The dissociative tendencies that are set in motion by trauma complicate other problems, which may have interfered with personality integration, such as pathogenic relationships with parents or physical disabilities. Sex-role socialization, for example, often leads females to inhibit certain activities as "not me." Anger, aggression, or sexual excitement may conflict with one's representation of oneself as a "nice" girl. A part of the self may be suppressed or altogether repressed from consciousness. Dissociation, however, typically involves even more rigid compartmentalizations of mind and body. In MPD, for example, the alternating personalities may have distinct facial expressions and characteristic body postures that concretely encode particular kinds of memories. Such discrete psychobiological patterns include measurable differences in EEG, in responses to medication, or in disease syndromes, although all the alter personalities occupy the same body.

Research on severe dissociative disorders offers new insights into a host of phenomena traditionally labeled "hysterical" (Braun, 1986; Putnam, 1989). Conversion reactions, for example, can now be understood as the body's way of remembering trauma. The so-called "belle indifference" classically associated with hysteria can be seen as a direct consequence of the dissociation of mind and body.

In recent years, multiple personality disorder, even though still comparatively rare, seems to have captured the imagination of the public. Books describing famous cases, such as *The Three Faces of Eve* (Thigpen & Cleckley, 1957), *Sybil* (Schreiber, 1973), and *When Rabbit Howls* (Troops for Truddi Chase, 1987) became best-sellers. Not only the unusual character of MPD as a disorder, but the sensationalism characteristic of some media accounts have aroused the skepticism of many clinicians, who consider the disorder to be factitious or an artifact of hypnosis. Although my own cases have convinced me of the reality of dissociative phenomena, including MPD, I also appreciate the skepticism. The recent burgeoning of popular literature and media attention given MPD is somewhat reminiscent of that 19th-century period when dissociation was part of the zeitgeist. Insofar as this development stimulates research on a sometimes incapacitating disorder, it is positive. Unfortunately, the focus on dramatic cases of MPD sometimes has had the effect of obscuring more common dissociative problems, which probably afflict larger numbers of women.

Amnesias and fugue states, for example, can be a reaction to any severe stressor, including isolated instances of assault in adulthood. Traumatized women sometimes report puzzling symptomatic acts suggestive of fugue states: Shoplifting in a woman who has no previous history of antisocial behavior suggests the possibility of a dissociative disorder, particularly if a severe stressor can be identified. Absentmindedness, which may provoke fears of organic impairment, also points to the possibility that a woman is experiencing transient, psychogenic fugue-like episodes.

It should be noted, too, that a number of disorders not primarily classified as dissociative often have dissociative features. The numbing response that sometimes leads to a diagnosis of depression has already been mentioned. Sexual problems may involve the inability to tolerate sexual stimulation without blanking out dissociatively. Eating disorders are often characterized by behavior patterns with dissociative features; both bingeing and purging, for example, sometimes occur in trance-like states. Whether dissociative responses occur as isolated symptoms or as part of a more severe dissociative disorder, however, it is useful to evaluate them as reactions to extreme, possibly trauma-induced anxiety.

Borderline Personality Disorder

Among the personality disorders reported to occur more often in women than in men, borderline personality disorder deserves special consideration. During the past two decades, this particular problem has become a focus of intense debate and research. It has been conceptualized most systematically by psychodynamic theorists, who emphasize issues like developmental arrest and ego defects that interfere with the regulation of affect and behavior.

Following Mahler (1968), psychodynamic clinicians have pointed to difficulties in separation and individuation in the developmental histories of borderline personalities (Adler, 1985; Gunderson, 1984). Some, particularly Kernberg (1975), have emphasized a process of "splitting," which prevents the integration of contrasting good and bad representations of internalized objects. Kernberg concludes that this problem arises in part from constitutional factors. Others, such as Masterson and Rinsley (1975), stress the etiological significance of early difficulties in the mother-child relationship.

Recently, Herman and van der Kolk (1987) have discussed the extent to which descriptions of borderline personality disorder are congruent with those of post-traumatic stress disorder. Disturbances in affect regulation, hyperreactivity to mild stimuli, irritability, dysphoria, and disturbances of identity are reactions considered characteristic of both types of disorder. These observations have led the authors to conclude that childhood trauma is an important antecedent of borderline personality disorder and that the significance of trauma helps explain the predominance of the disorder in women.

Herman (1986) reports data consistent with that previously found by Carmen et al. (1984) and Rosenfeld (1979) to the effect that abuse is a common but often neglected feature of the histories of hospitalized mental patients. Of those patients in her sample diagnosed as borderline, 67% had a history of abuse in childhood or adolescence. The recently discovered role of trauma in borderline pathology suggests opportunities for integrating developmental and psychobiological studies. Herman and van der Kolk envision a productive synthesis in this regard. The possibility that differential effects of trauma at different developmental stages may account for important variations in the severity as well as the type of symptoms observed in later life certainly merits exploration.

But although such a synthesis may be desirable, a number of difficulties impede it. Not the least of these is the traditional psychodynamic view of child development, which pictures the mother as the primary caretaker and thus the primary source of psychopathology. The psychodynamic focus on the significance of the first two or three years of life in the development of severe psychopathology also poses problems. Much childhood abuse, probably the most damaging, does occur at an early age. But abuse is a problem across the life span. Psychodynamic theories have scarcely begun to examine the role of the father in normal development; explorations of the effects of paternal abuse may be long in coming.

Other factors not usually much studied by psychodynamic clinicians, such as substance abuse, family violence, and social barriers to female individuation and independence also probably contribute to the kinds of pathology diagnosed as borderline. It is certainly not impossible to integrate studies of such variables with a psychodynamic point of view, but the task that looms is imposing. Abuse is not merely a developmental liability, but a problem of disordered families and disordered social arrangements that can only be adequately conceptualized when the complexities of female socialization are taken into account.

One final comment bears mentioning. For many years, feminists have been pointing out that some forms of behavior are considered more pathological in females than in males. This phenomenon may be especially pertinent to females diagnosed with borderline pathology. Trauma has been implicated in a number of disorders — including depression, anxiety disorders, and dissociative disorders — prevalently diagnosed in women. Borderline personality disorder, however, is a diagnosis that seems to be made on females who show a number of characteristics considered particularly undesirable in women. Such individuals exhibit the kinds of difficulties in impulse control more readily accepted in males. They tend, at least part of the time, to be excessively demanding rather than self-effacing, behaviorally active rather than behaviorally constricted. Insofar as their problems are a result of abuse, their identification with the aggressor is often more obvious than that of more inhibited and passive female victims. In many ways, they differ markedly from the "good hysteric" Chodoff (1974) identified.

Such considerations certainly do not detract from the importance of the discovery of the relation between abuse and borderline pathology. They merely suggest further avenues of research on the differential effects of abuse, as well as on how social stereotypes affect diagnostic evaluations of women.

PART I
Shocks, Dilemmas, and Double Binds

CHAPTER 1
Psychobiology and
Post-Traumatic Pathology

T HE SHOCK OF sudden trauma throws body and mind off balance. In extreme cases, typically those involving severe physical injury, this sudden destabilization can lead to circulatory collapse and death.

Most violence against girls and women is not fatal, however, although the daily papers remind us how often it can be. Much victimization leaves no obvious physical scars. Victims often recover to various degrees spontaneously. Yet, even if the body survives, subtle or dramatic alterations occur, some of which resemble a kind of psychic death: An emergent identity may die; a sense of aliveness may be temporarily or even permanently lost. Self-observing victims, perceiving mysterious internal changes, sometimes report an alienation from self and others that depletes them of meaning and vitality. Primitive minds used to describe a "loss of soul" (Ellenberger, 1970). Shengold (1989) has discussed abuse as a kind of "soul murder."

Yet, where there is life, even life without much hope, survival is often maintained not only by processes of physical repair but by persistent attempts at psychological reparation. Individuals who repeatedly experience alterations in self-experience, for example, sometimes begin constructing their identity over and over until the pattern of their life resembles a patchwork mosaic. Other victims of trauma, depleted of energy for reconstruction, may languish in a lethargic state that feels dead, or, becoming psychotically depressed, may develop the delusion that they really *are* dead.

The shock of an initial trauma is, to a great extent, a function of its novelty and unexpectedness; the unprepared victim has had no chance to strengthen her defenses. Responses to repetitive trauma, on the other hand, are complicated by anticipatory reactions ranging from almost reflexive avoidance reactions to elaborate self-protective fantasies and carefully planned behaviors. One common response to an initial trauma is a conscious determination to prevent a recurrence. This is an adaptive response if it works, but if it does not, if prevention is impossible, a repeated, predictable, but inescapable shock can have even more destructive effects than the original one.

Many basic responses to trauma are a part of an ancient evolutionary heritage, hard wired, so to speak, into the central nervous system. Others are an outcome of changes in brain structure that are, from an evolutionary standpoint, comparatively recent. Such changes have introduced a remarkable degree of variability and plasticity into the human species. The first line of defense against trauma is reflexive. But the human brain is not a slave to reflex; it can, to some extent, both monitor and modify the body's reactions, even behavior largely mediated by the hard wiring of the autonomic nervous system (Rossi, 1986).

A major premise of this book is that trauma responses can be modified. Healing can replace hopelessness. It is easier to facilitate positive change, however, if the negative effects of trauma are acknowledged and understood. A burgeoning literature on these negative effects is making it possible, in effect, to know the enemy.

EMERGENCY REACTIONS

For purposes of the present discussion, trauma will be defined as an injury to mind or body that requires structural repair. The emphasis on structure in this definition suggests that a main effect of trauma is disorganization, a physical and/or mental disorganization that may be circumscribed or widespread. Recovery, then, involves a process of reorganization that attempts to restore wholeness to body and/or mind.

From a psychobiological standpoint, trauma reactions can be understood in terms of a broader class of stress reactions from which they are distinguishable not so much in kind as in severity and duration. Such reactions illustrate both the creative potential and the adaptive limits of the human organism. Healing may leave scars, and severe or repetitive trauma may exhaust capacities for recovery, but under the most favorable conditions, processes of repair can strengthen a structure that was originally weak, making it less vulnerable to future strains and stresses.

One of the pioneering investigators into the psychobiological parameters of trauma responses was Walter B. Cannon (1953) who conceptualized a group of "emergency reactions" in terms of physiological departures from a steady state termed *homeostasis*. Departures from homeostasis activate compensatory responses as the body attempts to protect and repair itself and to restore balance. Metabolic processes are orchestrated to distribute energy optimally to those bodily systems involved in defense: We are energized for fight or flight, for example, but not for consumatory responses such as eating. The survival value of such reactions is greatly increased by the immediacy with which they are triggered.

Subsequent research on emergency reactions has focused on a characteristic array of behavioral as well as physiological responses, many of which are mediated by the autonomic nervous system, particularly the reticular activating system of the brain stem, the hypothalamus, and the pituitary gland (the HPA axis) (van der Kolk, 1987, 1988; Zuckerman, 1991). Stressful events alter the internal neurochemistry that regulates thinking as well as behavior at many levels of organization, including the rate of cerebral blood flow (Matthew & Wilson, 1990) and the turnover of central neurotransmitters such as norepinephrine (noradrenalin), dopamine, serotonin, and acetylcholine (Axelrod & Reisine, 1984; Rose, 1980; Zacharko & Anisman, 1991). Most such alterations are temporary, but extreme trauma may result in microstructural internal changes that permanently affect neurochemistry (Goddard et al., 1969).

Homeostasis, as originally conceptualized, was viewed as a steady state. It is more accurately viewed, however, as a *predictable pattern of variability*. Variability is a normal characteristic of biological systems: Body temperature, blood pressure, states of arousal, and other internal states fluctuate in periodic cycles regulated according to ultradian and circadian rhythms (Rossi, 1986; Thayer, 1989), which we associate with sleep and wakefulness. Sleep itself is a complex variable state and sleep disorders are among the most frequent of post-traumatic symptoms (Ross et al., 1989; van Kammen et al., 1990).

Stress can also disrupt other biological rhythms, including the complex system of hormonal control that regulates the female menstrual cycle. Symptomatic changes such as amenorrhea have been linked to stress effects (Berga & Girton, 1989; Blankstein et al., 1981). Exaggerated brain sensitivity to rising levels of estrogen at puberty has been offered as an explanation for certain aspects of anorexia, although exact mechanisms and the role played by stress remain unclear (Young, 1991). Swartzman et al. (1990) review data suggesting that lowered circulating levels of estrogen during periods of stress potentiate menopausal hot flushes.

Words like "defense" and "recovery" tend to emphasize the aftereffects of trauma. As survival mechanisms, however, emergency reactions are not merely reactive; they have a proactive dimension that is particularly relevant to the complicated defenses of human beings and to post-traumatic symptoms. In the course of evolution, a complex warning system has developed that prepares us for danger even when none exists. Any novel stimulus, even a harmless one, triggers an increased level of autonomic arousal that may, if the stimulus does prove dangerous, develop into a full blown emergency reaction. This novelty response is one we associate with startle. The startled animal moves reflexively to orient itself toward the novel stimulus, which may turn out to be merely interesting. The organism is energized for exploratory as well as defensive behavior, and attention is directed toward gaining further information.

There is an adaptive advantage to this novelty response—it is not merely defensive or pathological. Increased arousal not only energizes but, at optimal levels, facilitates learning and problem solving (Hebb, 1949). In humans, for whom novelty reactions are connected with symbolic processes, challenges, even risky ones, can be pleasantly stimulating. One outcome of successful coping is an increased sense of competence and self-esteem.

But trauma, in contrast to interesting challenges, overtaxes the mechanisms for responding to new or dangerous situations. As a result, these mechanisms may be pathologically altered in ways that subsequently interfere with normal, everyday coping. Systems regulating arousal seem to become hypersensitive, too easily switched on and too difficult to moderate or turn off. The wear and tear of this hypersensitivity takes its toll in physical symptoms and a general depletion of energy. The psychological consequences may affect social interaction in ways that precipitate new stresses and isolate the individual from social support systems.

In the 1930s, Hans Selye, a student of Cannon, identified a pattern of psychobiological changes that develop in response to continual demands on the adaptive capabilities of organisms (Selye, 1956). According to Selye, this pattern, which he labeled the General Adaptation Syndrome (G.A.S.), evolves through three phases: an alarm reaction, which energizes the body for action; a stage of resistance, which is in many respects the opposite of the alarm reaction and may represent an attempt to reinstate homeostasis; and a state of exhaustion, the end point when energy reserves are depleted and breakdown occurs. Selye's analysis provided a valuable model for investigating a wide range of chronic illnesses and disabilities, and his pioneering work continues to guide the study of so-called psychosomatic illnesses. Following Selye, the extent to which mind and body are systemically organized in environmental contexts has increasingly replaced traditional controversies about nature vs. nurture and biology vs. environment (Taylor, 1987).

EFFECTS OF INESCAPABLE SHOCK

Trauma impacts on several dimensions of psychological adaptation including

1. learning and memory
2. addiction, immunity, and stress tolerance
3. identity formation and personality integration
4. fantasy

The effects of a traumatic event on any of these psychological dimensions is not a simple function of the event itself, however, but a complex function of the individual's control over what happens. In animals as well as humans, whether an aversive event is escapable or not has been found to be a major predictor of whether the ultimate effects are negative or positive (Murburg et al., 1990; van der Kolk et al., 1985; van der Kolk & Greenberg, 1987).

The negative effects of inescapable shock (IS) include deficits in learning to escape new adversities, decreased motivation for learning, chronic subjective distress, and alterations in the immune system which increase vulnerability to disease (van der Kolk & Greenberg, 1987). Escapable shock, in contrast, is not associated with such deficits.

Both experimental animal subjects and people react characteristically to inescapable shock (IS) with a response pattern that has sometimes been interpreted as learned helplessness (Seligman, 1975). Previously defeated mice, for example, assume a posture of defeat even before being attacked again and also develop stress analgesia (Miczek et al., 1982). To an outsider, such victims appear to have given up and retreated into passivity.

In human beings, however, apparent passivity may be deceptive. Once active coping mechanisms have proven ineffective, internal adaptations are often instituted, many of which seem to involve deflecting attention from the inevitable trauma. In humans, these adaptations can include a rich array of fantasies.

Inescapable shock tends to produce lasting and deleterious psychobiological changes. Krystal (1990) reviews a number of studies that indicate that IS exposure has massive effects on noradrenergic activation. Noradrenergic systems can become so sensitized that, subsequent to IS, even mild stressors evoke extreme activation and the behaviors associated with it. Environmental factors can either increase or moderate IS effects. Such factors as a history of maternal deprivation or previous IS exposure, for example, increase individual vulnerability, whereas such factors as previous successful escape experiences and the presence of supportive peers can moderate or protect against negative effects.

In contrast to inescapable shock, controllable aversive events produce a very different pattern of responses even at the neurochemical level. Inescapable shock results in the depletion of norepinephrine and dopamine, for example, but with escapable shock, norepinephrine levels are not lowered and may even increase to enhance adaptive coping (van der Kolk, 1987). Being in control also has important effects on the complex cognitions and self-appraisals of humans. As Janoff-Bulman (1985) has observed, victimization heightens negative self-appraisals, but actions that foster a sense of personal control have positive effects.

This perspective has far-reaching implications for human behavior. It suggests, for example, that self-injury is inherently paradoxical, since it is apparently escapable. The paradox suggests potentially useful insights into the self-injurious behavior that so often appears as a symptom in trauma-tized individuals. Far from being a display of masochism, it is in some instances an attempt to escape from pain through positive coping, by replacing the uncontrollability of inescapable trauma with an experience of personal control. This hypothesis, along with a recognition of the phe-nomenon of addiction to trauma, which will be discussed subsequently, is especially relevant to the lives of women, whose choices have been systematically constrained and whose seemingly self-defeating behavior has often been facilely dismissed as evidence of so-called "female masoch-ism" (Waites, 1977–78).

Learning and Memory

Trauma impacts on learning and memory in a variety of ways, affecting exposure to or avoidance of information as well as the encoding, storage, and retrieval mechanisms of memory itself. To the extent that information input is traumatic, avoiding such input is a straightforward strategy for moderating stress. The simple conditioning of reflexive patterns of avoid-ance may enable the victim to escape confrontations with traumatic re-minders. The production of endogenous opioids produces analgesic and even anesthetic effects, which facilitate this shutting out of external stim-uli. As a further protection, complex cognitive defenses, such as denial and paranoid projection, may also be utilized to regulate the flow and dis-tort the meaning of incoming information about traumatic realities.

Such patterns can have massive effects on coping behavior. The victim may, in effect, try to live in a cocoon, walled off from a world perceived as dangerous. But a cocoon can eventually prove dangerously maladaptive, since avoidance patterns, which are originally instituted to make shock controllable, often have the ultimate effect of reducing control. In addi-tion, the avoidant individual misses out on important learning and the enhanced self-esteem that comes from effective coping. This situation can leave her vulnerable to inescapable repetitions of trauma.

Avoidant patterns are difficult to change, not only because the vic-tim cannot easily be desensitized to trauma-related cues, but because avoidance is to some extent a built-in feature of basic psychobiological responses to extreme stress, an automatic feature of the numbing and constriction phase of the trauma response. Avoidant patterns are also com-plicated by hypersensitivities that may reflect permanent neurobiological changes in stress tolerance.

For example, trauma sometimes alters patterns of coping in such a way that the victim responds to any subsequent increase in arousal, even a slight one, as a danger signal. Everyday challenges disappear from experience, and even a moderate new challenge precipitates a crisis. When this happens, novel situations are not explored in that state of optimal arousal and the focused attention that facilitates learning. Novelty itself becomes threatening. The internal warning system, originally a normal survival mechanism, has gone awry and is now a problem rather than a solution.

When this response pattern develops, exploration of novelty and the new learning exploration produces is preempted by patterns of fight or flight that can become a serious handicap. If tendencies to fight are increased, the belligerence of the aggressive individual often leads to new dangers of retaliation from those attacked. If flight tendencies are heightened, the behavioral constriction of the avoidant individual results in a new array of problems. Either pattern is likely to become a serious psychological and interpersonal liability.

Memory itself, and the integration of memories into coherent patterns, is often markedly affected by trauma. Any stage of memory—encoding, storage, or retrieval—may be involved. The noradrenergic system is intimately involved in short-term memory: Norepinephrine (NE) depletion decreases memory storage while NE stimulating agents have been shown to increase retention (van der Kolk, 1987). Memory effects may vary during different stages of the trauma response, depending on whether the victim is in a stage of heightened arousal or in a stage of constriction. Fair (1988) has described one-take memory formations, which sometimes result under conditions of stress.

In other instances, the memory of a traumatic event is obliterated by amnesia, and the affected individual develops a gap in her accessible memory, which may vary from a few seconds to months, or even years. Traumatic amnesia can be especially problematic in children, since it interferes with the integration of important cognitions about the self and the world.

Context is an important feature of long-term memory storage as well as retrieval. Retrieval has been shown to be facilitated when matched to the state in which material was originally learned (Parkin, 1987). Experimental studies of such state-dependent learning suggest weak effects, but Parkin (1987) concludes that the phenomenon is possibly more relevant to clinical settings. Clinicians most typically encounter state-dependent trauma effects in the dissociative disorders (Putman, 1989; Ross, 1989). In such cases, it sometimes becomes obvious that large memory systems have been organized on the basis of specific traumatic events and the emotions specific to those events. State-dependent storage seems to organize these memory systems like files in a box or computer—information in one file may be completely sealed off from that in another and only retrievable when one knows the code necessary for accessing it.

What we refer to as memory is, of course, a vastly complex domain, not necessarily reducible to a single mechanism or set of mechanisms. Those who study memory differentiate types on the basis of process as well as content. Tulving (1983), for example, has distinguished between semantic memory, which is involved in the learning and usage of language, and episodic memory, which stores life events and gives them a temporal stamp. Clinically, we seldom observe disruptions of semantic memory except in cases of clear-cut organic pathology. Episodic memory, on the other hand, seems to be more vulnerable to disruption by trauma, perhaps because it involves the location of events in time, and time perception is itself often distorted during periods of extreme stress.

Memory is an aspect of life that we rely on to enhance our sense of personal control. Loss of control over memory is itself one form of inescapable stress and can be one of the most terrifying sequels to trauma. It can also be dangerous. Although amnesia can serve a self-protective function, it often makes the victim vulnerable to new kinds of stresses. It may lead to accusations that the individual who cannot remember is lying or malingering, for example. Such accusations contribute to the destruction of the victim's self-esteem and are sometimes used as a pretext for abuse administered in the guise of punishment for lying. This is particularly destructive to children whose reality testing may be otherwise intact but who, having been previously dismissed as liars, have no way of proving their credibility even when memory is intact.

Memory plays an important role in what is usually termed "reality testing." Memory for traumatic events can be extremely veridical (Fair, 1988; Terr, 1990), but if the events are unusual or outside the range of ordinary experience, veridical memories may themselves evoke feelings of unreality. And, since humans rely heavily on the perceptions, memories, and beliefs of those around them to support their own reality testing, denial on the part of other people constitutes a withdrawal of social support that can have profound consequences on one's beliefs and self-esteem.

In contrast to amnesias, some traumatic memories are indelibly imprinted on awareness. In the wake of trauma, they recur with eidetic clarity in unpredictable and uncontrollable flashbacks (Blank, 1985). When such internal memory images become overwhelming, they may blot out or be mistaken for present external perceptions. This development, too, may interfere with reality testing, particularly if it is compounded by the tendencies of others to dismiss the flashbacks as mere fantasies. Visual flashbacks are most frequently discussed, but Wilcox et al. (1991) report that persistent auditory hallucinations frequently accompany post-traumatic stress disorder. Other hallucinatory experiences, such as vivid smells, are also commonly observed in victims of abuse (Putnam, 1989).

Traditionally, hallucinations were considered a hallmark of psychotic decompensation. The discovery that many may be flashbacks — vivid memories of actual traumatic events — introduces a cautionary note into diagnosis. My own clinical experience indicates that dismissing memories as psychotic fantasies can have a devastating effect on a victim and even lead to actual psychotic decompensation.

All distortions of memory are likely to affect autobiographical memory, the integration of particular events into a coherent, temporally organized, and self-referential pattern, one's personal life story. Autobiographical memory is an important dimension of identity. It is characteristically disturbed in cases of identity fragmentation and the dissociative disorders, most dramatically in multiple personality disorder.

Addiction, Immunity, and Stress Tolerance

One internal protective mechanism associated with trauma responses is the body's production of powerful analgesics, endorphins and enkephalins (Jackson et al., 1979; van der Kolk & Greenberg, 1987). Stress induced analgesia has a tranquilizing effect that moderates pain and allows the organism to conserve resources in situations in which escape is not possible. But, as van der Kolk et al. (1985) have emphasized, endogenous opioids, like the externally administered substances — drugs and alcohol — that people deliberately use to numb themselves, are addictive. Repeated, inescapable shock thus leaves the victim vulnerable not only to substance abuse, but to habit patterns associated with the production of internal analgesics, a vulnerability described as "addiction to trauma" (van der Kolk, 1989; van der Kolk et al., 1985). Some compulsive or ritualistic behavior, including self-abusive behavior, can be understood in the light of traumatically triggered addictive responses.

Addiction to trauma, basically a psychobiological response, has extensive psychological and interpersonal ramifications. It is related to the experience of controllability and contributes to symptomatic patterns of self-injury. It becomes a major source of frustration for therapists and a major contributing factor in revictimization.

In cases of repetitive trauma dating from childhood, addiction to self-injurious behavior has sometimes become an ingrained pattern of self-regulation, complicated by dissociative defenses that isolate pain from awareness. In female victims, it has often been dismissed as a dimension of the masochism that many mental health professionals considered intrinsic to femininity. Like other addictions, it interferes with adaptive coping and tends to cloud the cognitive processes that might enable the victim to extricate herself from abusive contexts.

Addiction to trauma as a facet of normal self-regulatory processes gone haywire is illuminated by the intricate connections among several systems involved in stress responses. Currently, research is mapping a complex regulatory circuit among the endogenous opioid system, the HPA-axis, and the immune system (Borysenko, 1984; Locke et al., 1984; Plotnikoff, 1986). Ader and Cohen (1982) found that immunosuppression can be classically conditioned in rats, and a growing body of research suggests that acquired effects on immune functioning are also a significant aspect of human stress adaptation and vulnerability to physical illness (Vollhardt, 1991).

Psychobiological research is thus confirming the results of earlier correlational studies on the relationship between life stress and disease. In 1967, pioneering research by Holmes and Rahe demonstrated an increased incidence of illness following periods of high life change density; the magnitude of the change, rather than whether it was positive or negative, seemed to constitute a stress that threatened health. Recently, the internal changes responsible for observed correlations between life stress and illness have been more clearly described. Life stresses such as divorce and psychiatric illness, for example, have been found to decrease resistance to cancer and other illnesses through the suppression of natural killer cell activity (Kiecolt-Glaser et al., 1984; Locke et al., 1984) and through negative effects on DNA repair (Kennedy et al., 1990).

Effects on the immune system, like stress effects generally, are critically related to the dimension of controllability. Immune functioning impairment as a result of inescapable stress, for example, has been found to be associated with increased susceptibility to infectious diseases, autoimmune disorders, and cancer (Pelletier & Herzing, 1988; Shavit et al., 1984). Depression, which may be a complex psychological reaction to stress as well as a specific stressor, has also been found to be associated with immune function impairment (Calabrese et al., 1987). Even at the cellular level, the immune system is adversely affected by uncontrollable but not by controllable shock (Laudenslager et al., 1983).

In addition to the long-term health related effects of inescapable shock on the immune system, the central nervous system itself may undergo lasting structural changes, which then impair the individual's ability to cope with even moderate levels of stress. One change particularly relevant to repetitive stressful events is known as kindling (Goddard et al., 1969). Experiments have demonstrated that intermittent stimulation by electrical current or psychostimulant drugs that was initially too weak to produce overt effects can cumulatively produce major motor seizures. Van der Kolk and Greenberg (1987) have suggested that kindling phenomena may lead to lasting neurobiological and behavioral changes in children who are repeatedly abused.

Neurobiological changes may thus permanently alter both sensitivities and patterns of adaptation to trauma. In such instances, the challenge of psychotherapy is not merely to facilitate psychobiological change, but to help the individual adapt to her own vulnerabilities and, insofar as possible, to transform liabilities into assets.

Hypersensitivity, for example, can be used to advantage in some interpersonal and vocational situations and can enhance certain creative and artistic pursuits. To the extent that extreme stress intolerance remains a handicap, it is a problem that can be approached, like other handicaps, with the aim of finding practical coping strategies and maximizing positive strengths and adaptations.

Identity Formation and Personality Integration

The effects of trauma on personality formation and integration vary according to the nature and severity of the trauma, whether it is an isolated event or a repetitive pattern, the developmental processes on which it impacts, the victim's preexisting development, and the responses of others to the trauma.

Even extremely painful or life-threatening experiences, for example, mean something different when they are socially typical and shared or even valued by the general community. Initiation rites in so-called primitive cultures are a case in point (Van Gennep, 1960). So are the commonplace experiences that distinguish the street-smart inhabitant of a large city from the sheltered inhabitant of a middle-class suburb.

There are limits to this generalization, of course. The hazards of a dangerous environment should not be minimized or excused just because many people live in it with no obvious ill effects. Even where there are survivors, casualties are usually high in a war zone. And where negative effects are not immediately obvious, they may eventually become obvious. Too frequently, overlooking detrimental effects is merely a way of avoiding the dilemmas they pose for those who make social policy. Even so, when a danger is commonly shared, those who share it sometimes escape the devastating sense of social isolation that so often magnifies trauma.

The integration of identity is closely allied to the development and experience of autobiographical memory, a sense of personal continuity and consistency over historical time that forms the background for the individual's interactions with others and serves as a reference point for self-reflective activities. Autobiological memory is often distorted by trauma, most dramatically in the case of amnesias. Such distortions have subtle or marked effects on self-presentation and self-representation and on the integration of self-experience into that cohesive pattern we phenomenologically experience as a stable personal identity.

Schacter and his colleagues (1982) hypothesized that episodic memories are organized around personal identity. When an episodic memory system becomes dissociated from personal identity, the usual frame of reference for utilizing it is lost. Temporary amnesias or fugue states can then arise in which both memory and the self-referential system around which episodic memories are organized are altered.

The reorganization of behavior and self-experience that follows trauma may be based in part on the compartmentalization of episodic memories

and the self-referent patterns of thinking that are linked to particular memory sets. Phenomenologically, traumatized individuals sometimes report
memory loss with an intact sense of identity. But, in other instances,
memory persists, sometimes with extreme clarity, as in flashbacks, and
it is the sense of personal identity that is experienced as disturbed or
different.

The psychobiology of trauma underlies this compartmentalization, but
because compartmentalization has a defensive function, it may be cognitively reinforced and elaborated in some individuals. By isolating certain
memories from the general memory system that organizes a particular
identity, the individual can defend herself against the intolerable awareness that "The trauma happened to ME. It HAPPENED. I could not
control it."

In the dissociative disorders that are often a sequel to trauma, the
organization of memories along a time continuum typically reflects several
distortions of normal integrative processes. At any stage of life, victims
generally have difficulty integrating strange or frightening experiences
with their typical experiences and self-referential thinking. Dissociation
can be limited in scope, however, and many dissociative experiences consist of transient, comparatively circumscribed episodes of depersonalization, derealization, or amnesia. Discontinuities in memory systems and
in the experience of personal identity can be so subtle as to be almost
imperceptible; many are recognized only in the context of psychotherapy.

In childhood, however, prior to the consolidation of identity patterns,
dissociation as a sequel to trauma can have pervasive and profound effects
on identity development. A single, circumscribed or phase-specific trauma
may organize a consistent identity configuration that remains unintegrated with subsequent experience, resulting in the loss through dissociation of a chapter of one's life. Or repeated traumas and the particular
episodic memories and mood states with which they are connected may
organize a series of identity fragments that remain unintegrated.

In some instances, abuse is such a familiar and predictable part of daily
life that it becomes an organizing focus in identity consolidation. Being a
victim defines who one is. When this happens, survival itself becomes
paradoxical; to be someone other than a victim threatens the individual
with an identity loss that may precipitate panic.

A related identity configuration is that of the scapegoat, the child in
the family, the school, or the community who becomes a target for the
hostile attacks of other people. The identity of the scapegoat is shaped by
the fantasies and feelings of the victimizer, disowned and often denied,
but projected onto the victim, who is then blamed for abuse directed
against her.

The victim identity or its variant, the scapegoat, can be a stabilizing
and integrative factor in development in spite of the pathological behavior

patterns with which it is often associated. This is one reason some victims, particularly those victimized repetitively from an early age, cling to it. It may provide a strange sort of refuge from feelings of confusion and internal disorganization induced by trauma. The scapegoat knows who she is, however painful that identity may be. Her world is a predictable place. She is needed and wanted and can hope to receive at least some degree of care because her role is necessary to the psychological equilibrium of the victimizer.

In other cases of repetitive abuse in childhood, however, basic processes of self-regulation and self-definition are disrupted. As a result, a unified identity may never be consolidated at all. Rather than a unified whole, the individual becomes a mosaic of identity fragments. In some cases, for example, one part of the individual retains and may be continually aware of a vivid memory of abusive experiences, while another part or parts have total amnesia for it. These distinct parts of the self and the memories they hold are disconnected from one another, leading to characteristic discontinuities in self-representation. Dissociation thus comes to characterize whole identity configurations as well as isolated memories.

The splitting or fragmentation of identity is most dramatic in cases of multiple personality disorder (MPD). In MPD, distinct alter personalities are often organized around distinct traumatic memories — some alter personalities remember what others do not. Even personalities who remember the same traumas may have experienced and interpreted them differently.

In MPD, what begins as an automatic reaction to trauma — an unusual state of consciousness encoded as "not me" — seems to be elaborated into a more complex defense, the construction of an alter personality. In this process, the individual also often learns to control, to some extent, the switching process. Some multiples have insight into the development of this defense. One of my own clients explained, for example, that her alter personalities took turns experiencing lengthy episodes of ritual abuse. Each had to bear the torture for a while, but no one had to endure it for very long.

The inability to lose consciousness during extreme states of arousal seems to play a role in this process: However horrible, the abuse cannot be escaped by simply fainting away. *Someone* is continuously aware. Yet the victim can still deny that the *someone* is *me*. And, since the experience is so extraordinary, it is easier to believe that it cannot be happening to *me*. It is a short step to the idea that it must be happening to someone else. In cases of MPD, the someone else is sometimes given a distinct name and a set of characteristic attributes; it becomes an alter personality.

In multiple personality disorder, the effects of trauma on the intricate orchestrations of personality structure can be complicated by variable patterns of psychobiological processes in distinct alter personalities (Braun,

1983a & b; Brende, 1984; Putnam, 1984). Different alter personalities may show different allergic reactions, different responses to anesthesia and drugs, and different forms of addictive behavior. EEG patterns have also been observed to vary from one personality to another. These effects can greatly complicate treatment, particularly the use of medication or of anesthesia during invasive procedures.

Because MPD is such a dramatic disorder, it has received considerable media attention in recent years, much of which has been sensationalized. This attention has sometimes obscured the spectrum of dissociative disorders, which includes milder as well as more severe symptomatology. It has also contributed to controversies about how dissociation is related to other developmental disorders.

Serious disorders such as MPD are hypothesized to arise as a result of severe child abuse that interferes with the integration of a cohesive identity in childhood (Kluft, 1985; Putnam, 1989). But extreme trauma can destabilize or fragment an identity at *any* stage of integration. In addition to childhood, when basic patterns of personality organization are laid down, adolescence and early adulthood are especially important periods of identity consolidation (Erikson, 1980). The adolescent or young adult is also particularly vulnerable to certain kinds of sexual trauma, such as rape. Although later disruption of identity patterns may not have the lasting and debilitating effects of MPD, they can nevertheless have a profound and pervasive impact. They are often masked, however, by seemingly mature adaptations.

Fantasy

The complex memory disturbances that are sometimes a sequel to trauma have contributed to controversies over whether patients' reports of abuse can be believed or not (Ferenczi, 1932; Masson, 1984). Although there is no evidence that endogenous fantasy produces the characteristic biological and psychological patterns associated with inescapable shock, a body of literature dating from the early work of Maier (1949) indicates that there are certain reliably observable negative effects of actual trauma and that these are not confined to humans with their complex capacities for fantasy. It is scarcely surprising that trauma responses have such a long evolutionary history. It would be difficult for any species to survive without a built-in system for discriminating and remembering the difference between real and illusory dangers.

Actual trauma does affect fantasy, however. Effects of trauma on fantasy life vary according to the kind of trauma, whether it occurred as an isolated episode or a repetitive one, and, particularly, the developmental stage in which the individual experienced it.

Ironically, although real trauma does shape fantasy, one common post-traumatic symptom is an impoverishment of fantasy life (van der Kolk, 1987). Following shock, reflexive responses to trauma, mediated by subcortical mechanisms, sometimes seem to short-circuit the symbolic elaborations of higher cortical structures. For long periods afterward, nightmares as well as waking flashbacks may simply reproduce the trauma, a repetition that is itself traumatic. When this occurs, the victim is deprived of the adaptive uses of imagination, a deprivation that can leave her trapped in painful literalities.

Eventually, fantasy usually modifies such literal responses. Nightmares in which terrifying experiences are symbolically elaborated replace or occur along with repetitive flashbacks. Often, the individual begins to imagine herself actively coping with the traumatic event or devises strategies to strengthen her control and prevent a recurrence. Such forms of imaginative coping, actively guided, can play an important role in the psychotherapy of trauma (Dolan, 1991; Gil, 1991; Hannah, 1981).

Terr (1990) has reviewed the impact of trauma on childhood fantasy. For psychobiological and developmental reasons, visual experience is often an especially vivid feature of the recollections and fantasies associated with childhood trauma. Traumatized children, like adults, experience flashbacks and nightmares. In children, the eventual symbolic elaboration of trauma tends to mingle traumatic imagery with the fantasy formations characteristic of particular developmental phases.

Many post-traumatic fantasies can be described as "compensatory." Fantasies of rescue and revenge seem to be especially common. In children, fantasy tends to impel actions; post-traumatic fantasies are likely to be expressed enactively rather than verbally. In some instances, the fantasies elaborated following trauma remain compulsively focused on the trauma itself. Repetitive reenactments are a common expression of such fantasies. Frequently, a victim plays out the role of both victim and aggressor, using whatever toys or materials are at hand. Some enactments involve repetitive self-injuries that seem to be related to addiction to trauma.

In both children and adults, enactive therapeutic techniques can make use of the action tendencies as well as the vivid nonverbal imagery characteristic of traumatized individuals. They help victims to abreact feelings, master overwhelming events, and map alternative strategies for coping.

Some trauma-precipitated fantasies are constructed to conceal the experience of terrifying amnesias, to replace missing memories, or to screen intolerable memories. Fantastic "tall tales" can become a compulsive response to the awareness that one has forgotten, especially if one is punished for forgetting. The teller of tall tales, of course, is sometimes punished for lying. In the lives of abused children, trauma is continually multiplied.

As Putnam (1989) observes, it is not always possible for a therapist to distinguish between enacted memories and fantasy material, but the effort is nevertheless important. Even when memory is modified by fantasy, many biological as well as psychological symptoms often bear witness to the actualities of traumatic events. Pain in a body part may reference a memory of an actual injury dissociated from conscious awareness. In therapy, the complex relation between fantasy and memory can only be adequately explored when such realities are acknowledged.

Some therapists claim that psychological reality is all that matters anyway. But while this assumption highlights the fact that experience is always interpreted and processed, it easily becomes a facile excuse for denying or glossing over the effects of real abuse. From a therapeutic standpoint, helping a victim to confront terrible and, at the time, uncontrollable realities as well as to distinguish between fantasy and reality is a necessary step in strengthening the capacity to exercise real adaptive control.

Sometimes the most important contribution of medication to the treatment of post-traumatic symptoms is the calming of psychobiological reactions that interfere with fantasy formation and the other forms of symbolic thinking so vital to human adaptation. Conversely, medication that interferes with fantasy life may impede recovery. When creative fantasy life has been impoverished following trauma, the renewed ability to construct fantasies is an adaptation that sometimes points to recovery.

POST-TRAUMATIC STRESS DISORDER

Experimental studies of the effects of inescapable shock, even those done on animal subjects, have provided very useful insights into human health and pathology. But clinical concepts of stress-related illness and trauma effects have typically derived from other sources, the pragmatic requirements of diagnosing and treating human beings in health care settings.

Traditionally, even when clinicians looked for biological causes of psychological problems, there was little contact between the clinic and the laboratory. Historically, changing fashions in psychiatry emphasized either the biological or the psychosocial origins of mental illness. It was only in the 20th century that systems approaches to mind-body interactions made their appearance.

Clinical approaches to the psychopathology of stress reactions have historically been shaped by social emergencies. The stresses of war, for example, have provided some of the most dramatic examples of what happens when human beings are pushed beyond their adaptive limits.

In 1941, Kardiner described a trauma response syndrome which he labeled physioneurosis. This syndrome, as typically observed in soldiers, was commonly dubbed shell shock, battle fatigue, or war neurosis (for a review, see Trimble, 1985). Symptoms included increased vigilance for signs of external threat and persistent startle responses. The traumatic experience remained a focal point of attention for affected individuals; vivid recollections of it continued to intrude into daily life and dreams long after danger had passed. Increased hyperactivity was sometimes accompanied by explosive outbursts of aggression. In contrast to these symptoms of increased irritability, patients sometimes showed signs of constriction, social withdrawal, and estrangement or alienation. Kardiner's description was later incorporated into criteria for a new diagnostic category, post-traumatic stress disorder (PTSD) and incorporated into *DSM-III-R* (APA, 1987).

Post-traumatic stress disorder illustrates what happens when stress responses, which may have been originally adaptive, persist in nonthreatening contexts. Given the diagnostic criteria for this disorder, it is easily conceptualized as fundamentally psychosomatic in nature.

Underlying the observed symptoms presented as criteria for the PTSD diagnosis is an evident psychobiological pattern: Biological systems regulating arousal, such as the reticular activating system and the autonomic system, seem to have become deregulated. The wear and tear of autonomic hypersensitivity takes its toll in physical symptoms and a general depletion of energy for coping with everyday stressors. The psychological consequences may affect social interaction in ways that precipitate new stresses and isolate the individual from social support systems.

According to *DSM-III-R* diagnostic guidelines, the distinguishing feature of PTSD "is the development of characteristic symptoms following a psychologically distressing event that is outside the range of usual human experience . . . " (p. 247). Symptoms involve both those associated with the arousal phase of the trauma reaction and those characteristic of the numbing, or constriction phase. The traumatic event is reexperienced as a distressing intrusion into waking life or sleep. The disorder is also accompanied by persistent signs of increased physiological arousal, which are often intensified by exposure to stimuli that were associated with or symbolize the trauma. There is typically a persistent avoidance of associated stimuli or a numbing of general responsiveness.

DSM-III-R criteria specify that the diagnosis is not to be made unless multiple symptoms of both arousal and avoidance are observable and unless symptoms last for at least a month. Although symptoms usually appear immediately or soon after the trauma, onset of symptoms may be delayed for months or even years; delay should be specified in the diagnosis. Children suffering from PTSD often show a range of physical symptoms, such as headaches or stomachaches, in addition to other characteristic symptoms of increased arousal. Symptoms in any victim may be mild or severe, may interfere with many aspects of life, and may be complicated by self-injurious behavior or substance abuse.

During the 1980s, considerable research began accumulating on PTSD as observed in veterans of the Vietnam war (Kulka et al., 1990; Laufer et al., 1985). During the same period, clinicians working with female victims of rape and battering began to develop paradigms for understanding and treating women, and there was a revival of interest in the dissociative disorders. The most severe dissociative disorders can usually be traced to extreme abuse in childhood, and clinicians began to conceptualize the relationship between these disorders and PTSD (Coons et al., 1990; Ross, 1989).

In many respects, PTSD is a useful and welcome addition to the diagnostic schemas that usually guide clinical treatment. Unfortunately, some biologically-minded clinicians still search for the causes of all psychopathology in genes and endogenous toxins. Perhaps the prospect of altering genes seems more hopeful than the prospect of altering the developmental and social contexts that perpetuate abuse. At any rate, the study of trauma has somewhat counteracted this one-sided view of biology. The recognition of PTSD as a category of pathology has facilitated the move from either/or models of illness to interactive models and has provided a model for integrating biological with psychosocial data.

In focusing attention on the somatic as well as the psychological sequelae of trauma, the *DSM-III-R* description of post-traumatic stress disorder has also enabled clinicians to integrate their observations and interventions with a burgeoning research literature. In spite of continued controversies, physical reality is finally a respectable psychological concept, no longer eclipsed by philosophical debates or psychoanalytic evasions.

Yet, for all the utility of the concept of post-traumatic stress disorder, it remains in some respects limited as a framework for understanding the psychological aftermath of trauma. Like diagnostic categories generally, it aims for a specificity of definition that may exclude many of the more subtle yet significant effects of trauma. And for all the emphasis on objective events, *DSM-III-R* presents criteria that call for sometimes questionable clinical judgments.

The criterion that a precipitating trauma should be outside the range of usual human experience is a case in point: It necessitates judgments that are not based on clear empirical criteria and may be highly idiosyncratic, depending on the beliefs and experiences of (usually) middle-class clinicians. What constitutes ordinary experience varies drastically, according to whether one lives in a quiet suburb, a crack neighborhood, or a war zone.

This consideration is especially pertinent to the diagnosis of females. For many years, incest was considered a rare occurrence and rape was dismissed as a not necessarily traumatic event. Yet the increasing incidence of reported female abuse suggests that neither incest nor rape is as far outside the bounds of ordinary experience as many would like to think. And the effects of rape or incest on victims do not really depend on the statistical incidence of such abuse. The diagnostic requirement that the precipitating event in PTSD be unusual is also not always consistent with placing diagnosis on a clearer psychobiological ground. The fact that a traumatic event is commonplace does not necessarily preclude the long-standing autonomic effects which contribute to the kinds of pathology described as typical of PTSD.

The relevance of trauma to psychopathology obviously extends far beyond the developments specifically associated with post-traumatic stress disorder. Recognizing the limitations of the PTSD model, Finkelhor (1988) has presented an alternative model for understanding the effects of child sexual abuse. In addition to the kinds of issues emphasized by the PTSD model, he discusses the dynamics of betrayal, traumatic sexualization, stigmatization, and powerlessness that characterize victims.

Finkelhor's point is well taken. As helpful as it may be for therapists treating female victims, the availability and specificity of the PTSD diagnosis should not deter us from considering the whole range of psychological problems that derive from trauma in general and from female victimization in particular.

These considerations are relevant to more general ones raised by feminists concerning the utility of diagnostic categories as they are applied to women. Historically, the medicalization of women's problems has tended to reinforce sexist stereotypes and to subordinate women to the control of mostly male physicians and male institutions. Diagnosis has often been a pretext for treatment modalities that perpetuated the sexist status quo and increased women's vulnerability to future victimization. Even under the best of circumstances, psychiatric diagnosis has seldom dictated treatment approaches that empowered women to take control of their own lives.

Nevertheless, diagnostic categories continue to be an important source of statistical information about how women are actually being perceived and treated. And, as the psychobiological parameters of categories like PTSD are refined, they may encourage a needed focus on the effect of stress and trauma on women's physical as well as mental health. Whatever the limitations of the PTSD model, as a framework for examining the effects of female victimization, it is a positive step forward from the almost reflexive diagnosis of hysteria and depressive neurosis that formerly characterized psychiatric approaches to women.

CHAPTER 2
Female Dilemmas

U NANTICIPATED SHOCKS like rape overwhelm mind and body. Physiological reactions, including massive stress responses, can distort perception and memory as well as the sense of personal identity. Recovery involves an attempt to return to conditions as they were prior to shock. Often, victims deliberately try to forget about the trauma and avoid any cues that might call it to mind.

Some of the most traumatic and, for females, most typical inescapable stresses, however, do not involve unexpected shocks but repeated and expectable injuries. When trauma is part of the fabric of daily life rather than an isolated event, forgetting would mean losing access to a great deal of one's history. Some victims do just that—a whole childhood may be missing from their adult account of themselves. But in day-to-day coping, such extreme memory distortions are usually rarer than numbing, behavioral constriction, and blocking of affect.

In such cases, the victim does not deny or forget what is constantly happening. She merely seems not to respond to it. She is, in fact, responding in a pattern that resembles the numbing phase of PTSD. If repetitive abuse persists, emotional and behavioral constriction can become a way of life, an individual's typical response pattern. If it begins and persists in childhood, this pattern can eventually be so strongly built into character structure that subsequent favorable, nonabusive conditions do not modify it.

Such a characterological pattern perpetuates a vicious circle. Exercising the control still available to her, the victim learns to avoid new experiences that might tax her already stressed coping capabilities. But in doing so she isolates herself from the kinds of new learning that might help extricate her from an abusive context. As the effects of ongoing stress continue to accumulate, somatic symptoms rather than cognitive awareness may be her only clue that something is very wrong.

RESTRICTION OF CHOICE
AS A STRESSOR

In many instances, the traumatic context around which a victim organizes her life is not a specific or even a repeated shock, but an insoluble
dilemma. In contrast to the victim of shock, who clearly has no choice, the
victim confronted with a dilemma often has the illusion of choice. Stress
arises from the denied but eventually inescapable awareness that there is
really no way to avoid a negative consequence.

Learning to live with such dilemmas lays a foundation for coping that
can have a decisive impact on subsequent trauma reactions. When negative expectations have come to be an inevitable part of existence, specific
traumatic events merely confirm long-standing beliefs about personal powerlessness. But hopeless giving-up is only one trauma response in the human repertory. Unlike defeated rats and mice, human beings tend to assimilate their defeats to complex ideas about themselves, their abilities,
and their self-worth. Just as human beings evidently need to believe in
free will (Gazzaniga, 1985), they also seem to have difficulty in accepting a
Hobson's choice, one in which their own ability to select a positive alternative is foreclosed.

For females, experiences of choice and efficacy are often gender-
related. The prevalence of victimization itself constricts the range of
choices available to girls and women. Yet other female choices, which
might profoundly affect coping with victimization, are also limited not
only by individual capability, but by law and custom. The occupational
training and economic resources available to women, the availability of
child care, the quality of medical care, including mental health care, can
make a crucial difference in how a woman copes with specific abuse.

Restriction of choice itself often constitutes an inescapable stress for
women (Waites, 1977–78). The loss of illusions, including illusions about
choice, can be one of the saddest casualties of victimization. Recovering
from the shock of this confrontation, the victim realizes that she never
really had the kind of choices she believed she had.

In trying to recover from trauma and plan for a safer future, many
victims for the first time encounter the complexly intertwined dilemmas
of coping in a sexist society. The decision to move to a safer neighborhood,
for example, may require a better paying job, which is unavailable. The
decision to leave a battering spouse may mean a descent into poverty.
Confronting incest involves confronting the terrible truism that no one
chooses her parents, but that, nevertheless, society grants them continuing
power over children's lives and status outside as well as inside the family.

The advantages of continuing to look for a way out, even in the face of
great difficulties, are obvious. Those who persist are more likely to find a
way out, even if the adaptive solution is rare or risky. And women do

persist. Even those perceived as stereotypically passive often search for years for a positive solution. Their active search is often overlooked because, by the time they finally come to the attention of health professionals, their demeanor reflects the giving-up that follows a painful series of defeats.

Seligman's (1991) research on optimism suggests that a hopeful outlook is favorable to survival. Clinicians are usually well aware of the advantages of positive rather than negative expectations. Denial that does not interfere with coping has its advantages. But in women, denial has been traditionally denigrated as a hysterical response, a contributing factor in victimization. "La belle indifference," an attitude reflecting extreme denial, was considered a classical symptom of female hysteria.

It is also clear that compulsive denial of a dangerous situation can be very dangerous. Focusing on one's own control over the uncontrollable, too, is often accompanied by responses that compound negative effects. Among these are the sense of guilt and lowering of self-esteem that arise when persistence proves futile. Females, in particular, are vulnerable to self-blame even for situations over which they have minimal control. Self-blame involves the internalization of victim-blaming tendencies that are widespread in the culture (Ryan, 1976).

A major source of self-blame in women is socialization that insists that females bring mistreatment or pain on themselves, that they are by nature masochistic, irrational, or self-defeating (Caplan, 1985; Waites, 1977–78). Self-accusations are frequently an echo of explicit accusations by others: "This terrible thing did not really have to happen to you. It's all your fault."

Self-blame deflects the victim's attention from the external causes of her problem and encourages her to change her own behavior. But if she discovers that, no matter what she does, abuse continues, the self-blaming woman has nothing left to blame but some basic weakness or "badness" in herself—a conclusion that further erodes her self-esteem and increases her sense of helplessness.

Being human, however, many female victims do not simply give up when a terrible reality seems inescapable. There are several available modes of psychological escape. Reality may be denied. It may be replaced by fantasy. Or it may be dissociated.

The individual obviously out of touch with reality is likely to be labeled psychotic. But forms of denial that are socially acceptable are not necessarily labeled crazy. If some aspects of reality are denied, but many are pragmatically accepted, a woman may appear to others quite normal. If she keeps a clean house, takes care of her children, and speaks politely to her neighbors, for example, the fact that she was sexually abused as a child, is currently being beaten and raped by a spouse, and spends much of her life in a stuporous fog may pass unnoticed.

Whether such a woman passes for "normal" or not, however, abuse blights her existence. Adaptive decision making requires an ability to evaluate and cope with reality that is not clouded by either the residual effects of trauma reactions or socialized inhibitions and self-blaming. Whether a traumatic event is singular and never repeated or whether abuse is part of the pattern of daily existence, female victimization takes its toll not only in the physical and mental suffering of individuals, but in the quality of life of families and communities.

DOUBLE BINDS

Among the dilemmas that contribute to inescapable stress in the lives of women are a special class that can be characterized as double binds (Bateson, Jackson, et al., 1956). The double bind is a "damned if you do, damned if you don't" situation that often has an added twist—denial that the dilemma exists. Difficulties in coping with a double bind include not only the inescapability of negative consequences but mystifying behavior on the part of others that fosters an illusion of social support while actually perpetuating the conditions that make trauma inescapable.

Following the original analysis by Bateson and his colleagues, the double bind concept was used to explain the origins of schizophrenia (Lidz, 1973; Lidz & Fleck, 1985). Clinicians focused on the conflicting demands of parents and the child's inability to please one parent without being rejected by the other. They also emphasized communicational inconsistencies in parents, particularly inconsistencies between verbal and nonverbal messages.

Currently, although it is doubted that double binds cause schizophrenia, the significance of such binds in the origin of dissociative disorders is widely acknowledged (Beahrs, 1982; Spiegel, 1986). This shift in diagnostic focus should be considered in the light of the fact that, until quite recently, severe dissociative disorders were often diagnosed as schizophrenia (Bliss & Jeppsen, 1985; Putnam, 1989; Putnam et al., 1986).

Double Binds and Dissociation

One common response to double bind conflicts is dissociation. Dissociation is a psychological response with psychobiological underpinnings (Braun, 1983a & b; Ludwig, 1983; Sabourin et al., 1990). Ordinarily, inconsistent or contradictory messages arouse anxiety, particularly if decision making is crucial to survival. Dissociation enables one to moderate such anxiety and to deal with maddening contradictions by altering one's perception of them. The victim of a double bind can then substitute trance logic (Orne, 1959) for normal logic, process mutually incompatible messages as both true, and react simultaneously or sequentially without experiencing the anxiety that would ordinarily arise from a perception of inconsistency.

In a survey of victims of violence, Blackman (1989) found an extreme tolerance for inconsistency to be a prevalent characteristic of abused women. Dissociation may well play an important role in such tolerance. Lacking effective controls over chaotic circumstances or a means of escape, many abused women nevertheless manage to avoid going crazy, though this avoidance is itself risky.

As a coping mechanism, dissociation makes overwhelming and seemingly inescapable stresses escapable, allowing a victim to remain sane by eliminating the anxiety that could, if unchecked, result in a breakdown. It is thus one adaptive alternative to psychosis. But, when used extensively and indiscriminately, the coping mechanism itself leads to pathological outcomes. Because dissociation as a form of problem solving takes place in an altered state of consciousness, it is often separated from normal consciousness by an amnestic barrier. The dissociated individual thus remains unaware of, as well as untroubled by inconsistencies, even though an external observer might be amazed by them. If the inconsistencies are extreme enough, this coping mechanism may prove almost as maladaptive as a psychosis.

Because dissociation is so commonly elicited by double bind messages, deliberately suggested double binds are a convenient technique for inducing hypnotic trance. In a therapeutic setting, a client's habitual and sometimes dysfunctional way of coping with stress can thus be turned to advantage. By bringing an automatic defensive behavior pattern under conscious control, the therapist can maximize the adaptive uses of the dissociative process (Dolan, 1991; Rossi, 1986; Rossi & Cheek, 1988). These include not only the moderation of debilitating levels of anxiety, but the control of pain.

A less benign use of the relation between double binds and dissociation is illustrated by the manipulation of double binding imperatives in brainwashing techniques (Ochberg, 1980, 1988). By carefully blending double binding messages—minimal caretaking and occasional pleasures with torture, for example—captors are able to induce states of idealization and attachment in the captive that resemble pathological forms of infantile bonding. Such bonding has been labeled "the Stockholm Syndrome" after a notable example in which hostages who were taken captive by bank robbers bonded with their captors and saw their rescuers as the enemy. Similarities between such situations and the situations of abused children and battered women are notable. The Stockholm Syndrome has been offered as one explanation for why victims sometimes remain with their assailants even after escape becomes possible (Hilberman, 1980; Symonds, 1976).

Dissociation as a coping mechanism is certainly not confined to females. But the prevalence of double binds and inescapable dilemmas in their lives helps explain the prevalence of dissociative defenses and dissociative disorders in females. Typical styles of coping reflect typical developmental and cultural challenges. Given the contradictory demands and expectations typical of female socialization, dissociation is an expectable female coping technique. And, since the coping techniques and defenses learned in the course of ordinary socialization are often a main line of defense during a crisis, it is scarcely surprising that dissociative disorders are especially prevalent in women. The combination of sexist socialization and female victimization practically guarantees this development.

A recognition of dissociation as a coping technique characteristic of women has been incorporated into common stereotypes. When dissociation is extreme and dramatic, observers may remark on the craziness of "hysterical" women. When it is subtle and momentary, though habitual, it is jokingly denigrated as an aspect of female inconsistency—a woman has the right to change her mind; women are fickle. The truth that seems to lurk in the background of such stereotypes derives from female circumstances rather than female genes.

DILEMMAS IN FEMALE SOCIALIZATION

Several sets of dilemmas and double binds are particularly relevant to the lives of girls and women and impact significantly on the interaction between female socialization in general and specific responses to victimization. Among the most troublesome are:

1. dilemmas of female sexuality
2. scapegoating
3. dilemmas of female expressiveness
4. dilemmas of female dependency
5. role conflict, role diffusion, and role overload

Dilemmas of Female Sexuality

For females, sexuality is a fundamental source of double-binding imperatives. These derive not from the inherent inadequacies so often attributed to females, but from the consequences of stereotyped attributions and the enforced limitations associated with them. From birth, little girls are subjected to incessant but contradictory messages about their sexuality. On the one hand, a female cannot escape the fact that, in the world at large, her gender is often the most salient feature of her person. On the other hand, she cannot escape the unsettling discovery that, as a famous study by Broverman et al. (1970) so strikingly showed, those characteristics considered prototypically feminine by society are the opposite of those considered healthily adult.

Ever since Eve, human anxieties and conflicts concerning sexuality have been blamed on women. Females are constantly subject to the double binds produced not only by their own inner conflicts but by male ambivalence. The result is an inescapable but sometimes maddening mix of social imperatives: Be attractive, but not seductive; be noticeably feminine, but not provocative; be helpful, but not controlling.

The reactions of others to her gender are not nearly as controllable as females want and are taught to believe. Whatever a woman does, or whether she does anything at all, her body arouses reactions just because it is there. The assumption that she *should* be able to control how other people, particularly males, react to her can become a source of continuing anxiety.

Traditionally, for example, girls were taught that it was the female's role not only to limit her own sexual behavior, but to set limits for males. To do less was to run the risk of being labeled promiscuous, although, as Brownmiller (1975) and Dworkin (1981) have emphasized, this risk is hardly escapable anyway. Even after traditional standards were relaxed somewhat in the 1970s, women continued to be held responsible for any undesirable outcomes of sexual behavior, such as unwanted pregnancy.

The idea that females can and should control male responses to their sexuality is a time-honored rationalization for rape and assault (Burt, 1980). It has even been incorporated into psychological, particularly psychoanalytic, treatment approaches that label children as well as adults as "seductive" (see Sink, 1988).

The relation among having a female body, experiencing one's sexuality, and pleasing other people is, thus, inevitably problematic. In order for a female to please, she must please sexually, but whether this imperative requires muting or heightening the sexual cues associated with her body depends on the situation and is, in any case, subject to the moods and judgments of men. Just the right amount and kind of sexuality, like just the right amount and kind of perfume, stimulates positive evaluations by men. But men have varying requirements in this regard, and the same man may vary from one day to the next.

The denial of one's sexuality is no escape; it merely reminds the audience that one is not feminine, an evaluation likely to be associated with negative appraisals. Only men, it seems, can have their sexuality recede into the background of male consciousness and thus experience it as irrelevant to life in the workplace, on the street, or at the club.

The Sexual Body in Female Socialization

Socialization of children reflects the values of adult institutions. For children of both sexes, the body experienced eventually comes into conflict with the body appraised; they must learn to inhibit and control their physical impulses and channel them into socially appropriate habits. But for females, appraisal is more insistently directed toward achieving a pleasing appearance, more selectively focused on looks rather than actions than is the case for males (Banner, 1983; Freedman, 1986; Seid, 1989).

In contrast, even though he is expected to learn to control himself, the male's relation to his body is expected to remain centered on drives, appetites, and active impulses. Lapses of control are frequently tolerated as simple signs of masculinity: Boys will be boys. The well-adjusted male is not expected to spend much of his time gazing in mirrors, lest he be devaluated like Narcissus or have his sexual orientation called into question. When a man's image becomes a focus of interest, as it of course does in American society where image is so insistently associated with status, it is expected to confirm the power and authority of his body. A real man is a substantial entity, not a perfected illusion.

As a girl grows up, however, experience of her body—its desires, feelings, impulses—is often gradually eclipsed by appraisals of her body— evaluations of how it should and does look, interpretations of its drives and motives, whether these are enacted or not, and, sometimes, accusations about the female body as a disturbing factor in the lives of other people (Tevlin & Leiblum, 1983).

Large industries are based on female double binds concerning the body. The selling of the socially acceptable female image is extremely profitable, as is the selling of pornography. As Kilbourne (1990) has graphically reminded us, in fact, the marketing of beauty products is deliberately designed to heighten every female's anxieties about her body while insistently, though covertly, portraying even female children as objects for sexual exploitation.

The social mirror, the self appraised, is thus the source of a typical basic split in female identity. Throughout socialization, female pleasure is systematically linked to the eye of a beholder, so systematically that pleasing others often becomes a prerequisite for feeling good. The development of the female body image typically reflects this split. The experience of sexual pleasure is also profoundly shaped by it.

The importance of pleasing others is simultaneously accompanied by prohibitions against any uses of the female body that might arouse anxiety in others, particularly men. Such prohibitions extend beyond the common restrictions on masturbation to which children of both sexes are subject, to a more specific disapproval of the female who, for any reason, puts her own pleasure first. Even when enjoyment of her own sexuality is permitted or demanded, female sexual pleasure is often linked to the condition of pleasing someone else.

The characteristic split between the physical, appetitive body and the body image tied to social appraisal sometimes results in an experience of the body as alien entity. To the extent that bodily messages are inconsistent with desired appraisals, they often form the core of a negative identity, a bad and ugly self. The body becomes the enemy, and disturbed women treat it as such, punishing or torturing it.

Whatever the social restrictions on it or the intrapsychic splits that delete it from awareness, however, the body as a needy and feeling entity does not disappear. It continues to announce its needs; survival requires it. After puberty, especially, its biological states, changing cyclically, constantly remind the female of her sexual drives and reproductive potential. But, by this time, she has usually learned ways of coping with the dilemmas associated with her gender.

One not uncommon way of coping is through dissociation; it is possible to split off her awareness of internal feelings and needs from her insistent preoccupation with perfecting the external image. This development is most striking in anorexia or bulimia, conditions that have become epidemic in young women (Boskind-White & White, 1983; Bruch, 1973; Garfinkel & Garner, 1982; Orbach, 1978, 1986). In anorexia, hunger may disappear as a consciously perceived experience even though the body is starving. In bulimia, the body is indulged and starved in alternating compulsive rituals, which are frequently characterized by alternating changes in states of consciousness.

Typical forms of sex-role socialization lay the groundwork not only for disorders like anorexia and bulimia, but for other pathological responses to the body. In my own practice, I have observed several young women who became obsessed with plastic surgery. No matter what the outcome of past surgery—negative outcomes were undetectable to me—the clients ruminated endlessly about whether the outcome was good or bad, whether surgery should be repeated, etc.

Sex-role socialization sets the stage for a victim's responses to the deliberate abuse of her body. But, although socialization predisposes women to guilt and shame, such responses are not merely a result of internal dynamics. They arise from and are powerfully intensified by explicit accusations. The assumption that females are somehow responsible for sexuality in general, including male sexual responses, is related to a general psychological dynamic that plays a major role in female victimization—the use of the female as a scapegoat.

Scapegoating

Control of the body is an expected female function that requires eternal vigilance. The body itself, its biological imperatives, constantly threatens to usurp the perfected image. But men, too, control the female body, often compulsively, as the history of physical restraints on the female body across many cultures clearly illustrates. Women have been subjected to footbinding, chastity belts, genital mutilation, veiling, corseting, and cloistering as socially approved forms of control. It is a short step to the variations on tying, chaining, and cutting up which characterize pornographic literature.

The carefully controlled images females devise to protect themselves from victimization can never be a dependably safe haven, since the victim a rapist or batterer attacks is not a real woman, but a product of male fantasy. Fantasy combined with rage leads to a compulsive devaluation of females in general or one female in particular. Violence against women then constitutes a deliberate attack on the ideal image as well as on the body underneath (Waites, 1982). To the enraged or contemptuous assailant, female "badness" cannot be camouflaged: "The slut deserves a beating."

The devaluation of the body that accompanies abuse as well as her body's physical reactions to trauma tend to confirm a woman's belief that her body is the enemy and to intensify her alienation from it. At the same time, such reactions confirm fears of being out of control and arouse feelings of profound guilt and shame.

In his pioneering study of prejudice, Allport (1954) observed that the scapegoating of females "reflects the two basic ingredients of prejudice — denigration and gross overgeneralization" (p. 34). Misogynists treat women as a different species from themselves, an inferior species. Psychodynamic analyses of scapegoating emphasize the role of denial and projection in the process. A positive image of the self is maintained by denying one's negative attributes and attributing them to others. "It is not I who is weak, inferior, or blameworthy," says the scapegoater. "It is that other person so obviously different from me."

Explanations of the scapegoating of females usually cite developmental as well as social factors, particularly the mother's perceived power in the infant's life (Chodorow & Contratto, 1982; Dinnerstein, 1976; Lerner, 1974). From this perspective, the scapegoating of women derives from the child's earliest fantasies about the mother, which remain active in the unconscious of both sexes even after the child matures. Mother, in the infant's mind, has the power to give or withhold, to satisfy or frustrate. If anything goes wrong, it must be her fault (Caplan, 1989). Sexual desires for mother are inevitably conflicted, however; many males who never resolve such conflicts carry them into adult life and continue to blame and punish women for them.

Some infantile fantasies that contribute to female scapegoating derive from disappointment in women because of their perceived powerlessness vis à vis men. The "weaker sex" is, on the average, smaller, disadvantaged in any contest that pits her muscular strength against that of the male.

But, as Freud was the first to emphasize, her actual physical characteristics are only part of the problem. The reality of her physical body is interpreted and evaluated according to the symbolic structures that govern civilization, patriarchal structures that celebrate the male phallus as the ultimate token of power and authority. Once he discovers that the female lacks a penis, the little boy, according to Freud (1933), devalues her. She is perceived as a frightening, castrated creature, an uncanny object whose sexual organs, however stimulating, are always reminders of injury and powerlessness.

Describing the extent to which irrational infantile fantasy is a motivating factor in human behavior was one of Freud's enduring contributions. But no one, including Freud, ever assumed irrational fantasy is an acceptable excuse for victimization and violence. Nor is irrational fantasy a sufficient scientific explanation for violence against females. Whatever the discontents of civilization, all cultures channel the infantile impulses and socialize children into beliefs about reality. Modifying irrational fantasy, alleviating the child's anxieties, and providing a more realistic picture of the world is a major challenge of parenting.

In even the most civilized societies, unfortunately, the developmental antecedents of female scapegoating are not simply a function of irrational infantile fantasy, something kids outgrow like their fears of monsters under the bed. Scapegoating, rather, is frequently a part of the socially defined reality children learn to accept, part of a conscious belief system that is institutionalized. Female scapegoating, like the scapegoating of racial and ethnic minorities, protects male, usually white male, privileges. The power and prerogatives that derive from being born with a penis are not simply an outgrowth of biological imperatives; they are rationalized in philosophy, perpetuated in custom, and codified in law (Bernard, 1981; Fausto-Sterling, 1985; MacKinnon, 1989).

Female subordination and female victimization thus always reflect pervasive social realities. Private motives may lead a man to attack a woman. But socially sanctioned and institutionalized scapegoating can always be used as a rationale for it. Rationalizations are built into law and, from its inception, law has been an institution devised by men as a bulwark of patriarchal privilege (Lerner, 1986).

Because the scapegoating of females is culturally institutionalized, female children internalize scapegoating stereotypes about their own gender and evaluate themselves accordingly, to the continuous detriment of self-esteem. Like racial prejudice, the social denigration of women is transmitted through a host of implicit as well as explicit behaviors. It includes its own language, the language of pejorative epithets as well as a repertory of blatantly persecutory behaviors. As the target of slurs like "slut" and "cunt," the female is blamed for any destructive or dehumanizing act directed against her. Once assaulted, she is often tried in public as well as in court.

It is up to her to prove her innocence, but that is hardly possible, since she is guilty of having a female body, of being, as the medieval church used to say, "an occasion for sin."

The problem of scapegoating is related to the more general issue of stereotyping and the stereotyping of women in particular. But it is in some respects more difficult to eradicate. All stereotypes are irrational, but some are at least theoretically subject to empirical debunking. Scapegoating stereotypes, however, are based on the most emotionally intense and irrational fears and hatreds that plague humans, the cumulative anxieties that haunt adults as well as the primitive anxieties of children. As a result, they are extremely tenacious and difficult to correct. Scientific experiments can be devised to prove that females are not inherently inferior to males in their ability to drive automobiles, balance checkbooks, or function as brain surgeons. But there is no way to disprove the irrational assertion that "All women are bitches" because it is not grounded in any objective or empirically measurable attribute. It is merely the objectification of a cry of rage.

Socialization teaches both sexes to scapegoat women. But it teaches them to do so in different ways. Whatever their personal history, males are encouraged to externalize their aggression as part of their masculine sex-role socialization. When a man feels inferior or doubts his masculinity, an aggressive act is one way of reassuring himself that he is a real man according to accepted cultural standards. On the other hand, females are typically socialized to turn their scapegoating tendencies against themselves. The internalization of stereotypical negative images, including the image of the female scapegoat, lies at the heart of many behaviors clinicians have attributed to "female masochism" (Waites, 1977–78).

Scapegoating in general is a powerful dynamic in family life. Within the family, children of both sexes are readily targeted. Abuse is often directed at a particular child who is closely identified with the abuser and represents unaccepted parental impulses (Green, 1985). The scapegoated child becomes, in effect, an "out group" of one, a "black sheep." Since we learn to see ourselves as others see us, the scapegoated child usually internalizes negative self-appraisals, which play an important role in the development of a victim identity or other patterns Erikson (1980) has described as "negative identity" configurations.

The infantilization of females, the social tendency to scapegoat females, and the secondary status of females in the patriarchal family makes adult women as well as children into family scapegoats. The battered wife is a dramatic example. But ambivalence and the scapegoating it gives rise to are also enacted in more complicated scenarios. A not uncommon dynamic in incestuous families, for example, is the father's use of the wife as a scapegoat and the daughter as an idealized partner. The daughter in such a situation is presented with several double-binding messages. On the one hand, she is very desirable—"better than mother." On the other hand, although little girls are nice, grown-up women are "bitches." Either way—as a child victim of incest, or as an abused adult—she will be in a no-win situation.

Dilemmas of Female Expressiveness

Women are stereotyped as being emotional, in contrast to rational (Broverman et al., 1970). Their supposed emotionality is ambivalently valued and tolerated. Female emotional responses that soothe and please others are usually considered desirably feminine. It is acceptable for women to feel kind, loving, cheerful, sympathetic, and sexually responsive (within prescribed limits) to men. It is less acceptable for them to feel angry, defiant, hateful, aggressively ambitious, or blissfully self-absorbed.

Some research indicates that even in childhood, little boys are more aggressive than little girls (Geen, 1990). Male aggressiveness has been frequently attributed to biological factors (Maccoby & Jacklin, 1974). On the other hand, it is scarcely deniable that females are socialized differently than males with respect to aggression. Geen reports a study by Mulvihill and Tumin (1969) that indicated that a large sample of interviewed subjects agreed that it is normal and expectable for boys to fight.

Such aggressiveness is not acceptable in females. Some feminists have carefully distinguished between assertive and aggressive behavior, but there is evidence that others do not make such a clear distinction; even assertiveness in women arouses disapproval (Muehlenhard, 1983). Across the life span, females seem to be more socially acceptable if they are "sugar and spice and everything nice." As a result, females are likely to experience conflict when asserting themselves. Their own aggressive behavior tends to evoke feelings of guilt and anxiety (Brock & Buss, 1964; Schill & Schneider, 1970).

Such attitudes encourage little girls to experience their own inevitable anger and aggression as "not me" or "bad me." Any situation that tends to evoke an angry response then places the girl in a double bind. As an aspect of adaptive coping, assertive, even aggressive behavior can contribute to problem solving. But if aggression is disowned and denied, it cannot function adaptively. It may lead instead to states of behavioral inhibition and ongoing tension, which eventually take their toll in physical symptoms— headaches, backaches, and other symptoms of a "clenched" body.

Turning aggression against the self is often considered to be an important dynamic in depression. It is also a behavior pattern that is stereotypically feminine (Carmen et al., 1981). A study of psychiatric inpatients by Carmen et al. (1984) suggested that a major factor distinguishing between abused males and abused females was the expression of aggression. Males tended to become overtly aggressive, females overtly passive. Overt passivity, however, was complicated by the tendency of females to direct their aggression against themselves.

Self-mutilation is one of the most troublesome symptoms in abused females and reflects complex distortions in self-expression as well as the factors related to the discharge of aggression. The tension between expressing one's real self and hiding it and the pathological behavior patterns that express that tension is, in fact, likely to be heightened in such clients. Some forms of self-mutilation, for example, are as ritualized and as compulsively displayed as normal forms of female self-adornment. The victim attacks not only her body, but most especially the stereotypically correct female image and thus forces observers to confront something ugly and damaged and out of control. But self-injury, like a negative self-image, may also be compulsively hidden.

In other instances, a woman's ambivalence about expressing herself leads to behavioral inconsistencies, which are themselves interpreted as stereotypically feminine. Sometimes, for example, the experience of anger is not inhibited but dissociated; angry but unacceptable feelings are split off from normal self-awareness and discharged in periodic outbursts of frustration and rage—hysterical "fits." Such forms of dissociated anger in women encourage others to dismiss the legitimacy of their anger and to label them as irrational, "bitchy," the hapless victims of raging hormones. Unfortunately, an overt expression of female anger, even if dissociated, can put a woman at risk for retaliation. When that happens, she may then be blamed for provoking the violence of others.

When aggression breaks into awareness but remains unacceptable and inhibited, it contributes to low self-esteem and depression. It is also often accompanied by self-destructive behavior. Paradoxically, however, since turning aggression against the self is a stereotypically female coping mechanism, it can play a part in attempts to rescue self-esteem through martyrdom. Martyrdom is an expressive style that insistently displays a victim identity, sometimes in an attempt to discharge aggression against other people by inducing guilt in them. It is one of the few expressive styles available to the powerless and, as such, may be deliberately employed as a political tactic. But as a female style, it tends to perpetuate powerlessness and all the disadvantages of having a victim identity, including low self-esteem and revictimization. The martyr can never be sure that her abuser will experience guilt or, even if he does, that he will respond to his guilt in ways that benefit the victim.

Because of the way many women internalize and cope with these dilemmas of expressiveness, they are inherently at risk for certain inescapable stresses and inherently handicapped in recovering from the traumas they experience. Even after an inhibited woman begins to get in touch with and sanction her own negative feelings, she may continue to have difficulty integrating these feelings with effective actions. Lacking a history of learning to do so, she is faced with acquiring a new repertoire of effective coping mechanisms. At the same time, she is likely to continue to be confronted with social appraisals that devalue her aggression, even when it is adaptively expressed.

Social expectations about female expressiveness contribute to another problem for the victimized woman. Most females learn early that a pleasing expression is part of the pleasing appearance essential for approval. As a result, women do not simply inhibit negative affects like anger, they frequently display positive affects that belie actual states of anger, depression, or apathy. Statements about personal discomfort or anguish, accompanied by a disarming smile or a nervous laugh, are self-protective but self-defeating. They encourage others not to be threatened by female anger—"I'm really a nice girl, not a complaining bitch!"—and not to retaliate punitively. But they simultaneously announce that the woman's discomfort is not real, not to be taken seriously. Like the female victim's "No!" her statement that she is suffering can then be ignored or discounted.

Dilemmas of female expressiveness make for special pitfalls in psychotherapy. According to Lerner (1982), cultural pressures to please men and appear attractive to a therapist can function as a major barrier to self-definition for female clients. Women may also subordinate their own needs to their attempts to protect a therapist or bolster his ego (Lerner, 1983). The double bind females confront in therapy is not simply an imagined one. To the extent that the reality of a client's experience contradicts accepted sex-role stereotypes, it may be devalued by the therapist. A woman's expressions of anger may be labeled as part of the problem rather than part of the solution. Subordinating her needs to the needs of a spouse or children may be encouraged as a goal of therapy reflecting normative feminine adjustment.

The presentation of an attractive feminine image may hide a client's underlying problems or compound them. It may deflect attention from issues related to sexism and victimization and elicit an analysis of the client's "seductiveness," which ignores the double binds associated with female sexuality. Compliance and an attractive self-presentation may be taken as standards of female mental health, signs that the client is really working in treatment and is progressing. Messages that contradict the attractive image, such as overt signs of continued psychological distress or somatic symptoms that persistently defy medical intervention, may be screened out of awareness by both therapist and client.

The therapeutic problems that arise from female socialization to please others are especially compounded in victims of abuse. Child abuse, as Rush (1980) has pointed out, is the "best kept secret," and silence is a typical victim response to sexual assault and battering. Hilberman (1980), in an overview of spouse abuse, notes that many battered women have had numerous contacts with clinicians but have never mentioned the pattern of violence in their homes. Failure to acknowledge the problem is not simply a matter of denial. In the context of self-blame and victim blaming so endemic to female socialization, being a victim tends to evoke shame and guilt. It confronts the victim with an image of herself quite contrary to the attractive image she has been taught to maintain. And, for many victims, such an admission realistically arouses fears that an assailant or even other family members may retaliate against her.

These considerations have important implications for the therapist-client relationship. When victimization has been the norm rather than the exception in a woman's life, her expectation of continued victimization by the therapist is to some extent rational. This problem may arise especially when the therapist is male and the client female, since that dyad is likely to evoke all the patterns of dominance and submission associated with customary power relationships between the sexes. But, particularly for clients with a history of abuse, the relationship to other females has also usually been compromised. The mother who failed to protect, the female teacher who preferred male students, the female friend or neighbor who pointed an accusing finger rather than offering assistance are familiar figures in the lives of victims and color expectations about therapists of either sex.

As the therapeutic process unfolds, attempts by a client to prevent revictimization by hiding abuse behind a pleasing facade are merely an extension of coping patterns that, however pathological, have been necessary for survival. Effective therapy must acknowledge female dilemmas and the positive as well as the maladaptive dimensions of such survival strategies. In work with victims, trust cannot be a prerequisite to treatment. It is, rather, a hard-won achievement.

Dilemmas of Female Dependency

Dependency is a familiar explanatory construct in traditional discussions of female psychology. Particularly in psychoanalytic perspectives, it has long been viewed as one of the ways in which anatomy is destiny. But as Lerner (1983) has emphasized, there is now a body of research that indicates that girls are systematically socialized in forms of dependency that often have pathological dimensions. From a realistic standpoint, dependency reflects the actualities of the choices available to women as well as the constraints of sex-role socialization. It functions adaptively as well as defensively in relations between the sexes. A major function of female dependency, for example, is to protect men and bolster their self-esteem; in this respect, it may enhance female attractiveness. Female dependency can be burdensome to males, but however ambivalently they value it, it is strong testimony to male power and prestige.

Female dependency is grounded in and perpetuated as much by socioeconomic realities as by psychological ones. The continuing discrepancy between the earning power of males and females, the feminization of poverty, and the statistics reflecting the impoverishment of women and children following divorce (Arendell, 1986) point to inescapable economic contingencies in female life. The constraints on choice are both obvious and depressing for many women. A choice that means misery is hardly a choice at all (Waites, 1977–78).

Psychological dependency is seldom completely separable from economic dependency. Even when she overcomes her intrapsychic resistances, a woman's decision to leave an abusive context is often shaped by a powerful double bind. To leave the incestuous father who rapes her, the husband who beats her, or the boss who harasses her will mean the loss of economic support. This is seldom a simple matter of living frugally without luxuries; often it means a real descent into poverty. Thus, even if she leaves an assailant, the victim will not be free. Poverty increases the likelihood of victimization and revictimization, not only for the woman herself but for her children if she has any. Life without safe shelter, adequate food, and needed medical care is a continual struggle with inescapable stress.

The psychological dimensions of female dependency are complicated not only by socialization to adapt to patriarchal institutional structures, including economic structures, but by the female's role as caretaker. She is doubly dependent because others are depending on her. Nor is this dependence simply psychological. In recent years, the entry of women into the work force and the decrease in numbers of full-time homemakers has highlighted the economic as well as the social contributions of mothers to family life. Following divorce, many women become the sole source of economic support for their families, a factor in their impoverishment and downward social mobility. The lack of needed child care facilities attests to the fact that society feels that children should remain primarily dependent on mothers; whatever a mother's psychological and economic status, she is expected to care for them.

But although economic dependency is often the bedrock of female existence, the psychological aspects of female dependency that continue to be reinforced by sex-role socialization are perhaps a more insidious problem. While a little girl is growing up, her economic dependence and her special vulnerability because someday children will be dependent on her may be obliquely acknowledged, but the focus is more typically on status issues. She can scarcely escape the recognition that her own social status as well as her material comfort will depend on the status of a male partner. Her developing self-esteem reflects this contingency; whatever her actual achievements, attachment to a man may remain vital to her sense of self. Even the rare female who escapes economic dependency can scarcely elude this psychological bind: She will be valued not primarily for who she is and what she does, but for the male who chooses her.

Dependency is sometimes associated with passivity. In relations between the sexes, however, this apparent association is somewhat deceptive. It is the male who chooses, yet the female need not wait passively. On the contrary, she is expected to influence his decision by devoting ceaseless attention to being a desirable partner. The trick is to act without appearing aggressive, to manipulate while appearing passive, or, if he likes active women, to mold one's activities to his tastes. Women's magazines, romance novels, and the vagaries of gossip constantly school females in these manipulations. Female dependence and patriarchal society require them. Yet men are often angered by them, particularly if they fear women and see female manipulation as robbing them of their power.

The need to influence men through covert forms of manipulation, then, is one double-binding consequence of female dependency. Through the ages, it has been widely recognized that the really passive woman is in danger of being left out of the competition for male attention. When Jane Austen writes about female responses to this danger, we find it amusing. In modern life, however, we are sobered by the dilemmas confronting the woman who actively competes for male attention, either overtly or covertly. When a man responds to her by being sexually aroused but controlled and respectful, she is admired as an artful creature. When a man responds to her by being sexually aroused but out of control and contemptuous, she is vilified as being a female vampire, deserving of harassment, rape, or any other abuse she receives.

Her situation is complicated if a woman seems to be competing not *for* a man but *with* a man. At this point, she becomes a threat not only to male self-control but to male power and economic superiority. Citing Horner's (1968, 1972) studies of fear of success in women, McGoldrick (1989, p. 208) aptly observes that "The pressure on women not to take full advantage of independent living may be intense." Yet, the world is so constructed that the only escape from female dependence is through competition and the kinds of economic rewards that guarantee real independence.

Some theorists, such as Miller (1978), have argued cogently that the denigration of dependency as a weak/female trait results from a sexist emphasis on individuation and the devaluation of relationship issues which are usually central to female self-definition. Women who value relationships above career achievements and economic success have been caught in a recurring double bind. They have been seen as stereotypically and normatively feminine, but implicitly faulted by analyses such as those by Erikson that identify separation from family as the hallmark of mature adulthood.

But while an increased recognition of the positive values of relationship, relationship caretaking, and mature interdependence may become increasingly necessary not only to human happiness but to the survival of the species, the present organization of society continues to reward independence and self-interested behavior. The dependent female is at risk, as is the one who subordinates her own interests to the interests of relationships. Faced with an inescapable double bind, she not infrequently responds by vacillating between dependent and independent (or counterdependent) behavior.

Commuting between home and workplace, each organized by different value systems, she may change her behavior to suit the situation, conveniently ignoring inconsistencies. Confronting dilemmas in either setting, she may fall back on familiar patterns of defense, dissociating conflicts, absenting herself from an awareness of inescapable stress.

One of the paradoxes of female dependency is the lack of social supports actually available to women. The traditional nuclear patriarchal family has customarily failed to care adequately for the female caretaker; but, in the past, extended family systems, in which several females cared for each other as well as men and children, did provide some supports. In modern life, however, the extended family is becoming less and less available, although many daughters still care for their aging parents (McGoldrick, 1989). In the absence of a supportive extended family, a woman often has little more than herself to depend on.

Welfare dependency, constantly the target of political rhetoric in the United States, is one consequence of this situation. The welfare system, however, exists for children, not women, as a minimal response of a civilized society that claims to value human life. Welfare dependency is likely to be experienced by women as just another aspect of their vulnerability and degradation. The belief that mothers are really supported by aid to their children is based on the assumption by policy makers that adult women have no needs of their own.

When coping proves overwhelming, however, there is still help. A host of medications promise to moderate stress, and such medications are prescribed most frequently for women. Medication, in fact, now constitutes a major social response to female psychosocial dependency and the double binds to which women are subjected. Not surprisingly, the very word dependency increasingly refers to chemical dependency.

It is popular to view chemical dependency as a personal problem rather than a social symptom, and from a clinical standpoint this view has undeniable merits. Treatment is necessarily a personal intervention that requires individual commitment and responsibility. But the refusal to focus on the social contexts of individual pathology is ultimately detrimental to both individuals and societies; the recognition of this consequence has been a major contribution of feminist theory. Addiction as a woman's problem cannot be effectively understood or treated unless the stresses of women's lives are acknowledged and ameliorated. In therapy, as well as in life, the personal eventually becomes political.

Role Conflict, Role Diffusion, and Role Overload

Role conflict and overload have been inevitable consequences of the multifarious support functions expected of females. Caretaking has many dimensions. Husbands require it, children require it, houses require it, pets require it, schools require it, neighborhoods require it—the list seems endless. These diverse activities demand diverse skills and resources. They are not always easily integrated with each other; they may conflict. Scheduling and implementing them may be an exhausting juggling act. There are only 24 hours in the day, and, as the old saying goes, "Woman's work is never done." The supposed liberation of women has added to the number of tasks they are expected to perform. Entry into the male world of work has not lightened the burden at home.

Female caretaking is often unpaid or, if economically requited at all, underpaid. It seems not to be much valued. But the complaints that arise when a woman fails to provide it indicate how essential it is believed to be. As Chesler noted in 1972, failure to perform her expected caretaking functions as wife and mother is often taken as a symptom of mental illness in women and may be a pretext for hospitalization. Conversely, a woman's interest in resuming domestic activities may be taken by clinicians as a sign that she is getting better.

Role overload, with its attendant stresses, is exacerbated by female guilt. Because their self-esteem is shaped from childhood by the need to please and care for others, women find themselves in a no-win situation. It is impossible to please all of the people all of the time. Besides, the requirements of pleasing change—yesterday's favored meatloaf becomes today's disdained leftovers. Other family members can mess up a house faster than any one woman can clean it. Nature, which blows dust around or fills the yard with mud is also a constant enemy. Paid work may seem a welcome excuse to walk away from the house, but, lacking a natural disaster, the house will always be there when she returns, just as messy or messier.

When things are left undone at home, when things are out of control anywhere, women apologize a lot. It must be their fault. Many husbands tend to agree, and with some, unsatisfactory housekeeping or cooking is used as a rationale for wife abuse. Overwrought women may in turn abuse their children. Eventually, either way, they are likely to focus blame on themselves. Guests came and the living room was untidy. Bought cookies instead of homemade ones were sent to the school bake sale. The dog's flea collar was not changed on time. That such trivial issues could motivate breast-beating and a litany of self-accusations sometimes strikes observers, including therapists, as preposterous. Female misdemeanors are the stuff of situation comedies. They are, unfortunately, also the stuff of psychiatric records.

Ironically, as Friedan illustrated in 1963, modern technology has not liberated women from household chores, but has, if anything, increased them. Advertising has also raised standards of what constitutes a clean wash or a clean carpet. Many support activities that people used to expect — and pay for — have disappeared: the dry cleaner who makes home pickups and deliveries, the delivery person who brings in groceries. Even if such supports are theoretically available, women who work outside the home can seldom afford to pay for them. Even child care is frequently unaffordable.

The workplace is also a major contributing factor in role overload. The demands of the workplace have almost invariably been determined by the preferences of men. Jobs start and end to suit their needs. Work outside the home, being paid, is expected to take priority over the needs of a family. It goes without saying that a woman's needs, too, are secondary. If she becomes sick, she is lucky to have either paid sick leave or medical insurance; many women do not. If she has a baby, she must often arrange day care soon after giving birth. If she is caring for an aging parent, she must consider a nursing home whether she likes the idea or not. Paying the mortgage depends on her paycheck. If she does not pay the mortgage, she may find herself on the street.

Television ads announce that a successful woman is a superwoman, one who brings home the bacon and bakes the bread, while remaining sexy, energetic, untouched by human sweat or the common cold. When women cannot meet all the demands of the plethora of roles assigned to them, their self-esteem may plummet. When they persist in trying, they are subject to stress-related illnesses. When those around them blame them, they become targets of abuse.

Dissociation is one way of coping with the double binds of role conflict and role diffusion. An overstressed woman sometimes compartmentalizes her identity as she compartmentalizes her life. Dissociation as a response to abuse greatly facilitates such everyday compartmentalization. Multiple personalities are the most striking examples of this phenomenon. One alter personality may be created for the specific purpose of holding down a regular job, while another takes on child care, and another becomes a prostitute or the sexual consort of a spouse. The compartmentalization of the world itself facilitates this strange adaptation. Those who meet the woman in one role often have no idea of how she appears in other roles or settings.

Multiple personality disorder is an extreme response. But milder examples of this sort of compartmentalization and the dissociation sometimes accompanying it are not unusual. The female who hides abuse from herself and others sets the stage for a double or even multiple life. It is a small step from this situation to the construction of a fragmented or dissociated identity. Dissociated identities, in turn, can make role overload less stressful by removing from consciousness an awareness of fatigue or conflict.

Because the fragmentation of the female self to accommodate role overload is often, to outward appearances, adaptive, therapeutic interventions that stress wholeness confront women with a new double bind. One woman cannot do everything. What must—what *can*—be given up? Choosing wholeness is an act of self-assertion that may mean losses. But the gains can be worth the price.

CHAPTER 3
Trauma in Developmental Context

THE IMPACT OF trauma on development can be dramatically obvious and specific, as in the sudden loss of a previously intact function, or insidious but pervasive, as in the failure to thrive. It may involve simple habit patterns or complex cognitive and social skills. It may leave objectively measurable behavior patterns intact while disrupting such subtle phenomena as a sense of ego involvement or a zest for living.

One of the major organizing concepts in child development is that of stage-specific tasks and sensitive periods. Theorists as diverse as Erikson and Piaget have observed that the impact of environmental events on development is in part a function of the competencies the child has developed or is developing during the period in which the event occurs. As Alice Rossi (1981) emphasizes, too, biological as well as psychological maturation is frequently a critical, though unappreciated, factor in child development.

The infant brain at birth is characterized by a discrepancy between a well-developed subcortical system, particularly the limbic system, and the comparatively undeveloped cortical structures necessary for symbolic thinking. Only as these mature does the child become capable of experiencing and describing events verbally or employing fantasy as a defense against anxiety.

Although the development of the cerebral cortex eventually makes such complex symbolic activities possible, it is the social context that programs them. As parents communicate their feelings and ideas to their children, they are helping to construct patterns of communication that the child will use to move beyond the family into the wider world. They are, at the same time, building a bridge between their own inner world and the expanding inner world that is the mind of a child.

As a result of the differential development of specific cognitive and behavioral competencies, "the 'same' event is likely to produce qualitatively distinct meanings for children at different ages" (Shirk, 1988, p. 59).

Children abused in infancy, for example, might have problems related to disrupted attachment (Egeland & Sroufe, 1981). Abuse at age two might interfere with object mastery. Five-year-olds are at risk for disruptions of peer relationships and other social skills (Shirk, 1988).

Early developments form the foundation for later ones, and long-term effects of post-traumatic reactions may persist across several developmental phases, resulting in long-standing developmental delays or arrests. Basic mechanisms of learning and memory necessary for phase-specific tasks may be impaired (Eth & Pynoos, 1985; van der Kolk, 1987), with widespread effects on coping and personality development. Some studies suggest that many social effects of child abuse, such as increased aggression or social isolation, may result from pervasive intellectual deficits (Barahal, Waterman, & Martin, 1981). In some cases, however, cognitive development may greatly outstrip emotional maturation, a situation that introduces new stresses into the child's life (Harris, 1989).

In childhood as well as later, controllability is a major dimension of whether and to what extent an event is experienced as traumatic. Controllability, however, is an aspect of developmental competence. In the absence of physical control, human beings develop psychological defenses, which can moderate their anxiety. Children learn to tolerate and control many aversive events in their lives, and their ability to do so contributes to a sense of mastery and positive self-esteem, but the degree of psychological control available is a function of a developmental timetable. Young children are at risk for trauma not only because of their physical vulnerability but because they lack the coping and defense mechanisms that depend on biological and psychological maturation.

Altshuler and Ruble (1989), for example, review arguments that controllable situations may be best handled by approach behavior such as monitoring, while uncontrollable situations can be somewhat defended against through avoidance strategies. They found that, although both children and adults do use avoidance tactics in uncontrollable situations, young children are unable to use the kinds of cognitive distractions available to older subjects. Shirk (1988) notes, too, that children who develop skills in role-taking are likely to express their feelings cognitively, while their less advanced peers tend to develop action symptoms.

In therapy, traumatized individuals tend to regress to pivotal stages in their development, and their reexperiencing at such times reflects not only the traumas that occurred but stage-specific coping mechanisms. Clinicians frequently observe shifts in modes of expression as well as discontinuities in memory. A client with a severe dissociative disorder, for example, may shift from self-reflective verbal statements to impulsive behavioral enactments and back again within one therapy session. Her life story is compartmentalized not only in terms of content but in terms of cognitive and affective styles typical of different periods of her history.

Unusual traumas and disasters, such as a kidnapping or a sniper attack, are clearly uncontrollable and could be expected to produce the post-traumatic symptoms associated with inescapable shock. Fortunately, unusual disasters are seldom repeated and, over time, although the effects of a single shock may persist for years, many children eventually work through the trauma with minimal lingering ill effects (Terr, 1990). Many childhood traumas, however, particularly child abuse, are repetitive and predictable and the continuing inability of the victim to control them could be expected not only to produce typical post-traumatic symptoms, but to have massive effects on a child's developing self-esteem.

Barahal et al. (1981) found that, compared to children who were not abused, those who were abused were likely to believe that events were beyond their control. Just how this belief impacts on the development of specific coping styles in children is not clear from existing research. But clinicians are quite familiar with the client who rationalizes behavior in terms of the debilitating belief that there is just no connection between how one behaves and bad things happening. During psychotherapy, one welcome advance is the cognitive and emotional integration of the discovery "I really am an adult now; I have control now that I simply did not have as a child." For women accustomed to being infantilized or to living in states of child-like dependency, this recognition can be especially liberating.

Recovery from childhood trauma is complicated by the intricate ways in which trauma responses become woven into personality structure. Traumatization can also delete from consciousness large segments of one's personal history, making that history inaccessible for identity consolidation in adolescence or early adult life. Even after specific effects have dissipated, there is often a lingering sense of psychological impoverishment, a feeling of self-depletion or self-estrangement. Too often, the adult personality that eventually emerges is not a whole and integrated individual, but a superficial facade erected to camouflage feelings of inner emptiness or pain.

SYMPTOMATIC EFFECTS OF TRAUMA IN CHILDHOOD

In some respects, the responses of child victims to inescapable shocks resemble those of adults. Psychobiological responses and somatic symptoms, in particular, seem to characterize victims across the life span. For example, Nader et al. (1990) found that, shortly following exposure to a traumatizing event, many children develop symptoms of post-traumatic stress disorder. In their study, children highly exposed to a sniper attack—those actually present during the attack or closely related to a victim—

developed more acute symptoms, including somatic complaints, and continued to suffer for months afterward.

In childhood, however, disruptive symptoms are not merely an intrusion into a previously normal life — they may have a significant effect on developing competencies or even shape character development. Considering the pervasive impact of persistent PTSD symptoms in childhood, Nader and her colleagues note that crucial developmental processes such as cognition, attention, self-esteem, social interaction, and impulse control may be adversely affected. Unfortunately, emotionally avoidant reactions often lead children to suffer in silence. Moreover, effects of trauma, even contextually distinct kinds of trauma, may be cumulative. Children traumatized prior to the sniper attack tended to develop renewed PTSD symptoms after the attack that were related to their earlier traumatic experiences.

In an overview of childhood traumas, Lenore Terr (1991) has identified four commonly observed and particularly important outcomes of early traumatization: "They are: 1) strongly visualized or otherwise repeatedly perceived memories, 2) repetitive behaviors, 3) trauma-specific fears, and 4) changed attitudes about people, aspects of life, and the future" (p. 12). She notes that even those who were traumatized in infancy and cannot verbalize memories tend to play or draw visualized elements of the traumatic events. In the dissociative disorders of childhood, behavioral reenactments of traumatic experiences are sometimes disconnected from the verbalizations that increasingly organize thought.

Childhood defenses against trauma include forms of self-hypnosis that can compartmentalize memories for specific events or even whole identity fragments. Dissociation as a response to childhood trauma is facilitated by the high hypnotizability of children in general (Hilgard, 1979) and of some abused children in particular (Putnam, 1989; Ross, 1989). Spontaneous dissociation can produce symptoms ranging from bodily anesthesias, feelings of being invisible, and amnesias for certain memories, to full-blown cases of multiple personality disorder (Kluft, 1985; Terr, 1991).

Chu and Dill (1990) correlated the reports of childhood abuse experiences in adult female inpatients with scores on the Dissociative Experiences Scale (Bernstein & Putnam, 1986). They found that both the presence and severity of reported abuse is related to the level of dissociative symptomatology.

When dissociation is used as a coping technique in childhood, it can interfere with normal processes of personality integration, which are already incomplete or in flux. As a result, some expectable integrations may never be achieved at all. This development is probably an important aspect of those "developmental arrests" that have been the subject of much psychoanalytic discussion. Unfortunately, most psychoanalytically oriented approaches to these issues have centered on theoretical speculations about early intrapsychic processes and have failed to consider empirical findings regarding child physical and sexual abuse.

One of the most frequently studied specific childhood traumas is child sexual abuse. Browne and Finkelhor (1986) report that several typical initial effects of such abuse have been widely noted in the literature, including fear, anxiety, depression, anger, aggression, and sexually inappropriate behavior. More long-term effects which are likely to persist into adult life include tendencies toward revictimization, substance abuse, and sexual maladjustment. Briere and Runtz (1988), comparing female clients at a walk-in center, found former sexual abuse victims to be significantly more likely than nonabused clients to be currently taking psychoactive medication, to have a history of substance addiction, to have been victimized in adult relationships, and to have made suicide attempts. Dissociative experiences and sleep disturbances were also widely reported by abuse victims in this study.

As is the case with child abuse generally, the effects of child sexual abuse vary according to the developmental level of the child at the time the abuse occurs. Gomes-Schwartz et al., in a study of 112 preschool, school-age, and adolescent children who had been sexually abused, reported that, as a group, these children showed more signs of behavioral and emotional problems than the general population (1985). But problems were also age-related. Disturbed preschoolers, for example, showed cognitive impairment and severe stress reactions. School-age children exhibited increased aggression, impulsivity, destructiveness, and fearfulness. Adolescent symptoms included anxiety, depression, obsessive thoughts, and, in some cases, increased inhibition.

Retrospective data as well as developmental studies point to the pervasive and lingering impact of early abuse on later adaptation. Studies of psychiatric inpatients have recently discovered a high prevalence of both physical and sexual abuse in patient histories (Brown & Anderson, 1991; Chu & Dill, 1990). Previously abused individuals seem to be especially at risk for personality disorders (Ogata et al., 1990; Shearer et al., 1990).

In the last two decades, borderline personality disorder, in particular, has been found to be associated with a history of abuse. Formerly, considerable controversy centered on whether borderline pathology resulted from developmental arrest, pathological forms of splitting arising in infancy, difficulties in separation and individuation, or regressive processes (for a review, see Herman & van der Kolk, 1987). In actuality, adult personality disorders often reveal a mixture of atypical developments, including pathological ones, that reflect chronic patterns of coping with childhood trauma. It is not necessary to postulate spontaneous and purely endogenous processes to account for the resulting pathology, although genetic and endogenous developments may be a contributing factor.

Borderline personality disorder is only one of a number of diagnostic categories that are currently being reevaluated in the light of research on trauma. Studies of the interactive effects of such factors as temperament, developmental stages impacted by trauma, coping styles, and patterns of family interaction may eventually provide keys to understanding that were missing from previous conceptualizations of personality development and psychopathology.

INTERPRETATIONS

Because we are fundamentally social creatures, even a trauma experienced in isolation has interpersonal implications. Because we experience the world in terms of symbolic structures, even from an early age, trauma is not merely experienced but interpreted. The interpretive mind, a uniquely human adaptation, has its own developmental history. A child's perception of *what* happened is frequently quite accurate, and vivid veridical memories often persist long after a terrible event, but understanding *why* is harder (Kagan, 1984). The whys and wherefores of suffering have exercised philosophers throughout recorded history; it is scarcely surprising that children often find their own suffering incomprehensible or invent irrational explanations for it. Irrational interpretations can themselves distort developmental processes and complicate recovery.

Many interpretations concern control. From childhood, internalized beliefs form a protective shield against uncontrollable shock. Such beliefs need not be rational; often they are not. But even magical thinking can provide a temporary escape from stress. Some beliefs rationalize abusive behavior: "They hit me for my own good"; "People who love you, hurt you." Some reinforce dependency on the abusive family: "Blood is thicker than water"; "You can never trust an outsider."

Interpretations make experience meaningful. Traumatized children sometimes attempt to reinstate a sense of control by ruminating about the past, creating explanations of why terrible events happened or how future shocks can be prevented. Terr (1990, 1991) terms such explanations "omens" and considers them especially characteristic of single-blow traumas. Perhaps in the case of repetitive traumas, such explanations are eventually discarded as futile. Omens, however, are sometimes incorporated into the explanatory constructs of chronically victimized individuals and are sometimes systematized into belief systems, including delusional systems. Some abusive parents indoctrinate their children in beliefs that contribute to such explanations, particularly fatalistic beliefs: "Life means suffering." Sometimes parents encourage "omenizing" by providing irrational explanations to rationalize abuse: "This pain is a punishment for your badness/a test of your strength," or "I, the parent, am an instrument of a higher power."

Many traumas have a ripple effect. Since human children depend on their caretakers to protect them, even accidental and impersonally inflicted traumas often arouse painful feelings of disappointment and disillusionment that disrupt relationships. Any failure of empathy on the part of caretakers may compound the trauma itself, leading to a vicious circle of pain, blame, and social isolation. This secondary hurt, the failure of caretakers to protect, sometimes has more lasting consequences than the original injury. "Traumatized children recognize profound vulnerability in all human beings, especially themselves" (Terr, 1991, p. 14). This sense of vulnerability can persist long after more specific responses have dissipated.

When injury is intentionally inflicted, awareness of that fact can produce a host of irrational as well as more reality-oriented coping responses. Victimization is often staunchly denied by both victims and perpetrators. Victim-blaming is not only common as an individual response, but is sometimes socially institutionalized (Ryan, 1976). Victim-blaming offers a specific set of interpretations about the "why" of trauma, allowing the real perpetrator to escape responsibility and shaping cognitive distortions in far-reaching ways. In childhood, victim-blaming can lead to profound distortions of self-concept and contribute to the development of self-punitive and self-injurious behavior. Even after the child matures and is able to think more rationally, self-blame may persist as a characterological trait or as a dissociated part of the adult personality.

Victim-blaming sometimes has ironic consequences. After a victim has developed a scapegoat identity or incorporated self-punitive behavior into her self-concept, any effort to locate blame outside herself may threaten her with identity loss. Trauma involves many kinds of loss, in fact—the loss of needed care, the loss of soothing comfort, the loss of trust, faith, and cherished illusions. Depending on the stage of development at which they occur, such losses set in motion processes of mourning and attempts at reparation that can profoundly affect subsequent development. As Terr (1991) has emphasized, the shock of trauma interferes with childhood mourning and subjects the victim to prolonged states of grief.

At any age, recovery from trauma often involves not only a revised appraisal of realities, such as the actualities of victimization and abuse, but a process of grieving losses and a restructuring of patterns of regulating self-esteem.

At this point, it should be emphasized that painful events are an inevitable part of growing up. The kinds of trauma and post-traumatic disorders under consideration in this discussion, however, do not derive from inevitable frustrations of infantile impulses or from occasional parental mistakes. For the most part they are a consequence of growing up in a family in which unnecessary, dangerous, even life-threatening traumas are repetitively inflicted and seldom admitted as mistakes. In this kind of family, basic patterns of social interaction inextricably mingle care-giving with deprivation, protectiveness with brutality. In some cases, punishment follows indulgence as predictably as clockwork. In others, parental behavior is erratic and the only predictable thing about the abuse is its inevitability. Such family situations are not rare, but they are also not the norm.

In persistently abusive families, the most vulnerable children are overwhelmed and do not survive. But most children have a remarkable ability to make use of the care available to them, however meagre. If the psychological nutrients necessary for survival are contaminated, they are nevertheless assimilated like the polluted air or pesticide-contaminated food so many humans learn to live with. In such instances, abuse becomes woven into the basic patterns of existence. When that happens, the transmission of abuse from one generation to the next is more predictable than surprising.

Understanding child abuse is complicated by historical traditions ranging from cultural myths to psychiatric practice. As is the case with adult behavior, what is labeled pathological development in childhood is to some extent a function of stereotypical thinking, particularly thinking about developments that are gender-appropriate. Recognition of child abuse, too, is often impeded by post-traumatic and gender-typical behavior patterns that hide the problem, as well as by wishful thinking and common beliefs. The myth of the happy family, the family that is not dysfunctional, is a powerful force that continues to obscure the extent to which psychopathology derives from social, including culturally determined, origins.

THE FAMILY FORTRESS

The social context into which human babies are born relies on the family as a primary buffer against trauma. Research has shown that the family often does serve a protective function even in the face of terrible events such as war. For example, some studies have indicated that those children who stayed with their families during the London bombings of World War II fared better psychologically than those who were sent away to physically safer surroundings (Freud & Burlingham, 1942). The disruption of attachment is itself a primary form of trauma, which may intensify the effects of other stressors, particularly if disruption occurs at critical stages of development (Bowlby, 1973).

The common and often correct assumption that families protect the best interests of children is so expedient that it often becomes a barrier against recognizing the traumatic potential of families themselves. Idealizations of the family as a safe haven, rationalizations about the family as a bulwark of authority that preserves the social order, fantasies about the wild and incorrigible nature of children, and religious prescriptions like "spare the rod and spoil the child" protect traumatizing families from scrutiny. The practical difficulties involved in policing or changing the behavior of abusive parents also operate to restrain intervention. It is much easier to envision benevolent social policies than to finance and implement them. And sometimes the well-intentioned fumblings of bureaucracy can be as injurious as an intentional assault.

Other social factors, such as the family's right to privacy, help preserve the family as a fortress against external interventions. Pathogenic families often exploit this position by teaching the child to distrust the world outside the family, by limiting contacts with people who might provide the child with a different perspective on life, or by emphasizing that everything that goes on at home must be kept secret. Abuse, of course, is one of the biggest secrets (Rush, 1980). But a general atmosphere of secretiveness serves to enforce the child's dependency on family members as well as to hide abuse. Females, who are typically socialized for dependency, are doubly disadvantaged by the secretive family. The illusion that it is the only haven in a hostile world may keep them tied to it.

Secrecy serves another function. The family transmits to the child a particular view of reality and filters out competing views. In abusive families, abuse is often presented as necessary and normal and life without abuse becomes, in effect, unimaginable. Secrecy, which isolates the child from competing views of reality, reinforces the authority of parents to the extent that sometimes even bizarre beliefs are accepted unquestioningly. This problem becomes especially complex when ritualistic forms of abuse are rationalized in the context of family religious beliefs.

In recent years, the practice of Satanic rituals, which is sometimes familial in origin, has captured considerable media attention. But it should be emphasized that Satanism is by no means the only religious or philosophical pretext for child abuse. For centuries, severe corporal punishment was accepted discipline in many mainstream institutional traditions, including public schools, and psychological as well as physical forms of terrorizing children were philosophically justified as being in their best interests. Pilgrim children were routinely subjected to dramatic preachments concerning hellfire and damnation, for example. Witch-torture and burning, self-flagellation and self-mutilation are a familiar aspect of the history of Christianity. It should be noted, too, that female scapegoating has played an important part in many such practices; most of those burned for witchcraft, for example, were female (Morgan, 1989; Williams & Adelman, 1978).

The family that simultaneously isolates the child from extrafamilial contacts and rationalizes abuse in the context of a belief system erects a strong bulwark against external intervention. Nevertheless, even in socially isolated families, extrafamilial contacts cannot be restricted entirely. School is usually unavoidable and severe injury often brings children to the attention of emergency rooms or physicians. Reporting laws in many states, problematic as they may be, make it possible for teachers and other outsiders to intervene protectively. Unfortunately, though, unless such interventions are carefully orchestrated, they may result merely in an intensification of secrecy on the part of parents, even punishment of the child for causing "trouble."

Even if she never comes to the attention of authorities, an abused child often makes use of any normative contacts available to her. Attachment to someone outside the family can be a life-saving source of hope as well as an opportunity for modeling adaptive behavior. Positive use of such contacts can nevertheless lead to confusion and painful conflicts. Such a child, in effect, lives in two worlds, the isolated world of the family and the wider world beyond it. Being able to cope with two worlds is in itself a complicated achievement, one that attests to a child's adaptive competence. Paradoxically, however, growing up in an abusive household often reinforces the dissociative tendencies that make it possible to tolerate such inconsistencies. Even victims who develop extreme forms of adaptation like multiple personality disorder may appear normal in the world of school and work.

On the other hand, the child who cannot manage a double or multiple life may become psychotic. Even those who do adapt remain vulnerable, since defenses like denial and dissociation are always in danger of being eroded or breaking down entirely. At some point it frequently becomes clear that, of the two realities, the family's is the more distorted and destructive. But, since the family's reality was the first needed for survival, the first believed, the most deeply internalized, any challenge to it may be resisted as earth-shattering. For therapists, recognizing that abuse occurred in reality, not just in fantasy, is not enough to resolve such conflicts. It is the client's *sense* of reality that is at issue. The sense of reality is, of course, complicated not only by familial beliefs but by developmental and traumatic factors in the encoding and retrieval of memories.

Nevertheless, at some point in treatment, acknowledgment of the reality of traumatic events needs to be coupled with a recognition that, whatever she was taught about reality, the victim herself was not responsible for the events.

Patriarchy

The family fortress is a patriarchal institution. Most people acknowledge the universality of patriarchy; it is only the desirability or inevitably or meaning of patriarchy that is controversial. This issue is relevant to the present discussion because of the relation between patriarchal institutions, including the family, and the actualities of female victimization throughout the life span.

Patriarchal tradition assumes that fathers protect their households; children without fathers are considered at risk. As importantly, mothers without husbands are often considered inherently disturbed or pathogenic, and families headed by women are likely to be labeled disorganized or dysfunctional. The pervasive social significance of the marital status of parents has been traditionally reflected in pejorative labels applied to children whose families do not conform to the patriarchal norm. They have been labeled as "illegitimate" or as "children of divorce." The expectation that such children are at risk for pathology often overshadows attention to the pathogenic potential of abuse in so-called "intact" families. Abused children easily escape notice if they live in middle-class families headed by a seemingly good male provider.

The normative character of patriarchal institutions and practices has determined social, legal, and clinical responses to the issues of female victimization. Under patriarchy, many forms of abuse are explicitly prohibited. Incest, for example, is interdicted by law as well as by custom. On the other hand, the man's right to control his own household is considered a bulwark of social order. Traditionally, he has been expected not only to discipline his children, but to exercise authority over his wife. Historically, wife beating, like the corporal punishment of children, was sanctioned as a form of discipline (Davidson, 1977; Dobash & Dobash, 1979; Lerner, 1986).

The unquestioned acceptance accorded male authority in the home has often made it easy for men to misuse that authority, even to the point of transgressing specific laws, such as those against child sexual abuse. And the tradition that allowed a man to "discipline" his wife by beating her led to a tolerance for his physical abuse even after laws were enacted against it. Importantly, too, even when patriarchal law has theoretically interdicted certain kinds of abusive behavior, such as rape, it has reserved for itself the right to define and judge when abuse occurs (MacKinnon, 1989).

Clinical theories, which have evolved in patriarchal institutional settings, have often reflected social norms without much questioning them. They have tended to view the patriarchal context of child development as normal and desirable, and although such theories have often been presented as being value free, both theory and practice have tended to reinforce traditionally patriarchal values. From this perspective, challenges to patriarchy, either inside or outside the home, have been interpreted as pathogenic. Mothers who do not conform to traditional sex roles, for example, have sometimes been seen as endangering their children. Fathers who have not assumed a traditional patriarchal stance within the family or who have deferred to their wives have sometimes been labeled "castrated." The existence of physical or sexual abuse, when acknowledged at all, has often been downplayed as a rare aberration.

Statistics on family violence, however, attest to the pathogenic potential of the patriarchal family. Fantasies that all-powerful mothers control children's lives rationalize denial of the actual power arrangements within patriarchal families. According to Wyatt and Powell (1988), the most serious consequences of child sexual abuse involve fathers, genital contact, and the use of force. Most victims of spouse abuse are female (Hilberman, 1980). Holden and Ritchie (1991) report that mothers in violent marriages are likely to be generally more stressed than fathers.

Gender as a Risk Factor

But although the most serious abuse often occurs in the context of the family, gender-typical stresses form an important background to traumatic abuse both within and outside the family. Such factors as sexism, female physical vulnerability, and female scapegoating, which generally impinge on development, complicate the effects of specific traumas.

Girls assimilate their own traumatic experiences as well as those of their mothers to an evolving sense of what it means to be female. Since the disadvantaged status of females in the patriarchal family is reflected in most institutional structures, gender is a risk factor throughout the life cycle. Recognition of this depressing fact is sometimes incorporated into beliefs about the world in general as well as self-concept. In therapy, clients sometimes verbalize long-standing beliefs that gender in itself explains a history of abuse—it is normal for males to hit females; every man, when aroused, is a sexual beast, etc.

Whether a little girl is actually abused or not, she usually becomes aware, even in childhood, that her gender in itself puts her at risk for abuse. This awareness complicates positive experiences of herself, particularly her experience of her body. Contrary to phallocentric theories, which view the female body as lacking and the female mind as riveted on the wish for a penis, little girls enjoy their bodies, including their genitals, and take satisfaction in their gender—unless they are punished for doing so. Many little girls are wanted, loved, esteemed, and encouraged. Nevertheless, having a female body is risky. Whether a little girl confronts this risk in a disordered family, a dangerous neighborhood, or simply on a television newscast, her awareness of it is inevitably part of her emerging awareness of what it means to be female.

This recognition that gender is a special risk factor is so commonly acknowledged that most people probably take it for granted. For children of both sexes, growing up is typically guided by cautionary reminders of one's vulnerability that are eventually internalized as part of self-care: Don't talk to strangers. Don't go out alone or after dark or to certain places. For males, however, these cautionary restraints are annoyances to be discarded or rebelled against as adulthood approaches. For females, they are lasting and inescapable and are typically linked with another specific cautionary warning: Don't call attention to your female sexuality.

Paradoxically, the temptation to rebel against this last constraint is also strong, since girls and women are valued for their physical attractiveness. The result is a powerful double bind: Be attractive, but not *too* attractive. Don't be attractive in the "wrong" way or to the "wrong" people.

The social tendency to infantilize females, encourage or enforce their dependency, and blur the distinction between adult women and little girls is complexly intertwined with these risks. In many cultures, it is still generally recognized that an adult female, like a child, is only safe when under the surveillance of her family or the man she "belongs" to. Boys will be boys; they are expected to range freely and explore the world. Girls who stray too far may be considered fair game for predators, including rapists.

The tendency to see women as girls and vice versa is also a pretext for child abuse. To the exploitive male, the female child, like the female adult, exists primarily to provide pleasure for others — using her for sex is merely a response to what is seen as her basic reason for being.

As a result of social tendencies to infantilize and exploit females, the special risks associated with having a female body are lifelong. Growing older and wiser, achieving savvy and skills will not make them disappear. A woman cannot eliminate them simply by changing her attitudes, becoming more assertive, repudiating sexism, or even by always wearing running shoes and carrying a gun. She must learn to be realistically aware and self-protective and, if she is to avoid being overwhelmed by such dreary contingencies, to counter them with self-affirming coping mechanisms.

Little girls are usually taught to minimize the risks attendant on having a female body by controlling their own behavior. Frequently, they are also led to believe that they can control the behavior of males by not arousing sexual responses in them. This fantasy, that men are under the control of women, is as commonplace as it is contrary to fact. It can be a powerful source of guilt and shame in victims.

But, while it is true that, after infancy, male behavior is seldom much under the control of females, it is also true that some kinds of avoidant behaviors, such as being self-effacing or avoiding unprotected places can reduce risks. Paradoxically, these self-protective behaviors, if extreme, lead to diagnoses of maladjustment. When a woman's self-effacing style leads to her being interpersonally isolated or ineffectual in the workplace, it is likely to be seen as a form of self-defeating pathology. When her fear of unprotected places becomes extreme and extends to the whole outside world, her avoidant behavior is usually diagnosed as a disorder, such as agoraphobia. When she fails to avoid a dangerous situation, however, it is her lack of avoidance that is seen as pathological. Insofar as avoidance is prudent, it is usually appraised as appropriately feminine and healthy.

Gender as a risk factor impinges on child development in subtle or dramatic ways. The asymmetry of violent interactions within the family — males are most frequently perpetrators, females most frequently victims —

has profound consequences for patterns of identification in childhood. Throughout development, children integrate their own identity formation through increasingly complex identifications with their parents, most particularly with the parent of the same sex. Such identifications naturally reflect the child's observations of family violence. In violent families, normal patterns of identification are also complicated by patterns of "identification with the aggressor" (Freud, 1966), that is, a tendency to incorporate and enact patterns of aggressive behavior inflicted on oneself. Identifying with the aggressor, the child inflicts on himself or others what he has experienced.

Walker et al. (1989) found that both boys and girls from abusive homes showed more aggression and externalized behavior problems. However, my own clinical experience indicates that, because of the way the sexes are differently socialized to experience and express aggression, patterns of identification with the aggressor and the integration of these patterns with more normal identifications are likely to be gender-typical.

For male children, identification with an aggressive male can be dissociated, particularly if it is based on an especially brutal assault or was accompanied by sexual abuse. The male victim of sexual abuse may feel psychologically emasculated. One result is a feminized identification that is likely to be in conflict with and thus split off from identification with the aggressively masculine father. Usually, however, there is no implicit conflict between sex-role stereotypes generally and the aggression of his own father in particular.

The little boy's identification with the father in his ordinary functions can thus be readily assimilated to identification with father as an aggressor. If his father physically assaults him or his mother, the little boy feels violated and angry and must inhibit his own aggression because he is a vulnerable child. But his inhibited angry feelings remain consistent with his maleness. He may carry permanent scars from being abused, but if he expresses his anger aggressively, he will not necessarily be seen as disturbed.

In contrast, the female child who identifies with the man who aggresses against her is implicitly at odds with sex-role conventions and, frequently, with the submissive behavior of her own mother. To the extent that aggression is generally interdicted in females, as well as to the extent that she directly perceives it as punished in herself and her mother, she may come to experience her own aggression as forever dangerous. To the extent that identification with the aggressor means being like a man, she may experience gender-identity conflict.

Several stereotypical female responses to such conflicts are available. The girl may severely inhibit all aggressive responses. She may direct her aggression against herself. Or she may dissociate her experience of aggressive interactions, whether instigated by herself or others. Many female children learn to employ different response patterns at different times. Self-injurious behavior itself is often dissociated.

TRAUMA, ATTACHMENT, AND PERSONALITY INTEGRATION

The attachment behavior of primates, including humans, has been extensively studied. Disorders of attachment have been found to be associated with such pathological adaptations as anaclitic depression (Spitz, 1945), social alienation (Erikson, 1980) and sexual aberrations (Greenacre, 1970). Van der Kolk (1987) reviews data suggesting that early social deprivation in primates causes damage to maturing brain structures. The fact that loss of attachment is traumatic for human infants also makes them vulnerable to specifically human forms of pathology, such as the internalization of destructive beliefs and distorted symbolic representations of reality.

Many studies that present and evaluate data on attachment focus on the role of the mother in infant development almost to the exclusion of that of the father. Attachment studies often seem to imply that mothers are responsible for the most serious disturbances in infants, and easily lead to assumptions that reinforce traditional sex-role arrangements in the nuclear family, such as the mother's primary responsibility for child care.

Spitz (1957) has carefully reviewed the ways in which the infant's earliest attachment to the mother is orchestrated by complex psychobiological mechanisms that reciprocally modify the behavior of both. These include such reflexive patterns as the sucking and grasping of babies and the "letting down" lactation reflex in nursing mothers. Complex patterns of mutual cuing also appear early—parents vigilant to the infant's communications learn to recognize varied signals in different patterns of crying. For males as well as females, a baby's cry seems to have a strong demand quality, so much so that the inability to soothe it sometimes precipitates panic and abusive behavior.

As typically conceptualized, the mother's primary role in child development is not only to foster secure attachment, but to facilitate separation and individuation. Developmental theorists like Mahler, Pine, and Bergman (1975), for example, have described postnatal life as a continuation of a prenatal symbiosis; psychological birth is conceptualized as a gradual process. As development proceeds, reflexive patterns are supplemented and eventually replaced by instrumental learning. The child gradually comes to behave and experience herself as a separate, autonomous entity. And, increasingly, she relates to her parents as individuals separate from herself and from one another.

The process of separation and individuation involves a growing ability to tolerate distance from caretakers, which is, in turn, facilitated by the child's increasing capacity for self-care. This development is often conceptualized in terms of identification. In the most general sense it includes not only the acquisition of parental behavior patterns but a concept of the self as being a child of particular parents, of being like them as they are perceived and fantasied about, and of moving toward a gradual assimilation into the adult culture they represent (Erikson, 1980). Most theorists are agreed that secure attachment in infancy facilitates development and makes possible an eventually secure individuation.

Most research that has dealt with disrupted attachment has focused on detrimental effects in the child. When early attachment is precipitously disrupted, however, both mother and child may be adversely affected. Disrupted attachment can lead to maternal responses that impact powerfully not only on the mother's relationship to the child and her future behavior toward it, but on her own identity and self-esteem. And the popular emphasis on mothers as all-powerful determinants in child development complicates the normal process of individuation for mothers as well as children.

The Maternal Imperative

Mammals are so named because of a reproductive arrangement and, from a developmental standpoint, it is scarcely deniable that the mother is usually the child's first object of desire and attachment. Yet although the infant's primary psychobiological bond is usually with the mother, the patriarchal context is as vital a part of early development as the air we breathe. The mother in the nursery has herself been nurtured, socialized, and educated in a patriarchal culture. Her earliest interactions with her baby, like her behavior generally, are implicitly shaped by an inescapable adaptation to gender arrangements and the authority of patriarchal institutions (Ehrenreich & English, 1978). In some ways, this may be even more true of advanced cultures than of primitive ones. In modern American life, for example, the hegemony of women in the nursery and the folk traditions that guided it have been increasingly replaced by the prescriptions of scientific experts, typically male.

The earliest tie to the mother does lay an important foundation for subsequent relationships with others, including the father and the patriarchal institutions he represents. The earliest, most pathogenic, even life-threatening traumas often do involve abuse and neglect on the part of mothers. The significance of attachment to mother and the expectation of her protectiveness are such that, when fathers are abusive, mothers are often blamed for permitting it.

And many mothers do permit it for reasons of their own—a history of childhood abuse, economic dependency on an abusive spouse, or a need to use the child as a scapegoat. Sometimes a mother's tolerance for another's or her own abuse of her child reflects her deep-seated identification with the child victim. Sometimes it reflects the most dangerous aspects of her identification with an aggressor. Sometimes it reflects her rage at feeling trapped.

Self-Regulation

Development typically involves a gradual internalization of functions, including soothing functions, which are initially provided by external caretakers. States of arousal and sequences of organized behavior originally regulated by parents come increasingly to be regulated by the child herself. Self-regulation is thus a fundamental aspect of individuation, a complexly articulated competence that plays an important role in the development of self-esteem and self-concept.

Both self-stimulation and self-soothing are fundamental aspects of self-regulation. The satisfied baby who continues to suck her thumb is smoothing the path of separation that enables falling asleep by oneself. Eventually, a blanket may accompany or replace the thumb, or a particular soft toy may be incorporated into the self-comforting ritual. Winnicott (1965, 1971), who was the first to write extensively about the developmental significance of such "transitional objects," has described the part they play not only in separation and self-regulation, but in creative processes.

Self-regulating rituals serve a bridging function between present and past, between self and other, and, within the individual, between distinct internal experiences. They play an important role in the development of symbolic representations of the world and in linking symbolic representations with one another. Even in infancy, the world is not passively taken in, but actively apprehended.

When processes of self-regulation are pathologically distorted, the distortion is frequently reflected in the use of transitional objects. The child may be unable to utilize a transitional object at all or may develop a pathological version of such an object (Tolpin, 1971; Winnicott, 1971).

Genital masturbation is a form of self-regulation that includes both stimulating and soothing functions. At some point in childhood, masturbation often becomes a part of the ritual of falling asleep. As a self-regulatory activity, it acquires symbolic links to specific needed and loved people and is eventually enriched by complex fantasies about interactions with them. Traumatic overstimulation, however, can disrupt a child's ability to regulate her own tensional states. The psychobiology of trauma sometimes leads to severe or even permanent changes in homeostatic mechanisms. In such cases, attempts to restore balance sometimes result in compulsive rituals of self-regulation, including compulsive masturbation.

One aspect of such a distortion in self-regulatory behavior is what may be termed "the sexualization of soothing." The human contact normally associated with self-regulation has become compulsively associated with the experience of sexual tension and sexualized forms of tension reduction. This problem is compounded by adult interpretations of experience that insist that sexual contact with the child is a normal form of soothing.

Self-regulation can also become complexly entwined with the infliction of pain. Many patterns of child abuse mingle pleasure with pain or alternate comforting behavior and hurtful behavior. Sexual abuse, in particular, often involves such a confusing admixture. Other common occurrences involve the special gratifications that sometimes follow abuse. A battered child, for example, may be given a new toy. Pain may thus come to be inextricably linked to the basic experience of being comforted. Psychobiological processes involved in addiction to trauma can also complicate the association between pleasure and pain.

One kind of pathological distortion of self-soothing, which is frequently associated with trauma, is the fetish. A fetish has some features in common with the normal transitional objects of infancy, but illustrates what happens when states of arousal are extreme and normal forms of human attachment are disrupted. A major function of a fetish seems to be to maintain contact with a needed soothing object in spite of extreme states of arousal. The use of a fetish for sexual gratification is frequently related to early forms of traumatization that complicated social as well as sexual development (Waites, 1982).

A fetish has a symbolic as well as a self-regulating function. Like the transitional object, it can be understood as a kind of protosymbol based on nonverbal patterns of enactment as well as verbal ideation. Freud believed that the fetish used for sexual gratification represented the penis males, to their great distress, found lacking in women. But although many fetishes are associated with sexual rituals and may involve the reenactment of sexual trauma, others, such as those used by psychotic patients, often have idiosyncratic meanings, which are not obviously sexual.

The use of fetishes plays an important role in ritualistic behavior generally. In ritualized forms of sexual abuse, the fetish is often designed or chosen to disguise as well as express its connection with a disturbing memory. In this respect, fetishes serve a kind of "screening function." Required characteristics in a fetish usually include concrete particulars that cue memories of contact; a particular smell, for example, is often a requirement.

A major characteristic of a fetish is controllability. From the standpoint of symbolic representation, fetishism is often related to scapegoating. The fetish is the target of extreme negative feelings toward a needed female. It should be emphasized, however, that a sexual fetish does not represent a whole human being: It stands for a needed part. Sometimes the fetishist appears to be relating to a whole woman, but, upon closer examination, it is obvious that she is being treated like an object, a plaything undifferentiated from self-soothing fantasy (Waites, 1982).

Because of Freud's early conceptualizations and the phallocentric bias of many clinical theories, fetishism in females has been little studied. Yet it is obvious that females, like males, often become attached to special comfort objects and may use them in masturbatory rituals. Perhaps one factor complicating the development of sexual fetishism in females is the traditionally imposed inhibition of female masturbation. Restrictions on masturbation have combined with other inhibitions of female sexuality, and with the gender-related risks of female sexuality, to alienate many girls from their own bodies. If a female is socialized to believe that her body and her sexuality belongs to a male, the stage is set for a special relation to fetishism that reflects gender arrangements. The girl does not *have* a fetish. She *becomes* one. She then soothes herself and regulates her self-esteem by participating in male rituals.

Separation Conflict and Child Abuse

Fetishism is one of many responses to separation conflicts as these are exacerbated by trauma. Even normal individuation is not without such conflicts, but for some children, the process is complicated by extreme levels of anxiety and distortions in self-regulation. Unavoidable problems, such as a physical illness or disability in the child, natural or man-made disasters, or the loss of a parent through illness or death can intensify separation fears or precipitate pathological patterns of coping. Disorders of attachment are also often connected with child abuse.

Sometimes the prospect of separation precipitates panic in child, parent, or both. The frustrations evoked by a panicky child can precipitate abusive parental behavior. A parent may transmit his or her own ambivalence about separation to the child, intensifying the child's conflicts. Or a parent may respond to his or her own ambivalence about the child's separating by becoming either punitive or extremely permissive or by vacillating between these contrasting responses. In some cases, a clinging parent keeps a child tied indefinitely to home and family through complex patterns of behavior that include both indulgence and abuse.

One common contributing factor in such a situation is the parent's pathological identification with the child. The child is both needed and treated as an extension of the parental self and is thus not allowed to have an autonomous, individuated existence. Parents who live through their children are often extremely indulgent, but the gratifications they provide are the ones they, rather than the child, consider desirable. They sometimes verbalize their intention to make up for the deprivations they themselves experienced in childhood by giving their children every advantage.

As a result of their indulgence, such parents tend to see themselves as good parents. The child who disagrees with them is considered ungrateful, hurtful. They may reproach the child, intensifying and manipulating feelings of guilt.

Most parents identify to some extent with their children. Empathic identifications facilitate the normal processes of parenting. And many want to shield their children from their own frustrations and deprivations. Possessive parents who appropriate their children, however, are not genuinely empathic. The child's real wants and needs are, in fact, often denied and neglected, completely overshadowed by parental needs. Persistent attempts by the child to separate and become autonomous often precipitate panic in such needy parents. The stage is then set for forms of parental control which, in extreme cases, may include such physical restrictions as locking up, tying up, or bizarre forms of incarceration. Attempts to restrict the child's contacts with people outside the family are designed in such instances to prevent separation as well as to hide abuse.

The traditional clinical literature has usually described such pathologically possessive behavior in mothers—"castrating mothers," "schizophrenogenic mothers,"—and has sometimes interpreted it as an outgrowth of "penis envy." Lacking the coveted penis, the mother supposedly clings to her child, particularly her male child. But abuse as a response to separation panic is by no means restricted to mothers; fathers, too, defend themselves against separation conflicts by possessively appropriating, controlling, and abusing women and children. Fathers, in fact, often have more power to control and coerce, since control is an accepted aspect of their patriarchal authority in the family. Historically, women and children were chattel property (Dworkin, 1981; Lerner, 1986).

Although male possessiveness is widely acknowledged, the separation anxiety that often underlies extreme male possessiveness runs counter to sex-role stereotypes. Men are supposed to be strong and independent. Their separation from women is organized not only by developmental imperatives, but by social institutions. To protect his self-esteem, a man may steadfastly deny and repress his identification with dependent women and children. This is likely to happen—especially likely, perhaps—when his possessive appropriation of them is a defense against his own panic.

One pattern of parental behavior sometimes associated with abuse is what West and Keller (1991) refer to as "parentification of the child," a role reversal in which the parent depends on the child to take care of him or her. West and Keller interpret this development in the light of Bowlby's (1977) description of distorted attachment behaviors. The child learns, in effect, that the only way to remain close to the parent and receive minimal affectional supplies is by becoming the parent's caretaker. Such a role reversal, however pathological in some respects, preserves the child's sense of being in control. Nevertheless, it is often associated with heightened insecurity in the child and the difficulties arising from the pessimistic expectation that others will not care. Children who become premature caretakers may find themselves unable to ask for or accept needed help from others, a problem that complicates their response to therapy.

Bowlby's (1977) discussion of the parent-child role reversal, as is so frequently the case, emphasized *maternal* psychopathology—the depressed or inadequate mother who cannot give care but needs it herself. However, "parentification of the child" is a dynamic that can be inferred not only in instances of maternal abuse but from many descriptions of paternal abuse, particularly incest. A typical aspect of some incestuous experiences, especially those characterized by tenderness and seduction rather than violent coercion, is the father's claim to need something that only the female child can provide. Not infrequently, the little girl's caretaking extends to other maternal functions, such as cooking and cleaning. The idea of the incestuously abused child as caretaker is also sometimes reinforced by a mother's collusion in the incest. One girl, for example, was repeatedly ordered by her mother to go and calm her father lest his violence erupt to the detriment of the whole family (West & Keller, 1991).

Parental needs to be taken care of are often exacerbated when one or both parents is alcoholic and/or drug dependent. When family organization is chaotic, the ability of the child to care for both self and others may play an important role in the very survival of the family as a group.

Since most familial caretaking functions are provided by females, the "parentification" of the child is likely to impact differently on male and female children. When a male child is kept tied to the family in a suffocating way, it is likely to be viewed as a pathological situation, an acknowledged threat to the boy's individuation. But since caretaking is viewed as consistent with her gender, the little girl is likely to be praised and rewarded for it by those outside as well as those within the family. Until this century, it was not uncommon for the youngest daughter in a family to forego marriage and devote herself instead to parental caretaking. Daughters of note who cared for their fathers include Virginia Woolf, Anna Freud, and the famous psychoanalytic patient Anna O. (Bertha Pappenheim).

PART II
Diagnosis and Treatment of Trauma-Related Disorders

CHAPTER 4

Post-Traumatic Syndromes in Rape, Incest, and Battering

A LTHOUGH WE CAN isolate patterns of behavior specific to such forms of assault as blitz rape, date rape (Hartman & Burgess, 1988), father-daughter incest (Herman, 1981), or battering (Walker, 1979), the fact that different kinds of assault occur together in many abusive families and that many victims have been assaulted in more than one context attests to the general social and psychological dynamics that underlie the coercive control of females.

Social programming that makes all females vulnerable is often complicated by individual dynamics complexly intertwined with the tendency of children to bond with their caretakers (Bowlby, 1977; Waters, 1978) and the long-term dependency of children. In addition to the dominance-submission patterns characteristic of traditional sex-role socialization, for example, assaultive behavior often involves a pattern of symbiotic related-ness between a couple. Many observers, following the work of Mahler (1968), consider symbiosis to be a normal phase of early childhood develop-ment, which can be developmentally distorted in child victims in such a way that they remain vulnerable to victimization in adult life. Symbiotic aspects of bonding can also be regressively reinstated in adult victims and used as a mechanism of coercive control (Herman, 1992).

In the case of child abuse, the assaultive adult of either sex may be pathologically bonded to or identified with the child victim and may di-rectly sabotage any of the child's normal attempts to individuate. Not uncommonly this interaction has a patterning effect on the child's subse-quent interpersonal relationships. It does not lead necessarily to the seek-ing out of abuse, but it often increases the victim's tolerance for abusive relationships and decreases her sense of entitlement to personal safety. Since abuse in early life typically produces high levels of tension in the victim and distorts normal processes of self-regulation, it has other far-reaching consequences for development across the life span. Repetitive victimization may be a causative factor in many physical diseases as well as psychopathology.

In adult life, partners who are symbiotically attached to one another may feel panicky at the thought of separation. Sex-role socialization, however, tends to program males and females to behave differently when confronted by such panic. The assaultive male is likely to both deny his own dependency and to enforce continuing dependency in his partner (Walker, 1979). The assaulted female is likely to respond with submissiveness, complicated by the effects of shock and, frequently, physical injury. To the extent that the rage and retaliatory impulses she feels are contrary to her feminine socialization, she often dissociates them.

Other factors, such as the necessary dependency of children on their parents or the economic dependency of wives on their husbands combine with a lack of external social supports to keep victims tied to their assailants. But even when an adult woman tries to leave an abusive context, a pervasive social expectation of symbiosis between sexual partners, mythologized as romance, contributes to her problem. Once a woman has "made her bed," so the old saying goes, she should "lie in it."

Since rape, child sexual abuse, and battering involve the use of force by one person to achieve and maintain control over another person, they constitute an incontrovertible denial of the victim's choice and an inescapable overriding of her own capacity for control. The coping mechanisms employed by some victims may enable them to maintain a slight degree of influence over an assailant or to sustain the comforting illusion that they do have some control. But the stress of assault, whether experienced as a sudden shock or a repetitive torment, is actually inescapable. Consequently, it is likely to evoke the response patterns typically associated with inescapable stress. In many instances, the resulting symptom picture is recognizably that of post-traumatic stress disorder. Many assaults, however, particularly repetitive assaults by family members, also produce a wider array of post-traumatic symptoms, including distorted patterns of attachment, pervasive problems of identity integration, and belief systems that rationalize assaultive behavior.

Because victims differ in their vulnerability, coping mechanisms, and good fortune, they will differ in how quickly and completely they recover from the trauma of assault. Kilpatrick, Veronen, and Best (1985) found that the rape victim's distress at 6 to 21 days following the rape proved highly predictive of distress at three months after the incident. Based on a previous study they could infer that this early distress predicted responses four years post-rape. This finding suggests that apparent recovery from trauma may be deceptive. Long-term subtle effects, such as those related to PTSD, may persist unnoticed by observers unless specifically addressed in diagnosis and treatment.

Recovery for many is complicated by social tendencies to blame and stigmatize victims and to conceptualize their difficulties in terms of intrinsic pathology, such as female masochism or self-defeating behavior. Some of those concerned with helping survivors view the use of diagnostic categories as in itself a major form of revictimization (Ochberg, 1988; Stark & Flitcraft, 1988). They emphasize that pathology is usually a consequence rather than a cause of victimization and that professionals have typically used diagnostic labeling as a way of avoiding the social and political oppression of women. This analysis is to some extent valid and a needed corrective to the knee-jerk diagnostic assessments so often made on victimized females. Unfortunately, however, it fails to take into account the complex intertwining of victimization and victim response patterns, including chronic pathological developments, which may seriously distort adaptation across the life span.

From the perspective of the present discussion, the pejorative labeling and victim-blaming analyses that traditionally guided professional approaches to female abuse are a hazard to be carefully monitored. The study of such processes as addiction to trauma and self-injury, for example, can easily degenerate into a focus on the internal dynamics of the client that obscures the social context of her problems. Unfortunately, too, it is easy for helping professionals to become excessively preoccupied with diagnostic niceties and statistical compilations. Such preoccupations often involve an evasion of some of the most serious roadblocks to recovery, such as the persistence of an unsafe environment or social arrangements that perpetuate female victimization.

Even so, diagnosis can play a positive role in facilitating treatment and recovery. Explaining PTSD as a syndrome, for example, can reassure a survivor that she is not going crazy and help her understand her symptoms as a typical response to physical injury and psychological terror (Courtois, 1988; Dolan, 1991). By mapping the expectable effects of assault and the internal as well as external roadblocks to recovery, diagnosis can also helpfully guide professional interventions.

One of the uses of diagnosis is to facilitate approaches to treatment that focus on the relationship of body to mind in post-traumatic symptoms. The physical symptoms that are a consequence of abuse involve real and serious distortions of physiological processes, which can contribute to very real physical diseases. The negative impact of rape on physical health is indicated by the significant increase, following assault, in physician visits by victims (Calhoun & Atkeson, 1991). Somatic symptoms are also a common consequence of incest (Loewenstein, 1990) and battering (Walker, 1987).

Many physical symptoms of female victims were traditionally dismissed as "hysterical." Modern research and treatment is clarifying the extent to which they are psychosomatic. Not only unhealed injuries, but psychophysiological processes intrinsic to the organization of memories for painful injuries contribute to such symptom pictures.

GENERAL CONSIDERATIONS FOR
INDIVIDUAL PSYCHOTHERAPY

Effective therapy for survivors of assault needs to address both acute and chronic responses to trauma. Crisis intervention for victims of rape and battering are frequently antecedent to more long-term treatment. Such interventions can simultaneously focus on immediate issues related to self-care and safety and prepare the way for long-term therapy. Therapeutic interventions at all levels need to recognize the role of reality factors in victimization and victim recovery. The significance of personal choice is often at the heart of recovery, but glib approaches to choice, such as those that blame the victim or exhort her simply to leave an abusive context, are likely to be ineffective and, in some instances, to contribute to revictimization.

Therapeutic interventions will usually need to focus specifically on the practical problems involved in increasing the victim's control over her circumstances as well as her person. In many cases, survivors of assault require multiple services and different treatment modalities at different points in recovery. The utilization and coordination of adjunctive services can have a major impact on the outcome of individual psychotherapy.

Therapists can inform clients about adjunctive services while at the same time describing the focus and limits of their own involvement. It is helpful to frame psychotherapy as a continuation of the client's previous therapeutic accomplishments, to reinforce adaptive behavior that has already been facilitated, and to point out how ongoing therapy will differ from crisis interventions. The client should be asked about her own treatment goals and the barriers she perceives to achieving them. If she has felt victimized by previous encounters with helping agencies or professionals, it is important to review this issue frankly, to ask explicitly that the client bring it up when she feels it is relevant to the present therapy, and to recognize that issues of trust, some of which stem from revictimization, will be an ongoing treatment issue.

Most of those who work with survivors emphasize the need to clarify and delimit boundaries as an ongoing part of therapy. Assault involves a traumatic violation of boundaries that makes victims hypersensitive to such issues. Past betrayals have led them to expect new ones, and some constantly test boundaries in an attempt to discover whether or not the therapist is really trustworthy. Sometimes, too, hope is terrifying in that it requires a radical change in self-concept and world view. Clients who tend to view others in terms of simple split images—good vs. bad—are also constantly looking for the Achilles heel of the idealized therapist. They may interpret boundary issues in terms that prove the therapist's wonderfulness or confirm her incompetence.

Boundaries need to be discussed explicitly at the beginning of treatment, particularly if the client has had earlier therapies in which boundaries regarding such issues as touching or telephone contacts were not delimited. The therapist can be matter of fact about the boundaries of the present therapy, pointing out how they safeguard the client as well as the therapist. It is sometimes necessary to make it clear that the therapist will make no attempt to provide the kinds of direct assistance that the client has received or is currently receiving from other agencies, such as help in finding shelter, paying bills, or restraining the behavior of an abuser.

If there are any legal issues that are likely to impact on psychotherapy, it is important to explore both the issues themselves and the possible impact at the beginning of treatment. Exceptions to rules of confidentiality, in particular, should be stated and discussed. Laws in some states, for example, require psychotherapists to report the abuse of minor children. Legal precedents mandate the reporting of a client's plan to assault another individual. The client needs to be informed that such laws pose limits to confidentiality that are, nevertheless, specific; confidentiality is otherwise to be very strictly guarded. The client can count on the therapist to keep her secrets. Since some survivors have been betrayed repeatedly not only by assailants but by revictimizing contacts with helpers, the need for therapists to reinforce verbal statements about boundaries with consistent behavior is obvious.

In some cases, one of the most important issues to address initially in treatment is the therapist's inability to control the behavior of an assailant. This issue is likely to be especially important with clients who are in battering relationships or who suspect others of abusing their children. Divorced clients, for example, sometimes appeal to therapists for help in controlling noncustodial fathers suspected of abusing their children during visitation. The therapist can make it clear that she is on the client's side and can put her in touch with advocates, protective services agencies, and child therapists. Nevertheless, the individual therapist is limited in the kind of pragmatic interventions she can make. Her most effective intervention is helping the client assert herself strongly to protect herself and her children. For individuals who have been systematically cowed into submission, this task in itself is usually a matter of long-term, intensive therapeutic work.

Similarly, the therapist cannot stop a battering partner from battering — she can only help the client become self-protective. Helping the client understand that abuse is the responsibility of the assailant, and that others, including the client herself, cannot help him if he refuses help, is sometimes one of the most frustrating though most basic tasks of therapy. Differentiating those aspects of life over which one has control from those over which one is powerless is a demanding process, which almost inevitably leads to painful confrontations. Fantasies about changing the behavior of an assailant are frequently an attempt to avoid the grief of separation. Letting go and mourning is a necessary stage in recovery.

The therapist's inability to stop continuing abuse will arouse rage and overwhelming despair in some clients. The realization that the therapist, like the client herself, lacks omnipotence can trigger distressing memories of feeling betrayed by caretakers. It is an aspect of limitations and boundaries that most clients eventually come to understand; a few, however, take it as proof that nobody can really help or use it as a pretext for discontinuing treatment.

Medication

The usefulness of medication as an adjunct to psychotherapy is debatable, particularly among therapists with a feminist orientation. In some instances, medication is helpful as a temporary support. It may enable a client to continue coping during a crisis that would otherwise immobilize her. Medication is often useful for moderating acute symptoms of PTSD, particularly if they derive from single-blow shocks like rape. Many physicians (not just psychiatrists) routinely prescribe psychoactive medications. Many clients will already be taking prescribed medication at the beginning of psychotherapy, and some are convinced that medication is helpful or necessary. It is important for the therapist to be aware of any medication a client is taking and expectable effects, both positive and negative. Withdrawal from medication should always be carefully monitored, preferably by the prescribing physician.

Often the key word in reference to medication is "temporary." Clients need to be informed about possible negative side effects and the potential for revictimization through addiction to some medications, as well as such problems as drug and alcohol interactions. A decreased reliance on medication is frequently one of the positive outcomes of effective psychotherapy.

Some clients explain that they need medication because of a biological problem, such as a "chemical imbalance." For a few, this may be demonstrably true. Frequently, however, individuals who claim that they have a chemical imbalance have never had any physical tests that would warrant this assumption. It is merely a hypothesis used to avoid confronting the social and psychological dimensions of their problems. It also expresses the kind of either-or thinking—body vs. mind, instead of body *and* mind—that ignores the interactional features of human adaptation.

Both professionals and clients who attribute psychological disturbances to a "chemical imbalance" often underestimate the role of trauma in such imbalances and the possibilities of ameliorating internal imbalances through nonchemical interventions. A therapist can approach this problem by explaining that bodily responses are not simply preprogrammed by heredity, even when heredity is a contributing factor. The body constantly undergoes chemical changes in response to the environment. Stress-related chemical changes are, in fact, predictable and measurable. The best treatment of many such changes involves controlling the stressful environment and the individual's reactions to stress.

Some clients have been involuntarily medicated or have experienced negative side effects from medication. Not surprisingly, they are likely to be very wary of medication and to perceive it as a form of revictimization. Such clients often welcome more behavioral and holistic approaches to their symptoms. Many therapists, too, prefer to treat victims with methods that deemphasize medication in favor of such mind-body interventions as biofeedback or hypnosis. In cases of chemical dependency, nonchemical forms of treatment are particularly advisable. Nevertheless, where medication is indicated or desired, it is important to respect and carefully evaluate the client's need for it. The suggestion that her use of medication is a sign of weakness or a personal failing is most specifically to be avoided.

Hospitalization

With some clients, the issue of hospitalization arises. Clients previously diagnosed as having borderline personality disorder or those with severe dissociative disorders, for example, often have a history of hospitalization and treatment interventions that may include shock treatments, overmedication, and the use of restraints. They are likely to raise concerns about a repetition of such experiences. When symptoms are severe or chaotic and hospitalization has been a part of a client's history, the possibility of containing inevitable therapeutic crises within an outpatient therapeutic context has to be carefully evaluated. If the client is really out of control and has few external supports outside the therapy, the therapist can make it clear that voluntary hospitalization, like medication, is an available option.

It may also be necessary with clients who threaten suicide to explicitly review the contingencies that might lead to involuntary hospitalization. Many clients who self-injure are not really attempting suicide, but self-injury can sometimes have dangerous, though unpredicted consequences. The therapist can be matter of fact about these issues and avoid philosophical debates. As a professional, she or he is not only therapeutically concerned but legally accountable.

For many therapists, hospitalization, especially involuntary hospitalization, is a treatment of last resort. If the possibility arises, it is useful to discuss how hospitalization, either voluntary or involuntary, is likely to impact on the existing therapy. Some clients seem to become addicted to hospitalization and to use it as a resistance to confronting issues in therapy. Whenever the going gets rough, they leave the scene and enter a hospital, often a new hospital, where a new set of professionals starts over with them. This behavior is an aspect of revictimization and needs to be interpreted as such. Insofar as it fragments the treatment, it reflects the fragmentation of the client's life and proves to her that she is beyond help.

Some therapeutic techniques require a special therapeutic environment. Abreactive work, for example, requires special attention to the safety of the therapeutic setting and the need for controlling violent outbursts that might be dangerous to client or therapist. Abreactive work, in fact, easily becomes revictimizing if careful groundwork is not laid for it and it is not carefully guided. Given a strong therapeutic alliance and careful attention to the physical setting of treatment, however, such work can often be carried out without resorting to hospitalization. Hypnosis is particularly useful in providing the controls required for safe abreactions (Putnam, 1986, 1989).

The availability of hospital facilities suitable to the client's needs and the kind of relationship a therapist has with such facilities will also be relevant to any discussions about hospitalization.

Telephone Contacts

The use of telephone contacts in psychotherapy is controversial. Many therapists explicitly avoid such contacts. Brief telephone contacts can be helpful, however, if the therapist is comfortable with them and can limit them and if the client does not react negatively to them by losing boundaries or avoiding dealing with underlying issues in the therapy session itself. These are big "ifs." At the beginning of treatment, especially, it is best to be cautious. Particularly during initial phases of therapy or when flashbacks become especially troublesome, the client may simply need to arrange for extra therapeutic sessions. Just as *temporary* is a key word with respect to medication, so *brief* and *occasional* are key words with respect to the usefulness of telephone contacts.

Psychotherapy

A major consequence of abuse is fragmentation—fragmentation of self, shattering of social relationships, erosion of social supports. The challenge of psychotherapy is integration and the restoration of a sense of wholeness. Wholeness involves repair and growth, healing and health maintenance. The focus of psychotherapy is necessarily personal and particular, but in the process of personal integration, many victims confront the social dimensions of their individual problems. Therapy can impact on social as well as personal integration by empowering the victim to lay claim to her own authority, to create rather than merely react to the world she lives in.

My own approach to psychotherapy attempts to integrate perspectives from social learning, particularly those aspects of socialization that contribute to women's special psychological problems, with a focus on internal dynamics and interpersonal relationships. This focus involves an awareness of issues, including transference issues, that are especially significant in traumatized individuals. Verbal communication is the main, though not the exclusive mode of interaction. Adjunctive techniques are used when they seem indicated, can be integrated with the therapy as a whole, and are not likely to be disruptive. In practice, it is possible to integrate adjunctive techniques with more traditional "talking therapy" approaches if one remains flexible and sensitive to the overall pattern unfolding in therapy. I find enactive techniques, such as the use of drawing and play, particularly useful with adults victimized as children, as well as with children. These will be described more fully in a subsequent chapter.

Psychotherapy is a dialogue based on a contractual arrangement. Equality and mutual respect make the process possible. Nevertheless, there are acknowledged distinctions between therapists and clients. As a professional, the therapist is accountable for her knowledge and training and for the appropriateness of her behavior. As an unhappy or disturbed person, the client has the right to be unaware, needy, freely expressive, and regressed within the boundaries of the therapeutic context. The client has an obligation to respect the therapist's boundaries and vice versa. But the client has no obligation to take care of the therapist or the therapist's feelings. The therapist, in contrast, is a special kind of caretaker.

Several consequences evolve from this arrangement. It is up to the therapist, as the professional, to continuously monitor and control boundary problems. Clients will quite typically have problems with boundaries as well as experiences with care givers that compound such problems. Many constantly test boundaries and the therapist's consistency. They subject the therapist to the double binds that have constantly structured their own lives. When the client is self-injurious or suicidal, for example, the therapist may feel she is in a damned-if-I-do, damned-if-I-don't position with regard to hospitalization. Whatever the practical solution chosen, it is important to interpret the transference aspects of such double binds, to help the client understand their origin in early relationships, and to facilitate behavioral changes that will make her relationships with other people, including the therapist, less conflicted.

Effective psychotherapeutic techniques with survivors of abuse are based on a wide variety of theoretical orientations. For many victims of single-blow shocks, such as rape, crisis intervention and short-term therapy can facilitate recovery (Hartman & Burgess, 1988). With such clients, treatment can be quite specifically focused on the single unexpected trauma and the reestablishment of a previously high level of adaptation. Because so many women have internalized self-blaming tendencies and scapegoating stereotypes about females, however, any victim may need to focus specific attention on these typical "women's issues."

In many cases, long-term psychotherapy is indicated as an approach to repetitive traumatization in childhood or adult life. Responses to childhood victimization often lead to characteristic problems in self-regulation and social interaction that require systematic exploration. Behavioral change is not a simple outcome of insight and may, in fact, be facilitated though techniques like desensitization that require little insight. But insight is an important factor in self-esteem and the experience of self-control; most long-term psychotherapy aims to facilitate insight.

Insight-oriented therapy may, nevertheless, be supplemented with behavioral or cognitive techniques targeting specific symptoms (Giaretto, 1982). In many instances, those in individual psychotherapy find simultaneously working in groups of survivors especially helpful (Courtois, 1988; Leehan & Wilson, 1985). Groups vary from those focused primarily on support among survivors to those that emphasize particular theories and ideologies. The effectiveness of a group depends on how well the survivor feels matched to it, a variable only she can evaluate. The individual psychotherapist can provide some guidance in this respect, however. At different points in treatment, for example, the survivor may need different kinds of group experience.

Occasionally, a survivor becomes involved with a group whose orientation runs counter to the ongoing work of individual therapy. Certain political or religious groups, for example, may foster beliefs about loyalty to the group or a particular group leader or beliefs about female subordination, which seem to sabotage the client's moves toward autonomy. Being played off against an authoritarian group leader is only of many double binds therapists are likely to encounter in their work with survivors. The client's right to make choices in her life must be carefully respected. But in such cases, the therapist can be specific and consistent about her own orientation. Although therapeutic neutrality is basic to therapy, no psychotherapy is value-free. Victimizing groups, like other victimizing relationships, need to be discussed from the standpoint of revictimization.

Hypnosis

One technique useful in certain phases of psychotherapy with survivors is hypnosis. Some therapists are very wary of hypnosis, however, because it has been associated with questionable practices, such as stage performances and involvement in the occult. Others implicate hypnosis in iatrogenic symptoms or claim that such phenomena as multiple personalities are artifacts of hypnosis. The problem of iatrogenesis will be discussed more extensively in a subsequent chapter.

The use of hypnosis with females also raises special concerns because hypnosis has been popularly associated with authoritarian forms of control. In 1894, George du Maurier wrote a novel, later made into a movie, that portrayed this popular image of hypnosis—that of a compliant young woman named Trilby manipulated by the self-serving Svengali. Unfortunately, even in the 20th century, many women have had a Svengali in their lives. Being overwhelmed by controlling authorities is a familiar female experience. Sometimes, strict obedience to authority has been a condition of survival. Sometimes romantic love has been equated with entranced submissiveness. For these reasons, the effective use of hypnotic interventions with women requires careful attention to issues of autonomy.

Even so, hypnosis can be a powerful therapeutic tool, particularly in the treatment of dissociative symptoms. Procedures in which the therapist becomes a hypnotic guide to client trance states that were formerly spontaneous, uncontrolled, and autistic, can function as an important bridge to integration. Such techniques are particularly useful with victims of child abuse. Ebert (1988) has also found hypnosis to be useful in focused therapy with rape victims.

Some survivors decline hypnosis; some are not able to make very effective use of it. Many survivors of abuse, however, enter spontaneous trance states habitually and some, such as those with multiple personality disorder, are hypnotic virtuosos. In such cases, the therapeutic challenge is helping the client gain control over an uncontrolled symptom. Ericksonian techniques, which downplay authoritarian forms of induction in favor of more client-centered ones, are especially useful in facilitating such control. Dolan's discussion of solution focused therapy with survivors provides a helpful introduction to several procedures based on Ericksonian hypnosis (1991).

Other approaches to hypnosis, including formal inductions, can also be helpful in some cases, particularly with severely dissociated individuals. Sometimes in working with multiple personality disorder, for example, the therapist needs to take charge quickly in an authoritative way, as distinct from authoritarian way. If a client is very regressed or out of control, hypnosis can protect the safety of both client and therapist. Bliss (1986) and Braun (1980) have described the use of hypnosis in diagnosing and treating multiple personality disorder.

Physical Contact

The therapeutic alliance is, for most survivors, a new kind of mutual interaction. It is distinctly different from relationships with abusers. Nor is it an attempt to match unrealistic ideals about good parenting or to replace, in any concrete fashion, what the client missed in her childhood. These considerations are especially pertinent to therapeutic interventions based on ideas like "reparenting." The therapist is not and cannot be the client's parent, and attempting to do so can only confuse the client and possibly destroy the therapy. Part of being a real parent, for example, is being constantly on-call, an available source of physical support as well as emotional contact.

In practice, the client's presumed need for reparenting is taken by some therapists as a pretext for physical contact with the client. In most instances, however, physical contact is inappropriate to the therapeutic context and some forms of contact, such as sexual contact, are not only unethical and countertherapeutic, but illegal in some states. Body work involving physical contact, such as massage therapy, can certainly be a useful adjunct to treatment, but is best provided by someone other than the psychotherapist. Body work in the context of psychotherapy, similarly, is most helpful when it is least threatening, that is, when it does not involve actual physical touching between therapist and client.

Most survivors of abuse are extremely ambivalent about physical contact. In my own work, I usually do not engage in much of it. Although an occasional hug or letting a client squeeze my hand during a painful abreaction are acceptable with some clients, even such seemingly benign forms of contact have to be carefully evaluated. When clients seem to have an intense need for touching, transitional objects, such as stuffed animals or hand puppets can often provide an effective bridge between physical and psychological contact. From a therapeutic standpoint, the client's needs and fears need to be sympathetically interpreted. Tendencies to act rather than think or process material verbally need to be channeled into behavior, such as play, which can eventually be integrated with symbolic thought.

Physical contact is one of the major revictimizing pitfalls of psychotherapy. It is inevitably a countertransference issue as well as an issue for the client. Survivors of abuse, in particular, are likely to try to place the therapist in the kinds of double binds about contact that are familiar to them. Will contact hurt or soothe? Will it arouse painful memories or frightening sexual feelings or rage? Who is allowed to initiate and control contact? When is it all right to refuse? Aside from the possibilities of sexualization of contact, the issue of genuine feeling arises. The therapist's feelings about contact vary with her own moods and personal meanings. It is unfair to arouse a client's expectations of physical contact and then withhold it when the therapist is not in the mood for it. On the other hand, the feelings of the therapist are not the responsibility of the client, and it is inappropriate to spend time in treatment discussing the therapist's personal issues. It is simpler and more therapeutic to define boundaries, including contact boundaries, at the beginning of therapy and to respect them consistently.

For many survivors, one of the important discoveries in therapy is the extent to which sustained psychological contact with another person can be meaningful without being physical. For many clients, this experience has been painfully missing and mourned. Insofar as psychotherapy does involve aspects of constructive reparenting, it is this dimension of normal parenting—the establishment of a stable, nonexploitive, growth-facilitating relationship—that is therapeutic.

Mistakes

Therapists vary from day to day in how well they manage genuine helpfulness. The formal boundaries of the therapeutic context help shield the client from the therapist's imperfections and human frailties. But mistakes occur. Sometimes it is useful for the therapist to admit them to the client, particularly if the client confronts her about the mistake. Often, however, that would mean burdening the client with the therapist's problem or shifting the focus of therapy from difficult issues to the imperfections of the treatment process. In many instances it is best just to learn from mistakes, try not to repeat them, and move on.

Sometimes, especially in work with survivors, lapses in therapist empathy are simply a sign of therapist burnout. Avoiding burnout means acknowledging one's human needs as well as imperfections. Periodic time-outs are in order for therapists as well as for clients. When major or repeated lapses of empathy occur, it is usually a sign of a countertransference issue that requires careful and immediate attention. If the problem cannot be corrected, it may be best for both therapist and client for the client to change therapists.

Many clients can forgive occasional mistakes in the context of an otherwise helpful therapy. A few cannot. The discovery that therapists are only human, combined with the punitive evaluations internalized from abusers, can lead to therapeutic impasses and even tragic losses. On the other hand, learning to be humanly imperfect without suffering sudden extreme plunges in self-esteem is an important achievement in therapy, a form of behavior therapists can usefully model for clients.

SYMPTOM CONFIGURATIONS IN POST-TRAUMATIC SYNDROMES

For females, rape is arguably the archetypal image of inescapable shock (Brownmiller, 1975). As a category of traumatic experience, it subsumes other painful violations, such as incest. Briere and Runtz (1988), in fact, consider the post-abuse reactions characteristic of sexually victimized children to be a form of chronic Rape Trauma Syndrome (Burgess & Holmstrom, 1974). Even ostensibly nonviolent intrusions are often shocking, inescapable, and achieved through the threat if not the actuality of force. Thus, as Calhoun and Atkeson (1991) argue, " . . . any act of sexual domination can be regarded as rape" (p. 2).

The rape of children has often been rationalized as affection, dismissed as infantile fantasy, or excused as not necessarily harmful, but it is nevertheless a destructive violation, a form of coercive intrusion predicated on the power differential between victim and victimizer. Although rape laws define degrees of assault, and although violations like penetration and physical violence can be expected to produce the most severe trauma, it is the degree of terror and confusion in the victim that is correlated with post-traumatic pathology. The experience of being deprived of choice, of being immobilized and physically controlled, is physically as well as psychologically overwhelming. In both children and adults, rape is also often accompanied by other forms of violence, such as other forms of physical abuse and battering.

Repetitive rape, whether it occurs in childhood or adult life, tends to evoke active protest, although the expression of protest may be muted by numbing and withdrawal. A victim caught off guard by a first shock often tries to resist subsequent intrusions. When this happens, the level of violence may escalate; the victim learns that shock is inescapable and that submission is the only way to moderate it. But submission as a coping mechanism will not necessarily prevent violence either; the assailant's impulses are not really under the victim's control. Shock, then, really is inescapable and sexual cues become inescapably associated with helplessness, rage, and pain.

Even if a child victim's relationship with her abuser is characterized by tenderness, her experience of overstimulation and coercion tends to arouse feelings associated with violation. Even if an adult woman's sexual relationship with a battering partner starts out nonviolently, it tends, with time, to become contaminated by the physical violence (Schechter, 1982; Walker, 1979). In either case, overwhelming negative feelings become an expectable part of sexual interactions.

The study of the incidence of rape in battering relationships and in marriage generally is complicated by a legal tradition that considers sexual access to "his" woman to be a specific entitlement of the married male (Russell, 1982). Any woman who has an ongoing relationship with a man is likely to find that others interpret this relationship as an explanation for assault that releases the assailant from accountability. This is particularly true in instances in which the victim tries to hold the assailant legally accountable (MacKinnon, 1989). The attempt to prove she knew him is merely an indication of the extent to which a woman's relationship with a man is commonly taken as an excuse for his domination of her. Unfortunately, though, proving that the victim did *not* know the assailant will not necessarily help much.

Many victims of rape and battering fear for their lives (Calhoun & Atkeson, 1991; Russell, 1984; Walker, 1979). Ochberg (1988), borrowing a concept from Robert Lifton (1967) discusses how victims lose their "veil of denial" regarding death and become preoccupied with death imagery. Some of the most severe post-traumatic symptoms are connected with this response. Both initial responses to the trauma and long-term accommodations involve basic survival strategies—the automatic, gut-level responses associated with psychobiological emergency reactions, the cognitively elaborated coping procedures employed by vigilant inhabitants of unsafe surroundings, or the numbed endurance strategies of entrapped hostages (Herman, 1992).

Different modes of treatment and adjunctive services are appropriate for different forms of assault. However, certain symptom patterns are a common sequel to both physical and sexual assault and will need to be addressed sooner or later in the treatment of many survivors. They include:

1. symptoms characteristic of post-traumatic stress disorder (PTSD)
2. issues related to self-concept, self-esteem, and identity
3. pathological forms of attachment and interpersonal relatedness
4. tendencies to repetitively enact traumatic experiences and post-traumatic adaptations
5. dissociative pathology

Other common symptom configurations are those related to somatization and physical illness, substance abuse, and revictimization. These problems are often secondary to the more basic consequences of inescapable shock. Clients presenting such symptoms may require specific, focused interventions including medical evaluation and treatment, detoxification and addiction recovery, and helping the victim to extricate herself from particular revictimizing contexts, including institutional contexts. In such cases, the success of individual psychotherapy is usually contingent on the effectiveness of these adjunctive interventions.

PTSD Symptoms as a Sequel to Assault

Following the conceptualization of post-traumatic stress disorder, this diagnostic category has been increasingly used as a framework for understanding the symptoms that typically follow both physical and sexual assault (Briere & Runtz, 1988; Calhoun & Atkeson, 1991; Coons et al., 1989; Goodwin, 1990; Hartman & Burgess, 1988; Kilpatrick et al., 1985). Although, as a number of investigators emphasize, the PTSD concept does not easily account for all post-abuse symptoms, it is especially useful in describing and treating the characteristic psychobiological responses and the somatic complaints of victims. One of the challenges to modern research is the explication of how PTSD responses immediately following trauma become woven into personality structure in childhood and how

PTSD symptoms overshadow and distort preexisting healthy adaptations in adult life. It is also important in evaluating post-traumatic symptoms to recognize that they are not the whole picture and that, in adults especially, they may mask well-developed capacities for adaptive coping.

Post-traumatic stress disorder, as described in *DSM-III-R*, involves a set of symptoms that point to persisting disturbances in the biological systems regulating arousal and stress adaptation. Alternating symptoms of increased excitement and vigilance followed by numbing and behavioral constriction suggest a disturbance in basic biological rhythms, which may have far-reaching physical as well as psychological effects. It is sometimes possible in the course of therapy to reconstruct an original post-traumatic stress syndrome that was subsequently masked or modified by other symptomatic or characterological developments.

Traditionally, clinical interviews have often failed to elicit material concerning rape, child sexual abuse, and battering. In some cases, such material appears almost parenthetically in a case report and is not systematically related to the victim's symptoms or treatment. This omission can be avoided by gentle but specific questioning, which invites a victim to disclose assaults and to place them in the context of her presenting problems (Courtois, 1988). Questionnaires and checklists, which reference abuse issues, can also be helpful (Briere, 1989). The Dissociative Experiences Scale (DES, Bernstein & Putnam, 1986) is a useful tool for assessing the dissociative symptomatology often associated with abuse.

In some instances, a client's symptoms will strongly suggest a history of abuse that she no longer remembers. Childhood sexual abuse, for example, may not be uncovered for years. Thus, at the beginning of treatment, it cannot necessarily be stated that the client is reacting to an event outside the bounds of typical experience. In such cases, the interviewer can carefully elicit context factors that will subsequently clarify any abuse pattern that unfolds. In the safety of the therapeutic setting, the hypothesis that the client was abused can be presented to her in such a way that both her positive and negative reactions can be closely monitored. Occasionally, clients who have been precipitously told that they must have been sexually abused but do not remember it become panicky or are suddenly overwhelmed by flashbacks.

It is often useful to address PTSD symptoms at the outset of treatment. This is obviously true if the symptoms are an acute reaction to a known stressor like rape. One of the reasons for being alert to PTSD as a symptom cluster is that such an awareness can guide the therapeutic search for the original stressor. Even if the stressor is not yet known, stress-related symptoms can be targeted as a preliminary to more intensive therapy. It is also helpful to explain to the client that such symptoms can arise in response to frightening or painful realities and that the client's physiological reactions are typical of stress responses that affect her whole body, not something just "in her head." Even if the client cannot remember specific abuse, she can be reassured that she is not going crazy. She can also be told that forgetting traumatic situations is not unusual and that one goal of therapy is helping her to remember without being overwhelmed.

A hallmark of PTSD symptoms is that they tend to be immoderate. The going to extremes that is characteristic of many traumatized individuals has often been attributed to such factors as endogenous mood disorders or "splitting." Recognizing that the stress-induced deregulation of biological processes contributes to the extremity as well as the cyclical nature of post-traumatic symptoms sometimes enables the client to distance herself from the overreactions and institute deliberate techniques for moderating them. Such simple techniques as deep breathing can sometimes calm a spiraling panic reaction. Symbolic enactments can expose a client in a safe and gradual way to a terrifying stimulus. Controlled confrontations in a new and safe context can help overcome avoidance.

Other approaches to PTSD symptoms include stress inoculation training (Veronen & Kilpatrick, 1983), and biofeedback and relaxation techniques aimed at increasing immediate control at the onset of a symptom. Some clients can effectively be taught to meditate as a general form of healthy self-care. Patients with dissociative tendencies, however, sometimes respond negatively to relaxation and meditative techniques and may initially need to be carefully grounded in the here and now (Briere, 1989).

Heightened states of excitement are only one pole of the PTSD symptom continuum. Symptoms associated with emotional and behavioral constriction are equally problematic. Avoidance symptoms are especially refractory to therapeutic intervention because the lowering of anxiety that follows an avoidance is such a powerful reinforcing mechanism. Avoidance also produces a host of secondary but debilitating symptoms, such as social isolation and, in childhood, the failure to learn social skills.

In therapy, the relation between overwhelming stress and avoidance can be explained to the client and the therapist can reassure her that confrontation with anxiety-evoking situations will be supported and titrated. It is important to acknowledge that avoidance is not "bad." Some clients envision psychotherapy as a descent into hell that will involve a tortuous repetition of painful experiences. Complicated victim responses, such as identification with the aggressor, can lead such clients to structure psychotherapy as a self-punitive experience. It is important for the therapist to monitor and moderate such tendencies rather than becoming an accomplice to them. In some instances, moderation means temporarily supporting avoidance rather than urging confrontation.

In the context of therapy, constriction and numbing responses can be approached as attempts at control, which may diminish when more effective controls are in place. Both anxious overexcitement and constriction may be somewhat alleviated by reassuring the client that she will not be forced to move too quickly or to confront anything before she is ready. Symptoms of constriction can be explained as an attempt to gain "time out" from overstimulation; the solution to the problem is enabling the client to moderate and control time-outs, in contrast to reflexive avoidance or emotional shutdown. At certain points in treatment, desensitization techniques can be useful for facilitating confrontation with cues that have come to elicit phobic avoidance.

Other techniques for breaking through denial and numbing include abreaction and emotional flooding. These must be carefully monitored and contained, however, since they introduce possibilities for generating treatment-precipitated complications and revictimization. At all points in treatment, even when dealing with constriction and avoidance, it is important for the therapist to acknowledge and support the client's need for personal control. Support is therapeutically organized by careful attention to the therapeutic alliance (Courtois, 1988) and by explicitly demarcating the therapeutic context as a safe time and place.

After an intensive psychotherapy is underway, PTSD-related symptoms are likely to appear whenever a client begins to get in touch with painful memories and affects or finds herself in a situational crisis. At that point, it will be useful to have established a repertory of techniques for dealing with acute symptoms. Techniques that involve the reexperiencing and abreacting of trauma require a temporary tolerance for acute symptoms, but such tolerance has to be built up in the context of therapeutic support. Abreaction, in particular, becomes therapeutically effective only if what is abreacted can be eventually integrated within a coherent self. By learning to control her acute post-traumatic reactions, a client acquires techniques that will eventually allow her to explore the roots of trauma.

Sleep Disturbances

Among the most common PTSD symptoms are sleep disturbances. Such symptoms have been found to be prevalent in survivors of sexual abuse (Briere, 1989; Briere & Runtz, 1988; Sedney & Brooks, 1984). They may signal a hidden traumatic origin in many kinds of disorders. Sleep problems may involve distortions in any aspect of the normal sleep cycle — difficulties in falling or remaining asleep, nightmares, sleeptalking or sleepwalking, etc. Abuse-related nightmares typically consist of flashbacks that replay the trauma in literal detail or disguise it with symbolic elaborations.

Secondary reactions to sleep disturbances are also a problem; clients develop fears of going to sleep and fears of sleep deprivation that complicate their other symptoms. Fear as a conditioned response to sleep-related cues is complicated by the fact that child sexual abuse or violent assaults by a partner often take place in the bedroom. As a result, vigilant watchfulness becomes associated with the bedroom as a place, as well as with other sleep-related cues. Sleep problems offer an opportunity to explore the specifics of traumatic contexts. Simply discussing the sleeping arrangements and bedtime rituals of childhood can trigger important memories.

Sleep problems have such extensive implications for daily coping, such as holding down a job, that they often require immediate, practical interventions. Behavioral interventions ranging from desensitization to physical changes in sleeping arrangements can help. Temporary use of medication is also one practical solution. It can be especially helpful in calming the effects of sudden, single-blow shocks. Medication poses dangers, however, since dependency on prescribed medication as well as alcohol and street drugs is one of the most common forms of revictimization. One problem with sleep medication, too, is that it merely postpones dealing with the underlying cause of the distress. Some medications, for example, cloud consciousness in ways that interfere with treatment. Nevertheless, as a temporary adjunct to therapy, sleep medication can help the client through difficult periods.

One of the effective uses of hypnosis in psychotherapy is in facilitating nighttime sleep. The client can be taught specific self-hypnotic rituals to use at bedtime or after waking in the night. Such rituals can be integrated with the bedtime rituals the client already uses, such as a warm bath or soothing music. When hypnosis is also used for other purposes, such as abreaction, rituals for inducing nighttime sleep should be set off by specific contextual cues.

Ross et al. (1989) have proposed that some of the sleep disturbances characteristic of PTSD result from dysfunctional REM mechanisms. They hypothesize that REM sleep, which shows important similarities to the waking state and varies in circadian fashion, is a state of continuous alerting. According to these authors, the neural circuitry involved in PTSD sleep disturbances as well as that associated with normal REM sleep is associated with the heightened startle and anxiety reactions characteristic of trauma responses. One implication of this hypothesis is that PTSD-related sleep problems may be treated by pharmacological or behavioral approaches that target REM mechanisms. Psychotropic agents that have been shown to affect REM sleep include monoamine oxidase inhibitors, tricyclic antidepressants, and lithium.

This formulation illustrates the possibility of treating trauma reactions through interventions that directly affect basic body rhythms. From a clinical standpoint, however, several problems arise with it. One is the need for more confirming psychophysiological evidence. As Reynolds (1989) suggests, the sleep disturbances associated with PTSD may be an epiphenomenon rather than a basic part of the disorder. Another problem involves the role of disturbed REM patterns in recovery—are they merely pathological or part of the healing process? Answers to this question suggest different kinds of interventions.

The assumption that REM distortions are basically a pathological contributing factor in persistent PTSD supports therapeutic attempts to inhibit or alter REM mechanisms. However, some investigators have hypothesized that such REM patterns and other altered states play an adaptive role in the internal processing of stressful material. From this point of view, intrusive flashbacks are part of the process of modifying and integrating painful memories, a kind of psychological metabolizing process.

Insight-oriented psychotherapy has also traditionally emphasized the importance of uncovering and emotionally reexperiencing traumatic material, even when the role of actual trauma in that material was ignored. The assumption that painful remembering may be a necessary part of the integrative process has suggested therapeutic approaches that do not inhibit intrusive imagery but actually stimulate it. Imaginal flooding techniques in the treatment of PTSD, for example, are based on a hypothesized need for intense reexposure to the original stressful stimuli (Keane & Kaloupek, 1982).

The negative therapeutic reactions sometimes associated with abreactive techniques in various forms of treatment, including psychoanalysis, have nevertheless illustrated the dangers of emotional flooding. Some clients, rather than being healed by renewed exposure, are continually retraumatized. Perhaps the key to the successful treatment of post-traumatic overstimulation lies in the careful integration of supportive and uncovering techniques in the treatment process. Many PTSD symptoms, including psychobiological ones, cannot be simply suppressed or avoided. They are the confirming data that convince many victims that repressed or dissociated abuse really occurred. Often, too, they are connected with important autobiographical memories that the client needs to integrate into her view of herself and her history.

Although the temporary suppression of such painful memories through medication or behavioral techniques may be indicated at some points in treatment, the goal of integrative therapy is to replace uncontrollable forgetting or remembering with controlled access to one's memories. In practice, this goal can often be achieved through a controlled confrontation in a safe setting and a careful emphasis on integration in the wake of any traumatic reexperiencing. In this process, one role of the therapist is continually to monitor and guide the relationship between painful confrontation and mastery.

Self-Concept, Self-Esteem, and Identity

Disturbances in self-regulation, self-esteem, and self-representation are common sequels to trauma. In some instances, the sense of self is shattered; in others, it is scarcely allowed to develop at all; in still others, it is deliberately and skillfully shaped to help sustain an abusive context and to guarantee the prerogatives of an abuser. Self-esteem is also related to abuse, particularly familial abuse, in complicated ways. A victim may derive a strange sort of pride from her ability to stand it. In certain cases of ritual abuse, victims are actually programmed to take pride in this ability.

The most debilitating disturbances in self-esteem are those resulting from childhood trauma, particularly repetitive traumatization in an abusive family. But even the individual with a "normal" upbringing and a supportive family can seldom escape distortions of self-concept and lowering of self-esteem following shocks like rape or battering. It is difficult for any victim, no matter how healthy prior to an assault, to altogether escape the negative effects of victim-blaming and sexist socialization.

Sometimes it is only after victimization in adult life that a woman begins to perceive the pervasive influence of such factors on her early self-development. She may then discover that, without realizing it, she has internalized scapegoating stereotypes that impede her recovery. She may also find that, in spite of her seemingly normal upbringing, common female dilemmas have frequently placed her in no-win situations that resulted in shame, guilt, and lowered self-esteem. She may be dismayed to uncover patterns of dependency, economic as well as social and psychological, which make it difficult to disentangle herself from an abusive context without suffering new insults.

Whether a victim is a stranger or an intimate relation, her explicit devaluation by the assailant is a typical part of an assault. She is likely to be attacked with verbal epithets as well as physical blows. If she has a low opinion of herself to begin with, the verbal attack echoes her worst self-accusations. Ironically, her responses to the attack itself may compound these. Her rage, for example, is contrary to female sex-role socialization; her wish to retaliate runs counter to her idea of herself as a "nice," pleasing feminine person. Stigmatization is thus often an inextricable part of the victimizing process. Self-stigmatization, in turn, is a response to socially prevalent trends in female sex-role socialization as well as to specific responses to abuse, including identification with the aggressor.

Such women find themselves up against the dilemmas of female sexuality and female expressiveness, as well as the powerful dynamics of scapegoating. The stigma attached to victims of assault is based in part on the explanation that "she asked for it" and in part on the devaluation of the abused woman as "damaged goods." Russell (1984) discusses the loss of status suffered by victims: "The same behavior that gives status to males (promiscuous sexual relations) endangers status for females" (p. 164). Loss of status for females, however, is not a simple function of a woman's actual behavior, but of social attributions. Reputation—that valuable female asset—is contingent on the opinion of others.

Child victims, who have not yet integrated their diverse and sometimes confusing experiences into a coherent identity pattern, are especially vulnerable to the verbal manipulations of assailants. Child sexual abuse, for example, frequently involves indoctrination. The child is presented with an explanation of the abuse that rationalizes it in terms of victim behavior or characteristics: "You really want it, don't you?" "I saw the way you were looking at me (or yourself)," "You are so bad (or good) I can't help myself." Indoctrination into secrecy reinforces the victim's guilt and isolates her from supports that might relieve guilt and bolster her self-esteem. Accusations that the victim is lying, which may come not only from those she reports abuse to but from perpetrators, are also confusing and guilt-inducing. In some instances, they may even erode a child's developing sense of reality.

Self-Regulation

One outcome of child sexual abuse is a distortion of basic forms of self-regulation that persists in adult life in such tendencies as the sexualization of soothing and the use of self-injury to regulate states of self-awareness. The sexualization of soothing is complicated by the childhood programming of a connection between sexual excitement and exploitation or pain. In such cases, the child learns to seek sexual interactions as a means of regulating her own self-esteem. Such interactions are frequently abusive because of the patterns of interpersonal relatedness the victim has learned and because of a conditioned tolerance for abuse. It is not that the victim is "asking for it." It is, rather, that she has not learned how to ask for, to insist on, something else. Even when a new sexual interaction is not abusive, the victim who needs attachment to another person for her self-esteem may be devastated when the attachment is disrupted. The loss of a partner is sometimes experienced as a loss of self, which may evoke a suicidal panic.

The effects of repetitive abuse on the development of self-concept and self-esteem in childhood are currently being systematically studied. Kinard (1980, 1982) found that negative self-image, as indicated by responses to the Piers-Harris Children's Self-Concept Scale (Piers & Harris, 1969), is predictably associated with severity of abuse. Putnam (1990), discussing the effects of state-dependent learning on identity formation, contends that the fragmentation of self commonly seen in incest victims can be explained by failures to integrate experiences that occur in discrete states of consciousness.

One of the most typical and pervasive experiences of many abused females involves responses to being treated like a nonhuman object rather than a human being. Dehumanization is a common aspect of scapegoating. But it is also an aspect of idealization—the idealized female is superhuman, a perfect angel, a "living doll." These contrasting dehumanizing responses may be expressed in alternating patterns of worshipful attention and violent abuse. They are a legacy of infantile fantasies about perfect or imperfect mothers that pervade culture and have commonly served as prescriptions for relations between the sexes. Once the female is set apart as a creature needed but altogether distinct and different from the male, she is related to on the basis of male projections rather than as an autonomous and equal subject in a mutual interaction. Whether adored or attacked, she is possessively controlled in an attempt to regulate the male partner's self-esteem. She functions, in effect, as a fetish (Waites, 1982).

The female appropriated in this way is likely to experience her partner's ambivalence toward women as a reflection of her own ambivalence. His stereotypes often match hers. But if she tries to extricate herself from the stereotypes in the course of therapy, she confronts the force of them in reality as well as in fantasy. Her partner needs her and will not let go. Being needed and the favorable attention she occasionally gets may be the only external supports for her shaky self-esteem. Functioning as a man's special object is thus essential to her own self-regulation. Only when other supports for self-esteem are in place can she be expected to move beyond the relationship with her abuser.

Objectification plays a particularly important part in the use of females for the production of pornographic material. Again, though children and adults of both sexes are exploited in pornography, females are especially vulnerable across the life span (Barry, 1979; Dworkin, 1981). They are simultaneously forced to be accomplices to illegal acts and intimidated by being told that they are criminals themselves and cannot appeal to authorities for protection.

Pornography dramatically documents the actualities of sexual and physical abuse. It may include photographing the victim in situations ranging from nude exposure to acts of torture. The victim is often posed and forced to exhibit a pleased expression even if she is in pain. If she is not in physical pain, she is nevertheless acutely aware of being degraded. Some adult victims are haunted not only by memories of being photographed in childhood, but by an awareness that such material may still be available and for sale. Their exploitation is thus a form of ongoing abuse rather than merely part of the past.

One pattern of identification that is especially problematic in survivors is identification with the aggressor. It is especially problematic in females, since aggressive behavior runs counter to sex-role socialization. Thus, in many instances it becomes a split-off or dissociated identity configuration. When it is overtly expressed or integrated into female identity, it is especially likely to evoke negative evaluations from other people, including mental health professionals. The aggressive female is likely to be labeled "delinquent," "bitch," "castrating woman," or "acting-out patient." "Acting-out female patients," in turn, are often diagnosed as having a personality disorder or a gender-identity disorder. The source of their acting out, a history of familial abuse, is often glossed over.

Because of typical patterns of sex role-socialization, however, identification with the aggressor in female victims is often contained by self-injurious symptoms rather than directly acted out against others. Such symptoms involve an implicit internal split between the self as aggressor and the self as victim. The victim does not hurt other people; she hurts herself as she was once hurt. In the course of treatment, these patterns need to be carefully and continually clarified.

Psychotherapeutic Approaches to Identity Patterns

Diagnostically, a client's negative statements about herself or her readiness to blame herself for anything that goes wrong can alert the therapist to the possibility of a history of abuse, even if none is immediately remembered. Such negative self-appraisals originated somewhere. Culturally typical scapegoating patterns are a contributing factor, but the client's extreme internalization of them suggests an origin in her individual history. The client may imply that scapegoating was primarily verbal and emotional. But scapegoating as a dynamic is such a common pretext for aggressive action that therapists who encounter scapegoating stereotypes should be alert to more physical forms of abuse.

The challenge of psychotherapy is to acknowledge the authenticity of the client's existing identity configuration (or multiple configurations) while facilitating changes. Whatever has enabled the self to survive is valuable, and the client has a right to hold on to it. During therapy, as she explores other possibilities, a particular configuration may be gradually reshaped or replaced. But it should not be devalued or forcibly altered. As it changes or disappears, it may be mourned, like the childhood that gave rise to it.

In addition to ongoing dialogue with the therapist, Calhoun and Atkeson (1991) suggest guided self-dialogue as a treatment strategy. This involves deliberately teaching the abused woman to monitor her internal dialogue and identify statements about the self that are devaluing or maladaptive. Briere and Runtz (1988) suggest deliberate therapeutic attempts to externalize the victim's negative self-attributions, guilt, and shame.

Many therapists who work with victims emphasize the importance of moving from the negative view of oneself as a victim to the affirmation of oneself as a survivor. The therapist's affirmative attitude as well as the client's work facilitates this move. Survival can be simply acknowledged or explicitly discussed as an aspect of competence. For many clients, competence has never been affirmed and integrated with self-esteem. Those who have been manipulated by inconsistent or insincere flattery distrust even the acknowledgment of it. The therapist can point matter-of-factly to instances in which the client coped effectively or creatively. If she distrusts positive evaluations or persists in maligning herself, the roots of that behavior can be explored.

In working with aggression in female clients, it is important to acknowledge sex-role stereotypes that engender passivity and compliance and to examine their development and function. The legitimacy of the client's aggression and the creative role of aggression in coping can be explicitly emphasized, even as the problems of expressiveness that have caused trouble are examined. Exploring the origin of the aggression in abuse usually uncovers ambivalence. Even those who justify their own destructive behavior often deplore being like their assailant(s). Acknowledging the normalcy of anger and rage as responses to abuse also helps place the client's aggression in perspective. It is not crazy. It is based on inevitable, though socially unacceptable, responses.

Attachment and Relationships

Victimization can be both a cause and a consequence of disturbances in interpersonal relationships. Assaults like rape are stressful to relationships as well as to individuals. Tendencies to blame the victim make some people who are needed for support part of the problem rather than part of the solution. Tendencies to withdraw or dissociate in the aftermath of shock isolate victims from supportive relationships that might be otherwise available. Specific post-traumatic symptoms, such as sexual inhibitions or phobias, compound other relationship difficulties. Repetitive victimization in the context of an abusive family often programs pathological relationship patterns from early childhood. The individuation of the child-victim may be systematically distorted by symbiotic enmeshment with abusive parents, or the child may be carefully schooled in views about reality that isolate the victim from potential supports outside the family.

Many abused children are, in effect, hostages (Herman, 1992)—they are kept alive by being given minimal care. At the same time, their own attempts to individuate and develop mature patterns of self-care may be systematically thwarted, or they may experience alternating cycles of controlling involvement with a parent and neglectful abandonment that requires them to learn to care for themselves and others. They seldom learn about mutuality, trustworthy interdependence, and reciprocal helpfulness. They often learn to take what they are given, whether they want it or not, but not to ask for anything lest they anger parental benefactors.

In therapy, individuals who have lived as hostages to abusive parents or spouses may have to learn other kinds of interpersonal relatedness from the ground up. In this respect, group therapy can be very useful not only as an opportunity to learn about communication and social sharing, but as a framework for learning and practicing social skills. Women in general and former hostages in particular also need to explore authority as distinct from authoritarianism as a dimension of relationships. Some, for example, react to the authoritarian contexts in which they were abused by becoming compulsively permissive. Others, identifying with aggressors, become compulsively controlling. Learning to speak with the authority of her own experience without coercing others is an empowering step toward social as well as internal integration.

Battered women who seek help while still hostages cannot be helped unless their actual entrapment is acknowledged and relieved. Safe shelter is often the first order of business. Direct assistance by police and the criminal justice system is usually a necessary prelude to successful psychotherapeutic intervention. Medical evaluation and treatment is also important. Any woman who has been beaten should be medically evaluated for residual physical effects; this is especially true if she was ever beaten about the head. An amazing number of women who complain of persistent headaches have never been neurologically evaluated for residual effects of battering.

Even if a woman is currently being held hostage in the relationship, her interaction with her partner is typically based on an early voluntary involvement with him that was positive, even excessively idealized. In such instances, the victim's continued enmeshment in her partner is not merely a form of pathological bonding with an assailant but a response to the prospect of loss. The victim cannot confront the loss of the idealized relationship — she insists that love has not really died, but can be revived if she is good enough or subservient enough or perfect enough in her caretaking. The loving phase of the battering cycle is sometimes taken as proof of such a miracle. Both partners often engage in extreme forms of denial about the inevitability of future battering. Sometimes both seem addicted to an illusion that can be compared to certain forms of religious faith.

In order for the symbiotically enmeshed woman to extricate herself from an abusive partner, she must separate from him psychologically as well as physically and mourn the loss. Separation involves healthy forms of individuation that decrease her dependence and increase her self-esteem. If her symbiotic attachment to the batterer has been primarily regressive, a response to a partner's terrorism, the woman can be helped to get in touch again with the more mature adaptations that she had formerly achieved. If individuation has been thwarted from childhood, and she has never learned to relate in any other way, the battered woman needs to learn more mature forms of relating. This task may require long-term psychotherapy.

Mourning the loss of a relationship is a process that is almost always complicated by trauma. Normal processes of mourning involve confronting extreme levels of pain. If the mourned relationship includes good memories and affirmed an individuated self, however, the pain of letting go is mitigated, since something of the good remains and is integrated in the survivor. Relationships that were needed but involved much pain, however, are more difficult to mourn, and if an individuated self has never developed, normal mourning is often complicated by panic. Confronted with separation, the panicky individual fears and believes she cannot survive the loss. Yet clinging to the painful relationship, even in memory, hurts. In such cases, a victim may cling to isolated memories of pleasure; the very fact that good experiences were rare makes them especially valued and idealized. Sometimes a victim will assert that, however cruel her assailant, he was the only one who ever showed her any kindness, the one who cared for and protected her. The abusive relationship is the only model of "love" she has.

One role of therapy is to provide a new model of what "love" is. This issue is usually discussed under the rubric of transference. The psychotherapeutic context tends to elicit the client's typical relationship patterns and to revive early experiences in which the self was not yet individuated. Psychotherapy allows the client to explore her experiences of love and hate, attachment and loss in a special nonexploitive context. In this context, the role of the therapist as caretaker is real but bounded; the therapist is not a parent who controls or must be cared for, not a friend one meets for coffee, not a lover. Yet the working relationship that develops between client and therapist can be supportive, productive, and intensely satisfying for both. Ideally, it enables the client to distinguish between attachment as a positive experience affirming individuation and the kinds of coercive physical appropriation that may have typified her history.

Therapy thus enables the client to make use of and to internalize the authority (as distinct from authoritarianism) of a caretaker, the therapist, who does not herself require caretaking by the client. In this respect, therapy revives early experiences of need and dependency that were often distorted by abusive caretaking or the "parentification" of the child. This aspect of the process makes it possible for therapy to function as a bridge to individuation as well as to the exploration of individuated relationships beyond the therapeutic setting.

The possibility of a relationship that is not sexual or exploitive may be experienced as a novel discovery by clients who have no history of such relationships. Clients who have tended to sexualize all relationships and who have regulated their self-esteem by functioning as a sexual fetish may have a hard time learning this skill. Boundary setting by the therapist may be viewed as a form of neglect, abuse, or rejection. Typically, these attitudes will require interpreting over and over the abusive contexts that gave rise to them. It is not interpretation alone, however, but the experience of the therapeutic relationship that enables the client to integrate healthier forms of relatedness.

Therapists are best able to cope with transference issues, including regressive transference patterns, if they have worked through their own issues. An important part of therapeutic work involves the ongoing monitoring of countertransference, the therapist's transferential response to the client.

Enactment

Traumatization stimulates tendencies toward action. High states of arousal and the deregulation of body rhythms may lead to repetitive enactments of traumatic experiences, disguised to a greater or lesser extent by symbolization. Flashbacks can stimulate enactments as can situational cues associated with the original trauma. If the enactment is contained in play or symbolic constructions, such as art or writing, it may not cause interpersonal problems. Many enactments, however, are not contained but occur in uncontrolled or even dangerous ways. Destructive enactments are often labeled "acting out" by psychotherapists.

The traditional approach to "acting out" has been to try to contain enactments within the psychotherapeutic setting and to replace behavioral acts with verbalization. With certain individuals, such as those with diagnosed character disorders, this containment is often difficult or impossible. The compulsive urgency of enactments derives from states of arousal that are not so easily moderated. In many instances, too, the traumatized individual has a history that makes verbalization difficult. She may have been strictly indoctrinated in secrecy. Her childhood may have provided few opportunities for channeling feelings into symbolic constructions.

One psychotherapeutic approach to enactment is to facilitate safe enactments rather than suppressing action tendencies and insisting that the client confine her communications to verbal statements. Enactment, contained within the safety of the therapeutic setting, can then become a powerful therapeutic tool. In order for this to happen, the therapist needs to familiarize herself with expressive forms and nonverbal forms of symbolization and with ways in which these can be integrated with verbal communications. Enactment in the context of therapy contrasts uncontrolled, socially isolating behaviors with the healing experience of the therapeutic relationship. Therapeutic play is not just a matter of letting an abused child or adult enjoy herself or release tension. It is a bridge to symbolic thinking and personality integration. This facet of therapy will be discussed in more detail in a later chapter.

Dissociation

Dissociative reactions are among the most common symptoms of traumatization. They are related both to the psychobiology of the trauma response and to certain intentional coping mechanisms developed by those who have been repeatedly traumatized. In some instances, dissociation becomes an organizing factor in personality development, resulting in such severe syndromes as multiple personality disorder. The complexities of dissociation are the subject of future chapters.

SOMATIZATION, SOMATIC DISORDERS, AND SUBSTANCE ABUSE

Trauma is referenced in memory not only in modes of visual and verbal recall, but in physical and physiological responses. A simple trauma response, for example, is the reflexive flinching of victims who have been hit. At the first sign of threat, the muscles react to effect attack or withdrawal; fists clench, the whole body may shrink inward or cower. People who have been hit frequently are often chronically tensed to receive blows. Sexual assault, too, can produce chronic patterns of clenching or flinching. Not only are such patterns exhausting, but sometimes they lead to physical pain or damage. Grinding the teeth as a response to stress, for example, may result in headaches or orthodontic problems.

In many instances, assaults produce physical injuries that have lasting consequences for the health of the victim. These consequences are compounded by the victim's hesitance to seek medical attention. Her assailant, in fact, may prevent her from seeking help. When that happens, healing may be delayed or incomplete. Bones that are not set, for example, may not heal properly. Sexual abuse may result in injuries that are not only painful but make the victim vulnerable to infection.

Unhealed injuries may continue to cause pain long after abuse itself has ceased. Certain injuries leave victims vulnerable to chronic problems like urinary tract infections or arthritic pain in injured joints. Headaches are one of the most common complaints of victims. They are frequently part of the symptom picture of dissociative disorders. Medical evaluation may not reveal the cause of such headaches in any physical head injury, but sometimes this failure is the result of inadequate techniques for discovering the injury. Closed head injuries, in fact, may result in microstructural damage that only shows up in sophisticated forms of examination (Montgomery et al., 1991).

In the therapy of survivors, careful medical evaluation is indicated whenever clients report physical symptoms. Since any physical problem is likely to produce psychological effects, it is often useful to request that clients have medical checkups at the outset of treatment. This is especially important if they have not had any recent checkups or complain of specific physical problems. Once current medical conditions are treated or ruled out, the psychotherapist can proceed to deal with somatic symptoms in terms of their significance as memories or symbolic expressions.

Some survivors, however, are reluctant to seek any kind of medical care.

They may experience even routine procedures as unbearably intrusive. In some cases, they may have been victimized in health care settings. Psychotherapy is then necessary to help the client overcome her avoidance enough to be able to make helpful use of available medical procedures, which may ameliorate her suffering.

Substance abuse, including the abuse of prescription medications, is a common problem in survivors of physical or sexual abuse. Addiction requires special interventions, particularly if withdrawal symptoms are a problem. Psychotherapy cannot proceed unless addictions to drugs or alcohol are first resolved. The addicted client is often physically as well as psychologically impaired in ways that compromise her ability to form a therapeutic contract or alliance. It is possible, however, to begin individual psychotherapy once an addicted client is actively involved in a program to facilitate her recovery from substance abuse. Particular therapeutic boundaries regarding sobriety need to be explicit. The therapist may need to make it clear, for example, that she will not attempt to engage in therapy with an individual who is intoxicated or whose patterns of intoxication lead to repeated absences from appointed sessions.

Substance abuse, at least initially, often begins as a form of self-regulation and self-medication. Victims who cannot sleep, for example, may begin to abuse alcohol. Those prescribed drugs for specific somatic symptoms may use them indiscriminately to cope with or hide ongoing abuse. The problem is compounded by the disturbances in self-regulation, which are typically part of the symptom picture in post-traumatic syndromes. Often, too, substance abuse reflects an identification with an abuser who was alcoholic or used drugs. In some cases, particularly cases of ritual abuse, victims are introduced to or forcibly given drugs by abusers.

REVICTIMIZATION

Revictimization is a corollary of many post-traumatic reactions, including patterns of self-injury, tolerance for victimizing relationships, and ignorant, insensitive, misguided, or unethical treatments by caregivers. Revictimization is part of a larger social problem, widespread tendencies to blame the victim, to deny or excuse abusive behavior, and to neglect services needed by victims. Because of the complexity of this problem, it, too, will be treated more specifically in a subsequent chapter.

CHAPTER 5
Perspectives on Dissociation

DISSOCIATION IS A pervasive feature of everyday life, familiar to all of us in ordinary activities like daydreaming while we engage in routine or boring tasks, becoming so engrossed in a book or movie that we forget our immediate surroundings, or absent-mindedly mislaying our car keys when we are suddenly distracted by a ringing telephone. The word itself suggests something of a working definition: it is implicitly linked to the concept of *association* and indicates a disconnection of things once connected. Braun (1988) defines dissociation simply as "the separation of an idea or thought from the main stream of consciousness" (p. 4). Ross (1989) defines dissociation as "the opposite of association," and goes on to explain that "Any two psychic elements may be in a dynamic relationship with each other, in which case they are associated, or relatively isolated and separate, in which case they are dissociated" (p. 87).

THE DISSOCIATIVE CONTINUUM

As a feature of diagnosed psychopathology, dissociation is not restricted to any particular disorder or set of disorders, but is part of the symptomatology observed across the diagnostic spectrum. In this regard, diagnostic classifications like *DSM-III-R*, which selectively isolate a group of "Dissociative Disorders," are unsatisfactory and somewhat misleading. Clinical manifestations of dissociation range from simple disconnections of motor functions that are usually integrated (so-called "conversion" disorders), to the dissociation of emotionally toned and uninhibited behavior from intentional behavior (disorders of impulse control), to the dissociation of sexual behavior from cognitive control, affective pleasure, or personal awareness (sexual dysfunctions), to name only a few. A number of investigators have contended that dissociation is also a major feature of eating disorders (Demitrack et al., 1990; Goodwin & Attias, 1988; Torem, 1986, 1987, 1988). Braun (1988) conceptualizes dissociative phenomena on four levels, that of Behavior, Affect, Sensation, and Knowledge, the first letters of which (BASK) are taken as the name for his model. Each of these four processes varies along a continuum from full awareness to an extreme splitting off from normal awareness, which he labels as *dissociation*. Dissociative episodes involve a break in all BASK processes along a time continuum. Since all four BASK processes are involved in memory organization, such disruptions can result in the kinds of compartmentalizations of memory and identity found in the severe dissociative disorders.

Even in diagnosed disorders, however, dissociation is not simply a pathological response and cannot always be classified as symptomatic. It may, on the contrary, protect the individual both from overwhelming stimulation and from maladaptive responses that would lead to pathological symptom formation. Sometimes, for example, dissociation seems to encapsulate symptomatic behavior. Fetishism, which involves disturbances in the regulation and social orchestration of sexual behavior, is a case in point (Waites, 1982). Often the fetishist functions adaptively in many aspects of his life, so much so that he may never come to the attention of mental health professionals. The dissociative encapsulation of symptoms is also observable in certain somatic disorders. If not extreme, a chronic ache or pain for which no physical disease process can be isolated may contain traumatic memories, which, if allowed into consciousness, would be overwhelming.

As a normal coping mechanism, dissociation plays an important role in creative experience, ranging from the inspiration of poets to the charismatic orations of actors, preachers, and political leaders. The creative aspect of dissociation is often culturally institutionalized, particularly in religious or medical settings.

In primitive medicine, for example, healing, self-actualization, and self-transformation were usually closely aligned; dissociative states were invoked to further such desired outcomes (Ellenberger, 1970; Rouget, 1985). Ellenberger has surveyed the long history of dissociative trance states as a feature of both religious experience and pragmatic medical interventions. Shamanism, for example, often involved a beneficial induction of trance states in both healer and patient. Dissociated states are still commonly encouraged in charismatic religious sects. Initiatory experiences, such as "conversion," are an expected part of integration into some groups of believers. Such experiences are typically sudden and dramatic and involve activities that simultaneously integrate the individual into the group and set the group apart from the uninitiated (James, 1983). Healing is a major focus of many charismatic sects.

The social uses of dissociation are not restricted to religious settings nor have they been banished to secret cults and clandestine rituals. In many diverse contexts, dissociation can be conceptualized as a programmed form of social regulation tied in with carefully orchestrated patterns of self-stimulation and self-soothing. Ritualistic group behavior, such as singing, chanting, and dancing has throughout history been an accepted, even prescribed means of organizing groups. Such practices and the dissociative states they facilitate are a dimension of crowd behavior that enlivens football games, rock concerts, war games, and political rallies.

From a very different perspective, hypnotic techniques involving the carefully monitored induction of dissociative states in clinical settings, have found a place in medicine, particularly obstetrics, and in dentistry. Hypnosis also has a long history in psychotherapy (Ellenberger, 1970) and, after a period of eclipse, is again coming into increased favor, particularly in the treatment of post-traumatic and dissociative disorders. As a treatment technique, hypnosis can transform uncontrolled and maladaptive dissociative responses into a part of the therapeutic process.

Dissociation and Self-Regulation

From a developmental standpoint, dissociative capabilities may be articulated from the earliest infantile attachments and elaborated in normal as well as pathological forms of interpersonal relatedness (Brown, 1991). Helpful parents facilitate "time out" for themselves as well as their children through playful and soothing rituals. Internalizing such social behavior, children are increasingly able to regulate themselves and to integrate individuated identities. Abusive parents, in contrast, simultaneously augment anxiety and distort processes of soothing, making it difficult if not impossible for their children to internalize healthy modes of self-regulation. Dissociative pathology is one result of such distortions.

Even in normal individuals with no history of abuse, dissociation as a self-regulating mechanism is a typical feature of trauma reactions. In any context involving inescapable shock or stress, the process may function to moderate levels of stimulation and organize coping. Paradoxically, dissociation really can increase control over the seemingly uncontrollable. Even in situations of absolute immobility, it is possible to escape in fantasy if one can shut out distracting levels of pain or panic. Fantasy, in turn, can lead to creative strategies for surviving. In some instances a dissociative response can even be lifesaving (Beahrs, 1982).

The dissociative response may be brief or lingering, relatively simple or complex. Brief experiences of being "absent" from consciousness, or conscious but in an altered state lead to a sense that one is "different" or that the world outside is "different." Sometimes the mind is experienced as disconnected from the body; the individual may observe herself and the rest of the world from some point seemingly outside both—typically from above. Diagnostic labels for such experiences include "depersonalization" and "derealization." Dissociated fantasy formations elaborated as a response to repetitive trauma can also give rise to complex forms of personality fragmentation.

The relation between dissociation as a normal form of self-regulation and early symbiotic experiences with caretakers is illustrated by certain kinds of abuse in adult life. Any assailant can increase control of his victim by exploiting regressive symbiotic tendencies. A deliberate manipulation of the dissociative responses that often accompany regressive states can simultaneously soothe the victim and heighten dependency on the victimizer. Many abusive spouses, for example, are adept at instilling both terror and dependency in their partners. Absolute obedience is not enough; they want the terrorized partner to love and idealize them (Walker, 1979, 1987). Con artists are also masters of inducing entranced states of idealization in those they exploit. Charismatic political leaders can instill infantile states of dependency and idealization in their followers (Freud, 1921). Demagogic leaders may attempt to make hostages of their followers by simultaneously increasing social malaise and offering themselves as a necessary soothing solution.

A history of socialization for submissiveness as well as a history of abuse makes compliant hostages of many victims (Herman, 1992). The double binds implicit in these exploitive social manipulations—the victimizer arouses anxiety and then presents himself as savior and friend—trigger dissociative reactions, which keep some victims loudly singing the praises of those who hurt them.

NEUROBIOLOGY AND DISSOCIATION

Distinct kinds of associative disconnections are readily observable following certain kinds of brain injuries. The word *dissociation*, however, most typically is used to refer to functional disconnections that cannot be attributed to any observable physical injury. Recently, however, investigators have been modifying the distinction between organic and functional. There may, in fact, be underlying psychobiological mechanisms for functional dissociations, although these are not as obvious as the impairments of gross brain damage. The psychobiological changes associated with trance states and hypnosis are currently being studied though such technological aids as EEG and electronic imaging techniques (Dumas, 1977; Gruzelier et al., 1987; Sabourin et al., 1990). Increasingly, the organization of phenomenal ego states as we experience and observe them in ourselves is being discovered to correlate with variable patterns of neural organization in the brain itself.

One hypothesis about the neurological correlates of dissociative phenomena proposes that the encoding, storage, and retrieval of memories are state-related; that is, contextual factors, such as emotional or toxic states organize memories for events (Braun, 1984; Kluft, 1984; Ludwig et al., 1972). This is a useful hypothesis, although it does not account for all the complicated aspects of dissociative phenomena.

Double Brains and Multiple Minds

In recent years, the mapping of the brain and the study of individuals who, because of accident or disease, have provided "natural experiments," have clarified the relation between brain structure and function in human beings. The evolution of the human cortex has made psychological integration an increasingly complicated process. Some dissociative phenomena are evidently related to design features of the brain itself.

Neither the brain nor the mind presumed to reflect its organization is a unitary structure. Its components derive from the evolution of reptilian (subcortical), old mammalian (limbic system), and new mammalian (neocortical) developments—what MacLean (1990) has called "the triune brain." These developments are further complicated by the differentiation of the neocortex into two distinct hemispheres, each of which is specialized for particular types of cognitive operations. Verbal thinking and the inferences and interpretations associated with it have been viewed as a functional corollary of the dominant cerebral hemisphere, the left in most right-handed individuals (Buck, 1986). The right cerebral hemisphere, in contrast, is said to be associated with a type of holistic cognition Tucker (1981) has called "syncretic" and is also specialized to deal with emotional experience (Geschwind, 1979). Cerebral dominance seems to give the left hemisphere special powers of executive control.

The two cerebral hemispheres are connected by a bridging structure, the corpus callosum, as well as by subcortical connections. When the corpus callosum is severed surgically, as is sometimes done to control intractible epilepsy, the brain functions like two separate brains, each of which reveals the differentiations specific to it (Gazzaniga, 1985; Sperry, 1974). Such "split brain" patients appear superficially normal, but can be shown under experimentally controlled conditions to be behaving with divided minds; the right hand, literally, does not know what the left hand is doing.

In recent years discoveries about cerebral lateralization have led to creative syntheses of many kinds of data concerning laterality and human adaptation (Corballis, 1991). Popular simplifications about "left-brain" and "right-brain" activities and personalities have also been in vogue. But the very popularity of such hypotheses has led to cautionary warnings from neurologists and neuropsychologists. Split-brain patients are a medical rarity; natural developments, even pathological ones, are usually much more complicated.

Normally, the cerebral hemispheres are integrated with one another and with other components of the nervous system. As Geschwind and Galaburda (1987) emphasize, too, cerebral dominance is not merely a genetic given, but to some extent a matter of adaptational context. And in addition to asymmetries that are normal, such as specialization of the left hemisphere for language, asymmetries may be produced in the course of development by subtle factors impinging on maturation.

The right hemisphere, which plays a major role in emotion and attentional systems, is especially adapted to activities essential for basic survival. In fetal life, it develops earlier than the left hemisphere; the left hemisphere is thus at risk over a longer period for certain detrimental influences and, as a result, is more likely to be impaired (Geschwind & Galaburda, 1987). If left hemisphere development is markedly delayed for some reason, a condition may arise which is referred to as "anomalous dominance." The brains of individuals with anomalous dominance may be more symmetrical than the brains of those who have not been developmentally impaired. One consequence of this development is that the resulting brain formations may be associated not only with deficits, but with superior capabilities: The influences that favor anomalous dominance may thus favor talents associated with developments either in the right hemisphere or in adjacent parts of the left hemisphere.

These considerations are particularly relevant to the study of trauma. The complexities of cerebral lateralization and dominance may interact with other basic psychobiological processes to produce a wide variety of individualized neurological responses to trauma. When trauma occurs during a crucial developmental period, particularly during the first few years of life when basic neural structures are maturing, the result may be microstructural anomalies that are not readily apparent but that have a profound influence on subsequent development. It is noteworthy, too, that this influence is not always in the direction of pathology, but sometimes results in positively valued talents. Further research is very much needed to clarify the relationship between trauma and neurological development.

Dissociation, as exhibited in hypnosis, has also been thought to be related to cerebral lateralization and variations in cerebral dominance (Bakan, 1980). Hypotheses about lateralization, dissociation, and the developmental effects of trauma are especially suggestive in connection with the serious dissociative disorders (Braun, 1984; Brende, 1984). Individuals exhibiting multiple personality disorder, for example, may have some alter personalities who are right-handed and others who are left-handed. If the effects of anomalous dominance postulated by Geschwind and Gallaburda are correct, the presence of microstructural anomalies may also account in part for the remarkable talents, particularly musical and artistic talents, often reported in multiple personalities.

On the other hand, the more we learn about the brain, the clearer it becomes that function is no simple correlate of structure but of the exquisitely fine-tuned variations in an organism designed to respond continuously to environmental challenges. Whenever we start to survey the workings of the brain, it becomes obvious how remarkably it has evolved as a mediating device, a bridge connecting the individual with the self, other individuals, and the world.

Beahrs (1982) has suggested a very apt metaphor for these developments. He notes that the brain seems to be in some respects like an orchestra; the music that gets played is not simply a function of the instruments, but of how they are orchestrated and conducted. If we pursue this analogy, the possibilities are intriguing. For example, the structure and quality of the instruments might roughly correspond to brain structures. But playing and conducting are learned skills. The music itself is a complex phenomenon that cannot be easily reduced to physical terms. It is, among other things, a created synthesis of form and feeling, an integrative process that unites individuals with themselves and with one another. In this sense, it is related to basic principles of self-regulation and social regulation that seem to be fundamental to adaptation. It is scarcely surprising that the ancients considered music — the music of the spheres — to be inherent in the cosmic structure.

Severely dissociated minds play music that seems strange by ordinary standards. They may themselves dance compulsively to it, like the dancing wanderers of the middle ages. But they have trouble finding and keeping partners. Sometimes the orchestration seems remarkable and creative. Often, though, the dance is exhausting and the music jars.

Brain Structure, Dissociation, and Gender

Modern developments in our understanding of the nervous system have inevitably invited speculations about issues that perennially exercise scientists and philosophers. Following any new discovery about biological differences between the sexes, some investigators make inferential leaps which explain sex differences in behavior as genetically programmed, inevitable, part of "the natural order." Not surprisingly, possible interactions between lateralization, cerebral dominance, and gender differences have also aroused considerable interest.

Most of these inferences about sex differences, however, do not stand up to careful scrutiny (Fausto-Sterling, 1985; Hrdy, 1981). Human behavior is too variable, biology too complexly intertwined with the external world, learning too demonstrably significant in the programming of behavior. Thus, proposals that the brains of females are less lateralized than those of males (Buffery & Gray, 1972; Levy, 1972) must be interpreted with extreme caution. Lateralization is not a simple issue, and even if there are structural differences between the male and female brain, the relation of such differences to behavior is far from simple.

The implications of new information about brain structure for the study of dissociative pathology are also far from clear. Hypnotizability, for example, is usually considered a major index of dissociative capability (Hilgard, 1986). But if there are sex differences in brain structure and function that impact on dissociative capacity, these differences are not indicated by empirical measures like hypnotizability. Since dissociative disorders are more prevalently diagnosed in females, something other than biological sex differences must be involved.

What is clearer is that, however the social context came into being, it is gendered. All cultures systematically transmit beliefs and habits as well as genes from one generation to the next. The brains we are born with have evolved to be exquisitely sensitive to such social programming. From birth, we are carefully indoctrinated by the institutions that nourish, protect, and in some instances, abuse us — families, schools, governments. Certainly, both post-traumatic and dissociative disorders are frequently observed in males — combat veterans, victims of abuse, or men who have survived political captivity or natural disasters. Perhaps the documented differences between males and females with regard to diagnosed dissociative disorders are based on the ordinary conditions females live in during times of so-called peace.

A pervasive feature of this ordinary social context is the ever-present threat as well as the experienced reality of violence against females. A cracked skull is a biological crisis as dangerous to men as to women, and biological changes associated with stress occur in both sexes. But in everyday life, adult women are more likely to receive blows to the head from people they live with — that is the ongoing context of domestic violence (Dobash & Dobash, 1979; Okun, 1986; Pleck, 1987; Schechter, 1982). And the stress associated with child sexual abuse impinges more prevalently on females than on males (Finkelhor, 1979; Finkelhor & associates, 1986; Straus, 1988).

Thus, until we have a clearer picture of the interactions among biology, psychology, and culture, we will not be able to interpret the observed prevalence of dissociative disorders in females in any simple fashion. Perhaps, if females do have characteristics, biological or psychological, that facilitate dissociation, dissociation is a survival mechanism especially needed by females, one that has enabled them to attend to the essential, multifaceted, but often stressful and undervalued support activities of culture — childbearing, childrearing, housekeeping, sexual servicing, etc. Insofar as dissociation helps people avoid psychosis, women, especially victimized women, have needed it for survival. Without it, the numbers of females incapacitated by psychiatric illness might have been considerably greater.

Consciousness

In addition to the hypotheses about neural and behavioral integration generated by research on split brain subjects, such research has also stimulated speculation about one of the oldest and most controversial features of mental life, the phenomenon of consciousness. Consciousness is an elusive construct. Intuitively, it seems related to the brain; modern research correlates it with variable psychophysiological states, such as those associated with sleep or wakefulness. But conceptual clarification remains confused by enduring controversies.

The construct of "the unconscious," as a kind of underside of consciousness is equally elusive, but has nevertheless had a powerful impact on psychiatry, particularly in the last two centuries. In 19th-century psychiatry, the idea of the unconscious was increasingly reified and popularized until the Unconscious became a kind of *deus ex machina*. After the advent of psychoanalysis, especially, the Unconscious was widely invoked to explain almost any mysterious or irrational behavior. It was typically presented as a kind of location in the mind to which socially unacceptable impulses were banished, a repository of primitive ideas and symbols, or a demonic instigator of "Freudian slips" and unintentional lapses.

Those who studied psychological phenomena closely, including Freud, were, of course, aware that the Unconscious was not really a place and that consciousness as a dimension of experience was much more complicated than popular dichotomies suggested. Anyone who carefully introspects can easily observe that consciousness is not a matter of either-or categories like waking and sleeping, but is a variable state. In addition to the normal variations that occur over the course of the day, altered states of consciousness occur in response to many situations, some deliberately induced, including alcohol or drug intoxication, meditation, religious ecstasy, and crowd "hysteria," to name only a few.

In recent years, in the wake of revolutionary discoveries about the brain, observations of dissociative phenomena as well as the results of neurological research have suggested new approaches to the concept of consciousness. The intricate structures of the brain are functionally coordinated in variable patterns that seem to correlate with many phenomenal states of consciousness. One novel hypothesis suggested by Gazzaniga (1985) is that, even in so-called normal people, the executive functions of the mind are not really under the control of one mind, but parcelled out among multiple minds. Beahrs (1982), in comparing the mind to an orchestra under the control of a conductor, has also emphasized that multiplicity is a normal feature of consciousness. In normal people, as well as those with dissociative disorders, several inner minds may be either integrated or dissociated from one another. Consciousness seems to involve focusing the searchlight of attention on one set of events, internal or external, to the exclusion of others.

These hypotheses are somewhat supported by observations on dissociative states. The intimate relation between consciousness and identity, for
example, is commonly acknowledged; in dissociative states, it is often
thrown into sharp relief. Individuals describing altered states of consciousness, for example, sometimes report "I was not myself." Or they sometimes
discover hidden dimensions of the self that were hitherto unsuspected
(Hilgard, 1986). Occasionally they even discover other selves; that is, the
ordinary unity of self-experience is replaced by an experience of duality or
multiplicity (Beahrs, 1983). When two or more selves are co-conscious,
they may even engage in dialogue. As an unfamiliar response this dissociation or fragmentation of consciousness can be very frightening. If it includes the actual hearing of internal voices, the individual may conclude
that she is going crazy.

In the context of psychotherapy, internal voices are frequently discovered to originate in external ones. Internal fragmentation as a response to
trauma typically reflects relationships with real abusers. It is the literal
nature of the internalized voice that seems especially pathological. Yet,
given the vivid memory features of trauma responses and the punitive
social contexts internalized by abused children, this, too, might be predicted. Abuse also results in pathological forms of identification, which
might contribute to the hallucination of significant figures with whom the
child is identified.

Just how this hallucinatory process comes about is rather mysterious,
but what clinicians have learned about processes of identification in general does shed some light on the problem. When relationships are confusing and painful, ambivalence is heightened. The child simultaneously
clings to and pushes away the abusive parent. Processes of identification,
which normally contribute to self-formation, are thus compromised. The
abusive external caretaker is internalized, but the internalization reflects
both the extreme intensity and the extreme ambivalence of the original
relationship. As parts of the developing self, such pathological identifications often remain unassimilated and unintegrated, like an indigestible
meal. Sometimes conflicting and ambivalently internalized identifications
become multiple centers around which discrete identity fragments crystal-
ize. The result is a group of disconnected, conflicted, or quarrelsome inner
selves.

One intriguing though highly speculative hypothesis about how stress
impacts on the development of the internalized self has been advanced
by Julian Jaynes (1976). According to Jaynes, consciousness evolved at a
particular point in human history following the differentiation of two cerebral hemispheres, which were originally experienced as a bicameral mind.
In those days, supposedly, the voice of external authority was such an
important organizing factor in social life that it was eventually internalized
in memory and, in times of crisis or crucial decision making, was recalled

with hallucinatory intensity. Thus, an external authority, the king, became an internal guide. Jaynes hypothesizes that the experience of the guide as an interior part of the self rather than a hallucinated presence evolved during a period of extreme social stress and disorganization. Eventually, self-reflective thought replaced obedience to external commands uttered by the gods or their kingly representatives. Internal dialogue eventually became a way of living in the world and is now intimately connected with those experiences we associate with the "self."

Jaynes' theory oversimplifies the relation between brain structure and self structure. Nevertheless, it provides an imaginative framework for thinking about the origin of such phenomena as consciousness, conscience, the self, etc. The human organism, as a biological development, is an open system, constantly reacting to, learning from, and transformed by social interactions. During evolution, human adaptation and the physical structures related to adaptation have increasingly depended on the integration of social capabilities, such as communication, and on the development of complex mechanisms for internalizing the behavior of caretakers. In the dissociative disorders, not only processes of integration but processes of internalization are apparently distorted. Jaynes' theory suggests that these distortions have an evolutionary as well as an individual history.

Jaynes' assumption that hallucinations were a common feature of early thinking, eventually replaced by an internalized self cannot be substantiated. But hallucination remains a commonly observed and not well-explained feature of the most debilitating mental disorders (Kluft, 1987). Hallucinations were traditionally considered to be a hallmark of psychosis and almost anyone who experienced them in the absence of a known toxic factor was diagnosed schizophrenic. But they are now also a recognized feature of post-traumatic and dissociative disorders (Bliss et al., 1983; Coons, 1984; Putnam, 1989). Some (Putnam, 1989) have pointed out that hallucinations in the dissociative disorders are different from those typical of schizophrenia. The difference has not been well clarified beyond noting that those with MPD experience their voices coming from inside while schizophrenics hear external voices. Internal voices intensify the illusion that there really are different people inside the individual with multiple personality disorder. But these different people are merely internalized constructs, after all, and their hallucinated presence is still unexplained.

From a developmental perspective, individuals with dissociative disorders may be caught in an arrested process of internalization that has prevented the integration of external models into a unified self-structure. When external models have been extremely inconsistent or social experience has been extremely fragmented, the internalization of experience mirrors the social inconsistency. But the physical world is a predictable place, with predictable physical laws making it possible to develop intact reality testing. In such instances, although objective reality testing remains intact, the confused social reality is sometimes organized internally through compartmentalizations that introduce order into the chaos. Basic psychobiological mechanisms and state-related learning, as well as complicated elaborations in fantasy structure these compartmentalizations. One possible outcome, in contrast to a unified identity, is a confederation of selves, each with a characteristic autobiography and characteristic styles and tastes.

In therapy, the struggle for dominance and control sometimes observable among such unintegrated personality patterns mirrors the struggle that originally took place between the individual and her caretakers. The internal authority that normally orchestrates variable minds was never integrated; the components of authority were too inconsistent, cruel, and unhelpful. As a result, the dissociated individual functions like an orchestra without a leader. Or the leader keeps changing in ways that the individual adapts to but that other people find bewildering.

However speculative these ideas, they can guide clinical investigation as well as clinical intervention. A first step in the treatment of severe dissociative disorders is establishing lines of communication between the therapist and the various personality fragments as a prelude to bringing distinct but dissociated internal parts into communication with one another. In this process the therapist functions as a bridge—therapeutic work sometimes resembles a kind of internal group therapy (Caul, 1984) and involves such processes as mediation and negotiation. An important part of the process is helping the client learn about reciprocal, mutually respectful forms of dialogue, as distinct from intimidating commands, submissive silences, and violently escalating arguments. Psychotherapy can thus gradually guide the evolution of internal authority as distinct from authoritarian forms of self-control.

TRADITIONAL CLINICAL APPROACHES TO DISSOCIATION

Modern approaches to dissociation are heir to a long and rich tradition of psychological investigation, some of which has been discounted, but much of which still informs psychotherapeutic practice. Some earlier approaches, eclipsed for most of the 20th century, are finally beginning to be integrated with modern approaches. To the extent that history can shed light on current controversies, as well as provide suggestive guidelines to practical interventions, it is useful to survey it.

There are several extensive reviews of the history of dissociation as a phenomenon and as a deliberately induced form of clinical intervention, ranging from the immensely influential work of Mesmer (Chertok & De Saussure, 1979; Frankel, 1990), through the clinical refinements of such pioneers as Despine (Fine, 1988) and Janet (Ellenberger, 1970), to the resurgence of interest in the last two decades (Bliss, 1986; Putnam, 1989; Ross, 1989).

Throughout history, interest in and encouragement of dissociative phenomena has waxed and waned. Hypnosis as a healing technique, which involved the deliberate induction of dissociative states, enjoyed considerable vogue during certain periods. But as medicine increasingly differentiated itself from religion and folk-healing and attempted to provide scientific rationales for its practices, the use of hypnotic techniques fell into neglect. As times and fashions have changed over the years, the very difficulties encountered in finding scientific explanations for dissociation and the sensational exploitations of hypnosis by stage entertainers have periodically led to disclaimers that hypnotic phenomena could be a scientifically respectable field of inquiry.

The study of dissociation and hypnotic phenomena was at the heart of the development of early psychiatry, particularly the work of the 19th-century clinicians who devised the first dynamic psychiatry (Ellenberger, 1970). Theories about the nature of dissociation played a prominent role in the explanation of that ubiquitous female complaint labeled "hysteria." One of the most influential clinicians of the 19th century, Pierre Janet, conceptualized hysteria as a form of somnambulism, a trance-like dissociative state, and treated the disorder with hypnosis, which he also recognized as a form of dissociation (Haule, 1986). Janet also emphasized the role of real-life trauma in the origin of dissociative disorders. Following Janet, prior to the growing influence of psychoanalysis, dissociation as it was exemplified in multiple personalities was widely used to develop conceptual models of the human psyche. In the United States, such models were popularized in the work of William James (1983/1890) and Morton Prince (1978/1906).

Psychoanalysis

When Sigmund Freud began to explore hysteria as a syndrome, he was influenced by contemporaries like Janet and Charcot. *Studies on Hysteria* (1893–1895), which he wrote in collaboration with Josef Breuer, included detailed observations of dissociative symptomatology in several hysterical patients. One of the most famous of these cases, Breuer's patient Anna O., dramatically exhibited many symptoms then considered typical of "grand hysteria," including extreme alterations in mood and self-presentation. She also showed clear symptoms of multiple personality disorder as currently defined in *DSM-III-R*. Breuer was able to describe and relate to two distinct personality configurations separated by amnestic barriers.

Observing that Anna O. experienced spontaneous trance states, Breuer made use of hypnosis to explore her symptoms. He effected a temporary cure, but it did not hold. Her relapse was probably complicated by an addiction to the opiates prescribed to calm her. But in spite of her temporary setbacks, Anna O.'s story did not end with incurable illness. The patient, whose real name was Bertha Pappenheim, recovered and became an influential German social worker (Kaplan, 1984; Rosenbaum, 1984; Steinmann, 1984). The striking contrast between her presentation as Breuer's patient and her later life is further evidence that she was probably a multiple personality.

Not only was *Studies on Hysteria* a landmark work in early psychoanalysis, but it marked one of several theoretical and personal turning points in the life of Freud. The history of his work was punctuated by a series of close personal and professional affiliations disrupted by acrimonious breaks and enduring enmities. Although the ostensible reason for such breaks was said to be theoretical disagreements, the political fallout from the quarrels was sometimes destructive and affected the development of the whole psychoanalytic movement. It resulted, in effect, in the splintering of psychoanalysis into numerous sectarian factions. Because of the growing influence of psychoanalysis on the practice of psychiatry and psychotherapy, these internal political developments had extensive ramifications for both diagnosis and treatment. The conceptualization and treatment approach to dissociative phenomena was especially affected.

In his early views of neurosis, for example, Freud accepted the etiological role of trauma. He also accepted Breuer's views about dissociation as a response to trauma and the role of hypnoid states in symptom formation. Even before he repudiated his so-called "seduction theory," however, Freud repudiated the theory of hypnoid states advanced by Breuer. In "The Aetiology of Hysteria" (1896), he put forward his own explanatory concept of repression. Since, at that point, he still believed his patients' reports of sexual abuse and considered abuse a causative factor in hysteria, he contended that repression was something that happened to *memories*. Subsequently, when he repudiated that seduction hypothesis, he contended that repression was a dynamic affecting *fantasies*, typically childhood masturbation fantasies associated with the Oedipal period of infantile development.

In breaking with Breuer, as he broke with other colleagues such as Wilhelm Fliess, Carl Jung, Alfred Adler, and (less ostentatiously) Sandor Ferenczi, Freud took great pains to demarcate the boundaries of his differences from them and to emphasize the uniqueness of his own theoretical approach. In repudiating Breuer's theory of hypnoid states, for example, he deflected attention from certain features of his patients' symptoms that would today be considered hallmarks of dissociation. So doing, he steered clinical observations as well as theory away from the study of altered states of consciousness. As he conceptualized the unconscious as a topological feature of the mind, infantile fantasy, in contrast to actual traumas, became the clinical focus of psychoanalysis. And with the ascendency of psychoanalytic theory, the phenomena characteristic of dissociative disorders as well as the "grand hysteria" that had stimulated the development of early psychoanalysis faded from the clinical spotlight.

Dissociation, periodically dismissed from clinical attention, nevertheless has a way of periodically returning. So it was with Freud. It eventually became clear to him that the distinction between conscious and unconscious was too simplistic and that the concept of repression was insufficient to explain certain features of memory and awareness. He developed a structural model of the psyche that supplemented the old conscious-unconscious distinction with the more differentiated concepts *id, ego,* and *superego.* The executive function of the mind, the ego, was assumed to mediate between the impulses of the id and the demands of external reality. The superego was differentiated from the ego as a repository of moral authority.

This theory emphasized the influential role of actual experience in human development. The ego is supposedly built up over the course of childhood through interactions with caretakers and culture. As it acquires organizing competence, it becomes an executive function of the mind. But it is constantly beset from within by primitive, sometimes antisocial, id impulses and by superego demands, as well as from without by the constraints of reality. In some cases, the ego may not develop the strength needed to mediate between these conflicting forces. Under extreme pressure, too, the unity of the ego can be compromised. From a structural perspective, the ego, in effect, can be "split."

In "Splitting of the Ego in the Process of Defense," for example, Freud (1940) explained that a patient can be of two different minds about a painful reality. Part of the ego accepts it; another part denies it. A similar process can be observed, according to Freud, in the development of fetishism. Fetishism is viewed as the result of a traumatic experience, the discovery that females lack a penis, which the little boy interprets as evidence of castration. Even though the fetishist's fantasy is based on a misperception, it is supposedly so traumatic that it distorts his subsequent sexual relationships with females. Following Freud, a number of psychoanalysts (Gillespie, 1940; Greenacre, 1953, 1970; Payne, 1939) pointed out that such a dire consequence was not simply the result of a single painful discovery but was based on early disturbances in ego development, such as those produced by traumatic overstimulation in infancy and early childhood.

Thus, although fantasy remained the etiological focus in psychoanalysis, Freud's structural theory opened the way for a new look at the role of reality in personality development. Both the ego psychology, which grew out of this theory, and current object relations theories, which also owe much to it, acknowledge the significance of actual events in psychic life. The relative lack of emphasis on certain kinds of trauma, such as female victimization, in psychoanalytic literature is not simply an inevitable outgrowth of psychoanalytic theory. It is rather the result of historical trends in psychoanalytic politics and the male biases that pervade scientific theories generally.

In modern psychoanalysis, *splitting* is a pervasive organizing concept. Object relations theorists associated with the British school (Melanie Klein, Fairbairn, Winnicott), for example, view personality as a structural development based on early processes of splitting and integration. Integrating self- and object-representations—healing "splits"—comprise a major part of psychoanalytic work (Dorpat, 1976; Kernberg, 1975; Volkan, 1976, 1981). A few psychoanalysts such as Dickes (1965) and Fliess (1953) have also taken a second look at Breuer's concept of the hypnoid state. At first glance, it might appear that psychoanalysts who talk about *splitting* and other mental health professionals who are currently investigating dissociation are discussing the same phenomena. Thus, some clinicians (Ross, 1989) use the term "splitting" and "dissociation" interchangeably.

For the most part, however, the study of splitting and the study of dissociation have evolved in different domains of discourse. Psychoanalysts are likely to view splitting as a process endogenous to early ego development (Kernberg, 1967, 1975; Stone, 1986). The role of actual physical trauma in splitting is seldom considered at all. The effects of child abuse, in particular, are scarcely mentioned in the extensive psychoanalytic literature on splitting. The increase in recognition that severe personality disorders, such as borderline pathology, are often a consequence of actual abuse may eventually change this psychoanalytic focus. But to date, there is little evidence that the time-honored psychoanalytic avoidance of issues related to female victimization is changing much (Masson, 1984).

Those who talk more explicitly about *dissociation*, in contrast to *splitting* have long focused on external precipitating factors and the effects of actual trauma. Although much of their work was eclipsed in the 20th century by the influence of psychoanalysis, it is currently coming to the attention of psychotherapists, particularly those concerned with post-traumatic and dissociative reactions. Attempts are also being made to integrate modern approaches to trauma with more traditional psychoanalytic perspectives.

Horowitz (1976) was one of the earliest to explore trauma from a psychoanalytic perspective and has remained one of the most influential representatives of psychoanalytic approaches. Other notable psychoanalytic contributions include those by Ulman and Brothers (1987, 1988), who have conceptualized trauma from the standpoint of Kohut's self psychology. In the investigation of multiple personality disorders specifically, a number of therapists are working within a psychoanalytic orientation. Cornelia Wilber (Sybil's therapist), for example, was one of the first to bring multiple personality disorder to the forefront of 20th-century public attention (Wilbur, 1984, 1986).

Unfortunately, integrating psychoanalytic perspectives with other points of view from social and developmental psychology or with modern feminist perspectives is impeded by institutional traditions in psychoanalysis. Although many of the early psychoanalytic pioneers were female and many psychoanalysts have focused on social issues, the impact of such perspectives on clinical training seems minimal. Social factors, including factors associated with sex-role socialization, scapegoating, and sex-discrimination are still largely the province of sociology and social psychology.

Some modern psychoanalysts are nevertheless attempting to integrate the study of women's issues with psychoanalytic concepts, particularly concepts about relationships (J. Miller, 1976). Going back to Freud's original insights about the impact of trauma on development also suggests a viewpoint for integrating psychoanalytic and feminist perspectives (A. Miller, 1984). Unfortunately, these needed integrations are in their infancy and have had limited impact on the training of professionals. The investigation and treatment of dissociative disorders, like psychoanalysis generally, remains a field still dominated by old controversies and traditional perspectives, which direct little attention to women's special problems.

Jung and Dissociation

As a prominent psychoanalyst, esteemed by Freud and designated his professional heir, Carl Jung was involved in many of the most consequential developments in the psychoanalytic movement. His break with Freud took him down a radically different road. Yet both during his involvement with psychoanalysis and after the break Jung was continually intrigued by the dissociative phenomena that were at the center of the early dynamic psychiatries (Ellenberger, 1970).

Jung was among the first to systematically apply experimental methodology, including measurements of psychophysiological responses, to the psychiatric problems so prevalent in his day. Taking his cue from the experimental psychology of associationism as well as the work of psychiatrists like Bleuler, Janet, and Freud, he attempted to map associational configurations he called *complexes*. Jung noted that complexes had a dynamic, that is, motivational component; those complexes connected with conflict could be excluded from consciousness and assume a life of their own in the psyche.

Like Janet and others, Jung recognized that the Freudian concept of repression was insufficient to describe such dissociative phenomena as co-consciousness. He recognized the existence of multiple personality configurations in the mind. He also conceptualized certain configurations, the archetypes of the collective unconscious, as basic and universal. Archetypes were considered to be grounded in the biological as well as the psychological makeup of human beings. According to Ellenberger (1970, p. 707), archetypes can be described as subpersonalities, which resemble satellites of the ego.

The specific development of individuals supposedly shapes the expression and integration of such universal archetypal tendencies. Jung viewed the unification of the psyche as an ongoing process of individuation that proceeds through the integration of opposites. In this process, the individual differentiates himself or herself from the control of collective images and integrates distinct and contradictory parts of the self into a unified whole. Pathology arises when individuation is blocked. In contrast to Freud, who viewed the first five or six years of life as the decisive developmental period, Jung considered development as a process extending throughout the entire life cycle. He considered the latter half of life a major period of individuation.

Jung's concept of inherited archetypes of the collective unconscious has been one of his most controversial contributions. But his focus on complexes and on the human tendency to personify experience has been widely influential and remains quite relevant to modern approaches to dissociation. The tendencies of human beings to personify psychic functions reflects the significance of social interaction in the origin of the self. When we feel afraid, or lost, or lonely, we join company with the people who have reassured and comforted us. And if no such people are available, inside or outside, we may invent them. Thus, the inner world is populated by fantasies as well as memories of people—named people, people with distinct physical attributes and behavioral styles. Similarly, although we discover who we are through social appraisals as well as our own actions, we constantly invent ourselves. When an invented self is socially recognized, it becomes real to others as well as itself. When others ignore or deny it, it may go into hiding. The inner world, thus, is an ongoing human drama, a repository of selves creating selves and selves relating to other people, both real and imaginary.

The integration of so-called personalities in cases of MPD involves not only the integration of multiple minds but the integration of the mind with the body. Jung, considering the practical dimension of psychotherapy, was quite sensitive to this issue; however inflated one may be in identifying with internal figures, including archetypal ones, adaptive integration requires coming down to earth.

Jung, in contrast to Freud, focused on nonverbal as well as verbal forms of expression in the context of psychotherapy (Stein, 1982). His recognition of different expressive modes in therapy anticipated certain observations now popularly discussed under the rubric "right-brain" and "left-brain" thinking. His therapeutic techniques, which included active imagination and artistic expression continue to enrich modern therapeutic approaches.

Such nonverbal techniques are particularly helpful in the therapy of post-traumatic and dissociative reactions.

MODERN APPROACHES TO DISSOCIATION

Many of the most important contributions to our understanding of dissociation have derived from the exploration, in both clinic and laboratory, of hypnotic phenomena. In spite of continuing controversies about the nature of hypnosis, the pragmatic utility of hypnosis has made it a valuable tool in general medicine as well as in psychotherapy. In the treatment of the dissociative disorders, many consider it an indispensable tool. Experimental research is currently clarifying both the psychological and the psychophysiological dimensions of hypnosis.

A modern pioneer in research on hypnotic phenomena has been Ernest Hilgard. His work is highly valued and widely cited not only by experimentalists but by those who focus more explicitly on clinical issues. One of his most important contributions was his conceptualization of "the hidden observer" (Hilgard, 1986), a covert part of the individual which processes information not available to the consciousness of a hypnotized person who is instructed to ignore a given stimulus. The hidden observer can be accessed through experimental techniques like automatic writing and automatic talking. Hilgard regards the hidden observer as a metaphor, but the similarity between the phenomenon and the existence of autonomous organizations in the mind such as are typically encountered in alter personalities is obvious.

Among the most important contributing factors in the modern investigation of dissociative phenomena has been the increasing incidence and recognition of severe dissociative disorders during the last 20 years. The modern conceptualization of dissociative disorders, like that of post-traumatic stress disorder, has been accompanied by a growing understanding of the pathogenic potential of actual trauma. Clinical and experimental observations increasingly indicate the extent to which the two types of phenomena — post-traumatic and dissociative pathology — are intrinsically related. Herman (1992) emphasizes the need for a new orientation that will integrate what we know about trauma reactions with diagnostic classification systems. Future revisions of the *Diagnostic and Statistical Manual* of the American Psychiatric Association will probably reflect such perspectives.

Popular interest in the dissociative disorders has also increased, stimulated especially by a number of biographical books about multiple personalities. The public has always been fascinated by multiple personality disorder (MPD), even when the phenomenon was considered a clinical rarity. The literature of the past two centuries bears witness to this fascination.

Multiplicity seems to make intuitive sense to many people. Multiple personalities are fascinating not only because they are rare and exotic, but because normal people can relate to them. It is easy for people with no special training to describe such phenomena as "a Jekyll and Hyde" personality. Cartoons depict splits between the good alter ego, who wears wings and counsels moral behavior, and the bad, devilish alter ego who urges self-indulgent behavior.

When *The Three Faces of Eve* (Thigpen & Cleckley, 1957) was written and eventually made into a movie, multiple personality disorder was considered exceedingly rare. Even when *Sybil* (Schreiber, 1973) became a best-seller, the disorder was still a clinical curiosity, seldom studied. But in the last ten years, the number of books about multiples has mushroomed, and multiples throng talk shows to tell their stories. To some extent, such phenomena have been usefully educative. But multiples are vulnerable to exploitation. It is part of the pattern of revictimization that brings grief to many abused people.

Fortunately, the recent interest in multiplicity has also stimulated considerable research. Accounts of MPD have burgeoned in professional literature. The development of *DSM-III-R* guidelines for the dissociative disorders has contributed to such research and alerted clinicians to signs of dissociation that might formerly have escaped attention. The renewed interest in dissociation also converged with a focus on other prevalently diagnosed disorders, particularly borderline personality disorder. Even so, dissociation, though an increasingly respectable clinical concept, has continued to be a controversial one. Many clinicians, particularly those trained in psychoanalytic perspectives, have been quite skeptical about the cases of MPD that began to receive so much attention not only in the popular media but in professional journals. Debate fueled research and attempts at theoretical clarification.

DISSOCIATIVE DISORDERS IN *DSM-III-R*

Like the diagnostic clarification of post-traumatic stress disorder, recent *DSM-III-R* guidelines for diagnosing dissociative disorders are an important step beyond earlier conceptualizations about female hysteria. The relation between trauma and dissociation is implicitly acknowledged in these guidelines. Future *DSM* revisions will probably make the relation between PTSD and dissociative disorders even more explicit.

The dissociative disorders described in *DSM-III-R* vary in complexity. The essential feature that characterizes them is "a disturbance or alteration in the normally integrative function of identity, memory, or consciousness. The disturbance or alteration may be sudden or gradual and transient or chronic" (APA, 1987, p. 269). The varieties of dissociative disorders included in the diagnostic list are multiple personality disorder, psychogenic fugue, psychogenic amnesia, depersonalization disorder, and a catch-all category labeled "dissociative disorders not otherwise specified." From the criteria discussed, it is clear that these specified syndromes are phenomenologically related to one another and that they are usually stress-related. For example, psychogenic amnesia and psychogenic fugue, as described, are not only circumscribed disorders but features of more complex disorders, such as multiple personality disorder (MPD).

The authors of *DSM-III-R* guidelines note that dissociative pathology is also often a secondary feature of other diagnosed disorders, including major affective disorders and schizophrenia. However, although the phenomenology of dissociation indicates that fugue, amnesia, depersonalization, and other dissociative responses are probably antecedent to more complex conditions, multiple personality disorder is the first dissociative disorder described at length in *DSM-III-R*. It is characterized by "A. The existence within the person of two or more distinct personalities or personality states (each with its own relatively enduring pattern of perceiving, relating to and thinking about the environment and self). B. At least two of these personalities or personality states recurrently take full control of the person's behavior" (APA, 1987, p. 272).

Psychogenic fugue, psychogenic amnesia, and depersonalization disorders, as subsequently described, are characterized by altered states of consciousness precipitated, typically, by trauma. Because these states are also characteristic of more complex disorders, the dissociative disorders may be confused with one another. Psychogenic fugue and psychogenic amnesia, however, can be diagnostically distinguished from MPD in that these simpler disorders do not exhibit the characteristic shifts in identity found in MPD and are usually limited to a single, brief episode.

As is the case with PTSD, diagnostic criteria for dissociative disorders provide a useful framework for clinical intervention and research. The criticisms that can be raised against diagnostic classifications in general are applicable here, however. Brief guidelines are inevitably schematic and do not consider the broad range of dissociative phenomena that can be observed in clinical practice. Specialists are attempting to correct this inadequacy. Research on dissociation as a feature of other diagnosed disorders, such as eating disorders (Ross et al., 1989; Torem, 1986, 1987, 1988) and somatiform disorders (Loewenstein, 1990) suggest both the significance of trauma reactions and the pervasiveness of dissociative mechanisms in many kinds of symptom pictures.

One potential problem with the *DSM-III-R* guidelines involves the emphasis on the most complex dissociative disorder, multiple personality, and the implication that other dissociative disorders are less frequent or less clinically significant. This emphasis reflects both the scientific and popular attention directed toward multiplicity in recent years. It may also derive from the controversial nature of MPD and the dismissive attitudes of many traditional clinicians who consider MPD a mere artifact of hypnosis or other therapeutic interventions. Therapists working with clear instances of MPD have often been put on the defensive. By making MPD the centerpiece of a *DSM-III-R* category, those who have specialized in treating it have legitimized their endeavors. Such legitimacy, in turn, has fostered a growing body of research on the dissociative disorders and a needed focus on treatment issues.

DISSOCIATION AS A WOMAN'S ISSUE

The cases presented in *Studies on Hysteria* were of young women. In Freud's day, the very idea that a male could suffer from hysteria was controversial. The extent to which dissociation is especially prominent in the lives of women has always been implicit in history and in statistics. One of the consistent findings concerning the dissociative disorders as they are currently diagnosed, especially MPD, is that they are most prevalently diagnosed in women (Putnam, 1989; Ross, 1989). The *DSM-III-R* diagnostic category "Dissociative Disorders," in fact, replaces a former classification called "Hysterical Neurosis, Dissociative Type."

In spite of history and recent empirical findings concerning the psychology of women, however, the significance of sex differences in experience and socialization has never been given much attention in diagnostic approaches to the dissociative disorders. Therapists and shelter workers, who have been increasingly sensitive to dissociative symptoms in female survivors of abuse have often approached such symptoms from a feminist perspective, but have often been cautious about the pathologizing and revictimizing potential associated with diagnosis. Among those who are focusing on severe dissociative disorders, Rivera (1987, 1988) has provided a cogent feminist analysis. Herman (1992) has also persuasively called attention to the link among trauma, dissociation, and violence against women. Much of the current burgeoning literature on dissociation, however, particularly the literature on MPD, makes little reference to the significance of gender.

Several reasons for this comparative neglect are apparent. After an upsurge of interest in women's issues in the 1970s, the following two decades were characterized by attitudinal shifts that some (Faludi, 1991) have attributed to a widespread "backlash" against women and to the assumption that sexism is no longer a major social problem. Two other factors are also notable. The *DSM* guidelines of the American Psychiatric Association, not surprisingly, are based on a prevailing medical orientation toward the treatment of psychological problems. And in spite of an increasing awareness of the impact of social factors on mental health, the medical model is still a disease model reflecting traditional attitudes about the origin and treatment of illness.

CHAPTER 6
Dissociative Disorders

D ISSOCIATED WOMEN MIRROR the fragmentation and contradictory organization of their external world, the inescapable double binds to which they have been subjected, and the traumatic assaults that have threatened their survival. Splits or compartmentalizations of the female self are commonly based on the dilemmas implicit in being female — the conflicting dimensions of female sexuality, the expressive female styles invented to cope with unacceptable aggression and anger, the split between competence and appraisal as sources of self-esteem, the kinds of role diffusion elaborated as a normal pattern in female caretaking. Typical dilemmas of female sexuality and female expressiveness in particular, can lead to a profound distrust of or alienation from the body. The result is often a basic dissociative split between the body as a biological entity, characterized by drives, appetites, and affects, and the body as a socially appraised image.

THE FLIGHT FROM THE BODY

Flight from the body as a dissociative reaction to trauma has often been prepared in advance by a tendency to be at odds with the body and to consign it to the status of a bothersome, even alien entity. Trauma compounds self-alienation in several ways. When an emergency galvanizes the body to defend its survival, attention is immediately directed to the external threat rather than to internal responses. The individual may only notice after the threat has passed that she is bleeding from a wound or has a broken limb. Emergency reactions also produce internal physiological changes that may persist but only come to the forefront of attention after danger has passed. Not infrequently, the heart seems to go on racing after a sudden startle or one feels lightheaded for a while. State-related responses in turn result in internal splits in memory and self-representation.

Pain, which may be experienced only after the danger is past, is also self-alienating. The part of the body that hurts becomes a nuisance, even an enemy. The frustrated wish to free oneself from pain can lead to a wish to free oneself from the body altogether.

In addition to self-alienating physical responses, some forms of abuse systematically alienate the victim from her body. The female body is often appropriated, controlled, and debased in ways that make the victim repugnant to herself (Herman, 1992). Some victims have had their bodies posed and abused and/or photographed in contrived displays. All such painful indignities contribute to the flight from the body and the formation of a disembodied self.

Becoming disembodied is a dissociative response that may initially be automatic but that can, with practice, become habitual. One response to the complex biological and behavioral changes that characterize trauma reactions is a feeling of being outside the body, looking down on it from above, or monitoring it from a distance. This perception is probably initially based on the psychobiology of trauma as it impacts on complicated cognitive processes. Once experienced, however, out-of-the-body reactions are strikingly memorable. Some individuals learn to induce the out-of-body state so that it anticipates rather than follows a stressful event. An uncontrollable shock is then controllable. The victim, in reality immobilized, psychologically leaves the scene by entering a trance.

In trance, the victim may merely hang suspended, unresponsive to external stimuli that would ordinarily be painful. Or, while in the altered state, she may elaborate complicated fantasies. Where abuse is inescapable, this psychological form of escape makes sense; why go through an unavoidable painful experience? It may even protect the body from the detrimental effects of extreme and unmitigated anxiety. But as a conditioned avoidance response, habitual detachment from the body can greatly complicate ordinary living.

Trance

Trance is a hypnotic phenomenon popularly thought of as a response to the induction techniques of hypnotists. Hypnotists themselves disagree about just what constitutes trance (Barber, 1972, 1978; Rossi, 1986; Sarbin & Coe, 1972; Spiegel & Spiegel, 1978). They are agreed, however, that, whether they are based on biology or merely a manifestation of social compliance, trance states can have a powerful effect on behavior. Trance is commonly, though not necessarily associated with heightened suggestibility as well as alterations in perception and self-perception. The utility of trance in many medical and dental procedures is based on the ability to induce profound anesthesia through suggestion. Hilgard (1986) has demonstrated that the anesthesia is not total, that some hidden part of the personality continues to be aware of pain. Nevertheless, from a practical standpoint, the usefulness of hypnotic anesthesia in invasive medical procedures and for the control of pain is well documented. The uses of trance in psychotherapy include relaxing the body, promoting healing, calming anxiety states, and facilitating memory and abreaction. Therapeutic trance is also helpful in enabling survivors to bring spontaneous self-induced trances under control.

Trance susceptibility varies in the population. There is evidence that trance is related to normal biorhythms, the circadian and ultradian rhythms that characterize psychobiological processes (Rossi, 1986). Normal variations in consciousness can easily merge with these extremes usually designated trance; the "common, everyday trance," in fact, is a basis for some clinically useful induction procedures, particularly in Ericksonian hypnosis (Rossi & Cheek, 1988). Trance susceptibility may be measured by such instruments as The Stanford Hypnotic Susceptibility Scales (Hilgard, 1986) or by standard induction procedures.

Trance may well involve primary forms of social organization and self-regulation, which are biologically orchestrated. According to Brown (1991), for example, trance capacity is related to brain functions that are specific to the human species and is elaborated developmentally as a basic feature of social communication. From early infancy, gaze and soothing verbalizations—important features of trance induction—coordinate parent-infant behavior. This parentally mediated soothing is eventually internalized in patterns of self-regulation. It also retains its interpersonal stamp and continues to function in social communication.

Social regulation eventually encompasses a variety of cultural rituals that unite individuals into cohesive groups. Interactional rhythms, such as the coordination of breathing, chanting, or singing facilitate trance as an organizing feature of group behavior. As a feature of self-regulation, trance often regressively recapitulates the earliest adaptations of normal mother-infant symbiosis. As a normal regressive response, this recapitulation provides safe time-outs in reverie and certain kinds of aesthetic experience. It can moderate everyday stress, foster a state of increased receptivity to creative inspiration, or facilitate the transition from waking to sleeping.

But like other forms of self-regulation, trance can also be pathologically elaborated. Contexts in which such pathological elaborations occur include traumatic overstimulation or stimulus deprivation. Abuse frequently alternates traumatic overstimulation with neglect and understimulation. This pattern may lead to ritualistic forms of self-stimulation and self-soothing that include trance, compulsive behaviors, and self-injury.

Once trance is utilized as a technique for coping with trauma, the utility of this response for reducing anxiety and pain can be powerfully reinforcing. Subsequently, it may then become the coping technique of choice for escaping otherwise inescapable stressors. Not infrequently, self-induced trances become spontaneous, automatic, and indiscriminate and result in patterns of avoidance that contribute to social isolation and be-havioral constriction. Certain individuals, in fact, seem to be "hypnotic virtuosos." When this facility at self-induced trance is coupled with severe abuse in childhood, the stage is set for the development of dissociative disorders like multiple personality disorder (Braun & Sachs, 1985; Frisch-holz, 1985).

Sometimes a client remembers the historical development of self-induced trance states: "I would stare at something until I felt numb. After a while, I did that even without thinking. I realized eventually that I could switch myself on and off like a light." In childhood, state-related learning and memory effects complicate such simple trances in ways that can have far-reaching consequences for personality development.

In some trance states, even though consciousness is clouded or de-tached from environmental cues, the mind may nevertheless be busy with fantasy. Trance-elaborated fantasies can be quite complex: "I couldn't stand being at home, but there was no way I could leave. But then I dis-covered I didn't have to live there. I could live in a place inside my head. I made up some special people to be with me. I guess I was sort of like Dorothy in *The Wizard of Oz*. After I invented this world, things at home didn't bother me so much. But I didn't learn much in school that year."

One of the goals in the treatment of dissociative disorders is helping the client gain increased control over automatic and uncontrolled dissociative responses, including trance states. What was originally an uncontrolled symptom thus becomes a useful aid to therapy (Dolan, 1991). Hypnotic procedures can be adapted to short-term psychotherapies as well as longer, more intensive ones. In the treatment of severe dissociative disorders, the role of self-induced trance in personality fragmentation will usually need to be clarified. Exploring the origin of trances in early relationships and early attempts to cope with trauma facilitates personality integration.

Autistic Trance States

Some pathological elaborations of trance are autistic. That is, they func-tion to isolate a traumatized individual from human contact. As a form of self-regulation, autistic trance states are the ultimate way of leaving the scene without physically escaping or dying. The withdrawn individual may assume a fetal position, rock back and forth in a corner, or simply seem to be completely unresponsive to outside stimuli. The mute refusal to re-spond which typifies such states may be accompanied by physical immo-bility or postural rigidity. These are symptoms classically diagnosed as "catatonia," a schizophrenic syndrome (APA, 1987, p. 196).

Autistic trance is not necessarily a sign of psychosis, however. Autistic responses may be elaborated as a feature of less disturbed adaptations

(Tustin, 1986). Autistic trance is also often a transient feature of trauma reactions, including confrontations with traumatic memories. Fortunately, too, individuals who voluntarily enter therapy are almost never whole-hearted in their autistic withdrawal. Even if one part of the personality system is profoundly withdrawn, some other part usually remains in contact with the therapist. It should be noted, too, that some kinds of extreme withdrawal are not genuinely autistic but have an important communicative function. They can convey to the therapist the need for time-out or distance when the client is overwhelmed by emerging material. Or they may be an indirect way of expressing frightening feelings, of symbolically killing the therapist, or of nullifying the therapy.

In dissociative disorders, autistic states typically alternate with a wide variety of other kinds of altered states of consciousness, including those characterized by richly embroidered fantasies. In multiple personality disorder, one or more alter personalities may be autistic, that is persistently out of contact, while others become temporarily autistic. Although the client's being out of contact can be alarming and suggest psychotic pathology, the existence of parts of the personality that remain related to the therapist and involved in the treatment process makes the situation less ominous than might be feared.

As a dissociative symptom, autistic states are usually self-limiting. The therapist may be frustrated at being unable to contact the client, but eventually the client comes out of her trance and initiates contact. The therapist can sometimes moderate such autistic responses by acknowledging the need for time-out and facilitating other ways of achieving it. Prolonged states of autistic withdrawal, obviously, sometimes warrant more drastic interventions, such as hospitalization. But in many therapies, even with severely disturbed individuals, the self-limiting tendencies of trance states and the existence of an ongoing therapeutic alliance with less withdrawn parts of the personality system makes the situation manageable.

Trance and Transference

Trance, as Roustang (1976) has emphasized, is often related to the transference manifestations that color most psychotherapy. Although it has not been discussed much in these terms by psychoanalysts, trance may be a typical feature of those regressive transference pictures Kernberg (1975), Kohut (1971, 1977), and other psychoanalysts have described as characteristic of narcissistic and borderline pathology. Symbiotic trance states are typically characterized by an intense, even compulsive preoccupation with another individual who is psychologically not well differentiated from the self (a self-object, to use the terminology of Heinz Kohut). Attachment to a needed other becomes necessary for self-regulation and threatened disruptions of attachment lead to states of panic. In psychotherapy, this intense attachment may be evidenced by extreme psychological clinging, by obsessive rumination about another person, typically the therapist, and by ceaseless attempts to gain the needed other's attention. The individual in such a state may show exaggerated compliance or heightened suggestibility; often such compliance alternates with defiant attempts to break free and assert autonomy.

Such transference pictures often appear stormy or even chaotic and can be exhausting to both client and therapist. But they nevertheless can facilitate the exploration of early relationship patterns, particularly relationships with abusers. They can also become a powerful resistance to treatment, particularly when obsessive preoccupation with the therapist overshadows all other material in therapy. Although the trance-like quality of such states is often overlooked, upon close examination, typical features of trance can be observed. The client herself may call attention to them, noting that she seems to be magnetically attracted to the therapist or some other individual by an overpowering force. This magnetic attraction is sometimes considered a mysterious and magical aspect of relations between the sexes. It is a common theme in literature and the movies.

In severely dissociated clients, particularly those with MPD, entranced obsession with the therapist or other significant figures and struggles against the attachment may take different forms in different personality configurations. This fragmentation of the transference usually reflects an original fragmentation of relationships in the client's early life.

In severe dissociative disorders, simply interpreting transference distortions, particularly those that take place in an altered state of consciousness, will not enable the client to resolve them or integrate her fragmented experiences of relationship. Transference is more fruitfully approached by clarifying developmental inconsistencies as well as uncovering, abreacting, and integrating trauma. Managing transference involves constantly differentiating the therapist as a real, nonabusive person distinct from the images of abusers projected onto the therapist. A corollary of such differentiation is paying specific attention to those aspects of the working alliance that foster consistency and unify the client's experience of the therapist. Over time, the relationship with the therapist bridges the many altered states, including trance states, that have fragmented the client's existence. This bridging process is a major facilitating factor in the client's eventual integration.

ABSENCES AND FUGUES

When a client first enters therapy, it is helpful to be sensitive to her habitual uses of trance as a coping technique. This is obviously true in instances in which a client has been the victim of a known trauma. But in some cases, trauma has been forgotten; characterological style is the major clue that trauma is part of the client's history. Although dramatic presentations sometimes alert the therapist immediately, most dissociative symptomatology is subtle, and comparatively few clients will have developed full-blown cases of a severe disorder like MPD. Often what appears most obvious is a personal style that has been traditionally denigrated as hysterical: absentmindedness, lack of clarity in memory or thinking, a glossing over of inconsistencies accompanied by a flighty "what, me worry?" kind of affective display. In the course of therapy, the habitual use of dissociative defenses may become increasingly evident in frequent forgetting of what either the client or the therapist has previously said. There may be little continuity between therapy sessions. The client herself may remark that after she leaves, she never remembers what happened in the session.

As a client's history unfolds in therapy, not only her habitual uses of trance but discontinuities in her development and identity become clearer. Sometimes, in addition to memories of painful events, past incidences of dissociative symptomatology are recalled. A particularly graphic instance of amnesia or even fugue may have interrupted the continuity of her history. Such extreme symptoms need not have been frequently repeated; in spite of severe developmental liabilities, the client may have nevertheless integrated a reasonably coherent identity. Sometimes only a later precipitating stress erodes a long-standing adaptation.

Absences, as they were called in the 19th century, are among the simplest dissociative responses. Since they often are brief and may simply consist of temporary time-outs from more active involvements, they do not necessarily constitute a pathological symptom. Even when they are frequent and habitual, they may be overlooked as simply a feature of a flighty but otherwise normal character. Sometimes, however, absences can be elaborated into more complex, even dangerous dissociative responses.

Alice*

Alice, who was in her late 40s, entered therapy in a state of great agitation, saying she must be going crazy. A few days previously, while in the housewares section of a department store, she had shoplifted a silver napkin ring. One minute she was looking at it. The next she was in the parking lot, clutching the ring in her coat pocket. It was all so sudden; she couldn't really remember doing it; something came over her. She was not caught, but as a religious person with no criminal history, she felt overcome with guilt as well as dismay.

Following the graduation of her youngest child from high school a few weeks prior to this incident, Alice's husband had moved out and filed for

*This case example, as well as all others in this book, is based on a composite of two or more cases and does not refer to any particular individual.

divorce. There had been signs that things were not going well in the marriage, even that he might be involved with someone else, but she had tried just to ignore them. Now, for the first time in 26 years, she was not wearing her wedding ring. Nor was she giving dinner parties. "I have no need whatsoever for a napkin ring," she said tearfully.

Alice's shoplifting episode was the first she had ever engaged in. Like a suicidal gesture, it could be interpreted as a cry for help. Her adult life had been organized around routine domestic concerns. Now her world seemed to be in shambles. She felt panic and a strange unreality. The symbolic significance of her theft was obvious to her even before the therapist interpreted it. She had lost one ring, her wedding ring, and stolen another. She had been famous in the community for her flair at entertaining; she wished she could once again lose herself in details like elegant place settings and silver napkin rings.

However, although Alice had never shoplifted before, the dissociative minifugue in which the shoplifting occurred turned out to be symptomatic of a more long-standing problem. Acting without thinking was her characteristic coping style. All her life, she had avoided conflict and unpleasant feelings by taking flight into domestic and social activities. Her always full schedule, which consisted of childcare, housekeeping, cooking, volunteer work, and entertaining left little time for self-reflection. People laughed good-naturedly at her absentmindedness: The umbrella or sweater left behind after a PTA meeting or Girl Scout banquet always belonged to Alice. Everybody thought of her as a very nice woman, though, a devoted wife and mother, an asset to her church and community. But after her husband left, her whole life seemed to screech to a halt. She felt too ashamed even to show herself in church. Housework seemed pointless. When she woke up in the morning, she hardly knew what to do with herself.

Since the shoplifting incident had forced Alice to seek therapy, it served a useful purpose. In therapy, she was able to think about the unthinkable, the loss of her marriage, and to plan for the future. This process involved confronting not only her situational crisis, but her habitual patterns of coping with conflict. In order to avoid anxiety, she had responded to anything unpleasant by simply taking flight from her own thoughts and feelings. Eventually, this tendency had resulted in her ignoring even the signs of her deteriorating marriage.

One of the feelings Alice was used to dissociating was anger. In therapy, her theft was eventually understood as an act of defiance and fury as well as a cry for help. She had always tried so hard to be good, and what had it gotten her? Maybe it was time to break the rules. Because she had been lucky enough not to get caught shoplifting, she was now able to explore less dangerous ways of expressing her anger and to integrate anger with her experience of herself. The rules constraining her compulsively good behavior had become a kind of straitjacket. Eventually, she learned to break them to her own advantage, without engaging in dissociative or antisocial behavior.

Alice's shoplifting was a symptomatic response to a situational crisis. It was a serious crisis and, had she gotten caught, might have had very destructive consequences. But Alice was not a seriously disturbed woman by most standards. Her character structure was in many ways typical of that often described in terms of "the good hysteric." She was attractive, feminine, socially outgoing, and likable, though somewhat fussy and flighty. Patterns of thought and behavior clinicians often label *repression* and *denial* were a pervasive part of her life, but seemed not to get her into trouble until midlife. At that point, she discovered that she had a big problem, that it was not really new, and that the only effective way to solve it was to confront it.

The dissociative features of Alice's character had produced many small blank spaces in her memory, but no really big gaps. Brief absences do not necessarily interfere much with the organization of a coherent existence. Her social circle tolerated these little lapses, was even supportive. If Alice lost an umbrella, someone usually returned it; if not, buying a new one was no great problem.

Some individuals are troubled by more extensively organized absences, however. They live a fragmented existence. Although they do not necessarily elaborate the complex fantasies characteristic of multiple personality disorder, they may lose episodes of their lives. Since dissociation can function as a strong defense against depression, for example, an individual may habitually absent herself from the awareness that she is depressed. If the flight from depression involves manic excitement, she may get into trouble through inappropriate behavior, such as giving away all her possessions or picking fights with people. Through dissociation, however, she may simply physically or mentally leave the scene of distress in ways that others scarcely notice.

Noreen

Noreen had not expected to be laid off from her administrative position at a small manufacturing firm. Her work was her life. The news, she said, hit her like a ton of bricks. Her mind was blank as she cleaned out her desk and started for home. But she did not reach home. Instead, she woke up the next day in a motel room near a city over 200 miles from where she lived. The television set was on, but she did not remember having watched anything. After a moment of disorientation, she realized where she was: She had stayed in this hotel when on vacation the previous year. Vaguely, as if it were a dream, she remembered driving there the night before.

As she began to collect herself, the world seemed unreal though strangely vivid. Colors were almost painfully bright and a blazing sun outside contrasted sharply with the cloudiness of her thoughts. Almost mechanically, she dressed, drove into the city and spent most of the day wandering past shop windows, buying an occasional scarf or pair of earrings. She knew she was avoiding thinking about something important. Yet, as she wandered, she was detached from both thinking and feeling, aware only of the sights and sounds of the city. At the end of the day, as suddenly as she had come there, she checked out of her motel and returned home.

Once she was home, the painful reality of her situation hit Noreen with full force. It was like coming out from anesthesia, she said. She perfunctorily took care of a few things, then settled into a depressed but obsessively ruminating state. Chain-smoking, she imagined how she ought to revise her resumé. Yet she had no inclination to move beyond the confines of her own apartment, where she kept the shades drawn and seldom even bothered to get dressed. When she finally asked her physician for medication, he suggested psychotherapy.

In therapy, Noreen talked initially about the situational crisis and her depressive reaction to it. In the course of exploring her depressive symptoms, however, her habitual use of dissociative defenses against depression became clear. As a child, she had frequently dissociated to escape from a home she described as a "battlefield." Her father seemed always angry and was often physically abusive to his wife and Noreen's older brother. Her mother was a "doormat" who tried constantly to please him, but never seemed to succeed. Noreen herself escaped physical abuse — she tried to fade into the woodwork — and handled psychological distress by "blanking out" or focusing compulsively on school work. Sometimes she rode her bicycle round and round the streets of the small suburb where she lived. Or she "watched" television for hours without really seeing anything. She did not elaborate many fantasies about herself except for the fantasy that, one day, she would grow up and leave home. Right after high school, she did leave, worked to support herself, eventually put herself through college, and embarked on a career.

As she had made a new life for herself, Noreen had tried not to think about the old life. Her layoff threatened this neat compartmentalization. The feeling of trapped helplessness she had so often felt at home suddenly overwhelmed her again. Her first impulse was just to get away and start over; yet it was no longer possible to do that. Dissociation only worked briefly to seal her off from the reality of her situation and her feelings.

Noreen had not been physically abused. Her father's attacks on her mother were nevertheless an inescapable stress from which she protected herself, like many children in violent homes, by becoming quiet and self-effacing. Her dissociative coping involved a trance-like absenting of herself from her surroundings or losing herself in a compulsive concentration on work details. After she grew up, she continued to live a constricted life but did not consider herself unhappy. In therapy, paradoxically, she had to discover her unhappiness before she could move beyond it.

When Noreen entered therapy, she had never had a sexual relationship with anyone and had no intentions of marrying. Nor did she have real friends. Her depression reflected a hopelessness about relationships as well as a response to the immediate stress of losing her job. She had been depressed on several occasions before, but most of her adult life she had functioned as a busy, very efficient workaholic. Her hopelessness eventually became a focus of therapy, as well as her attempts to escape inner thoughts and feelings by concentrating compulsively on work or just "blanking out." It was extremely painful to think or to remember or to feel. But only by getting beyond her trance-like haze and letting herself think and feel was she able, eventually, to develop a more hopeful life that included human relationships as well as work.

MULTIPLE PERSONALITY DISORDER

When absences are lengthy rather than brief, and when they are filled up with thinking and behavior that is distinctly organized though cut off from the mainstream of life, the resulting incoherence of personality can become a serious problem. Sometimes the mainstream even gets lost; life becomes a series of branches flowing in parallel. Individuals who are this markedly dissociated are seldom as lucky as Alice or Noreen. Sooner or later they get caught, in the sense that the multiplicity of their existence has serious negative effects. Multiple personality disorder illustrates what can happen when dissociation is extensive and extreme.

MPD is not only the most dramatic and potentially incapacitating dissociative disorder according to clinical guidelines. It is also the dissociative disorder most intriguing to the general public and the media. This public interest is not simply spurious. Child abuse is a growing public concern, and MPD seems to arise from the most horrific instances of child abuse coupled with a perhaps heightened facility for dissociative trance states.

However, in spite of increased public awareness of MPD and the increasing frequency with which the diagnosis is made, clear-cut, full blown cases of MPD are still not very common. Many patterns of dissociative symptomatology, even dramatic ones, do not fit the MPD diagnosis unless the diagnosis is stretched unduly to accommodate them. The temptation to stretch the diagnostic category, in fact, may be at least in part responsible for the increasing numbers of multiple personalities being diagnosed. At the same time, this sudden increase in incidence, coupled with what is known about the suggestibility and plasticity of so-called "hysterical" people makes many clinicians very skeptical about the very existence of multiple personality disorder.

Such a state of affairs, in which the most striking manifestation of a syndrome is controversial or seldom observed in pure form, often leads to an excessive use of catch-all categories. In the case of dissociative disorders, this category is "dissociative disorder not otherwise specified." Such anomalous dissociative disorders are commonly observed in the therapy of abuse survivors. More research needs to be focused on them. For example, fugue states, transient minifugues, oscillations in level of cognitive awareness, and trances that do not necessarily involve the formation of alter personalities commonly occur in trauma victims. Such variable ego states frequently led to variable self-presentations and may even be disconnected by amnesias without necessarily being organized into enduring personality configurations. Their treatment is a major challenge for most therapists who work with victims.

The controversies surrounding the diagnosis of multiple personality disorder are complicated by the history of diagnostic classifications and fashions, as well as by theoretical preferences. Formerly, the significance of childhood trauma in adult psychopathology was not recognized or was explicitly denied. In an attempt to correct for a preexisting bias, it is not unusual for people to swing to the opposite extreme. Currently, not only professional studies of child abuse but sensational media accounts are much in vogue. In therapy, it is certainly important to validate any client's memories of abuse. However, that does not mean that everything presented in treatment should be accepted at face value as literally true.

This cautionary note might go without saying if it were not for some of the wild tales that circulate, even among trained therapists. Stories of multiple personalities formed in utero or dramatic memories of splits that supposedly occurred in the first months of life run counter to what we know about developmental biology as well as developmental psychology. Such accounts merely increase skepticism about issues that are already controversial.

Stories of people who have hundreds or even thousands of alter personalities also strain credulity. Some individuals dissociate frequently, produce many named personality configurations, and are, from a diagnostic standpoint, "polyfragmented" (Putnam, 1989). But there are still only 24 hours in a day. It takes real time in the real world for a personality configuration in a complex system to develop a history. This point—that personality has a complex history—sometimes gets overlooked in discussions of multiple personality.

What are commonly referred to as alter personalities may spring up full blown like Athena from the head of Jove. But a fantasy construction is not the same thing as a personality. It is merely an identity component among many, which, under normal circumstances, would have been organized into a whole personality. Many experts on MPD have explicitly emphasized that alter personalities should not be treated as separate persons inhabiting one body (Putnam, 1989; Ross, 1989). The point must be reiterated because tendencies to think of alters as separate individuals are so persistent and widespread.

In the 19th century, multiple personality became a widely influential model of the human psyche. From a theoretical standpoint, we might all be viewed in terms of multiplicity (Beahrs, 1982). But multiplicity as a model of the mind should be distinguished from multiplicity as a diagnosed disorder. It is an oversimplification to view all cases in which a lack of personality integration is a major problem from the perspective of one structural model. The distinction between lack of integration as a factor in identity development and dissociation as a factor in the compartmentalization of personality structure is still useful.

Lack of integration may arise from any number of developmental antecedents. Pathological dissociation, in contrast, is a defensive development that keeps memories or fantasy structures separate. In practice, of course, many individuals have both kinds of problems. The developmental context that leads to reliance on dissociation as a coping mechanism also interferes with personality integration in other ways. However, in the clarification of such questions as the relation between borderline pathology and MPD and treatment approaches to different personality disorders, such distinctions remain important. The best scientific way to validate MPD as a phenomenon is to continually question the phenomenon and consider alternative explanations, including alternative diagnostic categories.

In therapy, a client's discovery that she has a variety of ego states, which can be given names, does not necessarily indicate MPD according to the *DSM-III-R* criteria—not until it can be demonstrated that at least two of these recurrently "take full control of the person's behavior" (APA, 1987, p. 269). It may merely indicate the existence of personality configurations that, prior to treatment, were never autonomous. Or it may reflect fantasies about being a multiple stimulated by reading or by the media, including fantasies that the therapist would be more impressed with the client if she were a multiple. Such developments, which are really transference manifestations, are not insignificant; from a treatment standpoint, they may be highly significant. But they cannot be taken simply as evidence for the prior existence of MPD.

Even so, open-minded therapists who work with survivors of abuse are likely to encounter cases in which the diagnosis of multiple personality disorder makes more theoretical and empirical sense than any other. In professionals as well as in clients, the acceptance of the diagnosis is a necessary prelude to effective therapeutic intervention.

In typical cases of MPD, one personality configuration presents as the "host," that is, the personality pattern that takes charge of important social behavior like holding down a job or seeking help from a psychotherapist. Having alter personality configurations that recurrently take "full control of the person's behavior" will usually mean that significant features of a multiple life, such as different circles of acquaintances, different choices in clothing, and distinct histories have been evident prior to treatment. Typically, the client will have experienced gaps in the coherence of her life that are referred to as "losing time." Clues will indicate to the host that, although she has amnesia for the lost time, she nevertheless spent the time behaving in some organized fashion. She may have taken a trip, planted a garden, established a sexual relationship, etc., during the periods in question. And although she does not remember, others do. This dismaying situation greatly complicates her life and may, in fact, be the impetus for entering therapy.

In most cases of MPD, two or more alter personalities are not only distinct in self-presentation—they are in conflict with one another. In therapy, it becomes obvious that not only trauma but conflict and dissociative modes of coping with conflict is a significant aspect of the client's history. Integrating distinct personality patterns, then, is not just a matter of abreacting trauma and integrating memories, but a matter of conflict resolution.

In daily life, conflict gets acted out in clearly demarcated periods in which rival alters take over. An alter who hates wearing dresses may find a new one in her closet. An alter who never drinks may find a liquor bottle on the coffee table. An alter who is dieting may find an empty box of fudge. Rival alters may even brutally attack one another. Suicidal behavior is often, in effect, attempted murder of a rival alter (Putnam, 1989). Unlike most people who recognize and are exasperated by their own internal conflicts, however, rival MPD alters often interpret one another's behavior as external and autonomous. That is, the someone who bought the dress, drank the liquor, or ate the fudge is actually believed to be someone else, "not me." According to this logic, killing off a rival alter will not mean killing oneself. In therapy, one of the most urgent tasks is addressing this delusional attitude. Once the personality system can acknowledge that the fate of one is inextricably linked to the fate of all other alters, a major step toward integration has been effected.

Although from a technical standpoint multiples are not psychotic, they typically exhibit other kinds of thinking that, technically, can be considered delusional. Alter personalities really believe themselves to be as they say they are. Thus, a person who appears to any external observer to be a tall, blond adult female may staunchly declare that she is a petite, dark-haired child. Many cases of MPD include alters who claim to be of the opposite sex. These "personalities" quite obviously originate in fantasy. It has been suggested that they are related to the imaginary companions many children invent (Baum, 1978; Benson & Pryor, 1973; Hilgard, 1979; Nagera, 1969). Upon investigation, they often hold specific memories of trauma; a particular alter is often invented to cope with a specific trauma.

In adult clients, many child alters are clearly encapsulations of regressed ego states. As such, they demonstrate not only the memories of childhood events, but regressive episodes that occurred at later points in childhood or adult life. Thus, for example, a five-year-old child alter cannot be taken at face value to represent the client as she really existed at age five. The five-year-old alter may have been created as a regressive response to a painful event that occurred in later childhood or adolescence. The defensive function of regression is obvious here. At any age, a traumatized individual may attempt to go back in time to a period prior to the trauma. Some child alters live perpetually in a state before certain traumas occurred. Many, however, encapsulate specific experiences of trauma; specific memories are frozen in them. In any case, being a child allows one to deny and evade the responsibilities of adult life.

Because child alters are composites of memory, fantasy, and regressive developments, they behave differently from real children. As Ross (1989) points out, for example, they often understand adult vocabulary and can exhibit mature forms of rational thought and behavior. On the other hand, as disturbed and regressed ego configurations, they are often unable to function like normal adults. Their thinking is typically concrete, colored by the affects and ideation associated with particular traumatic events as well as earlier developmental stages. In this respect, they exhibit the action-oriented tendencies as well as the interpretations typical of childhood generally and abused children in particular. These behavioral tendencies make enactive techniques especially useful in the treatment of multiplicity.

Individuals with dissociative disorders are typically highly hypnotizable. Self-induced trance states in childhood have been posited as the states in which the alter personalities of MPD are originally elaborated (Braun & Sachs, 1985; Frischholz, 1985). The hypnotic capacities of multiples have led some to insist that MPD is an iatrogenic disorder, an artifact of hypnosis. The question of iatrogenesis will be considered more fully in a subsequent chapter. For the present, however, it should be noted that in most cases of MPD there is evidence for the existence of discretely organized and autonomously functioning personality states prior to treatment. The MPD diagnosis enables the client as well as the therapist to make sense of a long but puzzling history.

On the other hand, the question of the suggestibility as well as the hypnotizability of multiples is complicated by well-known features of those dissociative disorders that were traditionally diagnosed as hysteria. The chameleon-like changeability of hysterical patients was well recognized in the 19th century, for example. Chronically hospitalized patients would often mimic the symptoms of new patients who came into the hospital. Freud described this phenomenon as "hysterical identification," a form of identification characterized by transience and superficiality rather than durability and depth. Unfortunately, hysterical identification was usually dismissed as a bothersome symptom rather than a behavior pattern that in itself warranted investigation. Psychoanalysis did not really shed much light on the phenomenon either. When Freud attempted to explain the dynamics of hysteria, he located the origin of symptoms in Oedipal fantasies. The hysteric's remarkable flair for mimicry was never really explained.

Mimicry, however, is a fundamental aspect of identifications that not only form the basis of personality structure but that unite individuals into cohesive groups. From this perspective, hysteria, including crowd hysteria, has always been a social disease. In MPD, the uses of mimicry are so dramatic that they may distract other people, including the therapist, from the client's underlying depression and social isolation.

Relationships in MPD

At any point in life, extreme and habitual dissociation disrupts social integration as well as internal integration. Severe dissociative disorders provide the most dramatic examples of such disruptions. The individual's internal world may consist of numerous compartments sealed off from each other by dissociative barriers. Internal division, in turn, inevitably affects not only identity integration but relationships with other people. Fragmented and inconsistent relationships, in turn, reinforce internal fragmentation.

This vicious circle can be so isolating that the dissociated individual is almost as out of contact socially as the psychotic individual. One factor in the tendency to diagnose extreme dissociative pathology as schizophrenia is the autistic withdrawal that characterizes some alters in the personality system. In contrast to schizoid individuals, however, dissociated ones often construct personality configurations that mediate between them and the social requirements of the external world and that assuage intense states of loneliness. As a result, the dissociated individual often seems much less socially withdrawn than the psychotic one. Even though important parts of the self may be quite hidden or permanently withdrawn, other relationships with people are as richly embroidered as the dissociated client's inner world. The relationship problems of dissociated individuals may thus escape detection, particularly in settings in which social or occupational role-playing rather than intimacy is the accepted mode of interaction.

Close observation, however, indicates that the dissociated woman is nevertheless isolated by her secrets, including secrets kept from herself or secrets that separate fragments of herself. In severe dissociative disorders like MPD, the secret self or selves is often protected by powerful guards, some of which may be alter personalities invented just for that purpose. This extreme defensiveness inevitably affects the depth as well as the consistency of relationships. All relationships are not necessarily superficial; some, particularly those based on intense attachments to abusive parents, may be extremely tenacious and intense. Other relationships, however, suffer from lack of history with and consistent involvement in other people. These more superficial and transient relationships may change as kaleidoscopically as the multiple's own identity presentations.

Sometimes, too, dissociation in children correlates with dissociation in parents. Dissociated relationship patterns are then basic learned patterns of relating to other people. Once learned, such patterns continue to shape relationships with people outside as well as inside the family, including other abusers. Even when the dissociated individual's relationships are characterized by enduring intensity they are nevertheless likely to have a quality some clinicians label *narcissistic*. That is, relationships with others are not well differentiated from images and experiences of the self. This situation is the expectable outcome of being brought up by parents who used and abused the child as an extension of themselves. Individuation is systematically thwarted by incestuous families, for example.

Meg

Meg, who was 27 years old, was arrested and then hospitalized after being disorderly in a bar. Although this incident was a repetition—she had been hospitalized before—it was a terrifying experience as she eventually remembered and integrated it. At the time she entered therapy, however, she did not remember much about it. Meg said she was not the sort of person who went to bars or became disorderly. It was hard to believe what doctors had told her about herself, including their diagnosis that she was a "borderline personality." Doctors can't figure her out, she said. One once told her she was schizophrenic, another that she was just "spoiled rotten" and making things up.

In spite of the seriousness of her recent symptoms, Meg insisted that she was not crazy, although she got depressed sometimes. She did not, in fact, give the impression of being psychotic or even very unstable. She was coherent and showed flashes of intelligence, although she was rather diffident in expressing herself. She admitted, however, that her remembered history was as full of holes as Swiss cheese. She attributed these memory problems to the shock treatments she had had during one hospitalization, and to nerves. Her mother had been a nervous woman, she said, who practically lived on tranquilizers.

Her parents lived in another state, and she now had little contact with them. She was vague in describing her father and could remember little beyond the fact that he had a bad temper. She had been briefly married several years previously but was vague about that, too. In spite of her psychological problems, she had managed to obtain an undergraduate degree, although her work history did not reflect her level of education. She had worked at various times on an assembly line, as a clerk in a clothing store, and as a pianist for a dance studio.

At the time of her most recent hospitalization, Meg had been finishing up a program in a health care field and had a good job in a local clinic. She came for therapy because she felt desperate to finish her training and keep her job. "Something always happens to mess things up," she said rather despairingly. If it was not a disruption like the hospitalization, it was some other health problem. She had a history of repeated urinary tract infections and pelvic pain that nobody seemed able to diagnose or treat.

The first year of therapy focused on establishing a working alliance and supporting Meg's stated goals of finishing her training and keeping her job. Although her story suggested a history of abuse and a severe dissociative disturbance, there was no attempt to uncover trauma until she felt stably situated in both the therapy and her daily life. Eventually, however, the focus of treatment widened. When the therapist began tentatively exploring her marriage, Meg began having nightmares. One day she called in a panic to say she had lost time, almost a whole day. When she came in for a special session, she was quite distressed. The therapist suggested a relaxation exercise to help her calm down.

Hardly had she begun the exercise when Meg went into a deep trance. When she began moving her lips, the therapist stated simply, "If someone is trying to talk, I'm listening. Wake up and talk to me."

The person who woke up seemed strikingly different from the one who had gone into trance. She was angry and tough and sprinkled her speech with expletives. Asked to identify herself, she announced herself as Maggie. She expressed contempt for Meg, contending that Meg was good for nothing except going to work and paying bills.

Maggie's life was organized around the kinds of activities Meg usually ignored. She liked to party, she said. She considered herself responsible for Meg's divorce. That jerk, her former husband, was never any fun at all.

Maggie knew all about Meg and several other alters in Meg's personality system. She also remembered things from childhood. She described her father as the man who had taught her to party. His sexual abuse of her began by age five and continued until she left for college, at which point he turned his attentions to her younger sister. He had a violent temper and hit her a lot, but could also be quite indulgent and sometimes gave her expensive presents. He openly preferred Maggie to her mother, often complained about her mother to her, and occasionally hit her mother in front of her. Her mother reacted like a zombie, "totally out of it."

Maggie was not quite sure what her father did for a living — some kind of sales, maybe. When she was in her teens, her father took her on business trips where he introduced her to drugs and sometimes passed her off as his girlfriend. Occasionally he involved her in sexual scenarios that included other people. She believed he had also sometimes sold her sexual services to acquaintances.

Shortly after Maggie put in her appearance, a terrified child alter called Ladybug introduced herself, followed close by a depressed adolescent, Velvet, who defined herself in terms of her sexual servicing of men. Subsequently, five other alter personalities, including three other children, came out one by one to meet the therapist. All claimed to be separate and distinct individuals. Most, however, were fragments who had not had a very complicated existence. Three alters considered themselves male. Maggie and Hal, two adult alters who had existed from childhood, had the most complex histories. They were able to fill in many missing gaps in Meg's story.

The alter personalities were, in effect, dissociated incarnations of Meg's secrets, memories, desires, and feelings. When Meg was initially told about them, she refused to believe in them. But she admitted that they explained puzzling aspects of her life. It was only in the course of a long therapy, which involved the gradual remembering, abreaction, and integration of a very traumatic history that Meg was able to claim the dissociated parts of herself as her own.

It was the sustained reliability of the therapeutic context as well as specific therapeutic techniques like abreaction that made this integration possible. Therapy focused not only on the client's traumatic memories, but on the conflicts implicit in all her relationships with people and the expression of these conflicts in the transference. Since childhood, Meg, who identified strongly with her depressed mother, had been as oblivious to her alter personality states as her mother had been oblivious to her and to her father's abusive behavior. Family life had involved an elaborate game of hiding and display that came to characterize Meg's ways of relating to everybody, including the therapist. The secret life of alter personalities thus reflected not only secret trauma but the internalization of characteristic family coping styles.

The game of hide and seek was a significant factor in Meg's adult experience of sexuality. Early in treatment, Meg seemed overtly inhibited, and Maggie and Velvet seemed overtly sexual, even provocative. Meg's marriage to an inhibited, detached man had been almost asexual, one reason Maggie had sabotaged it. Yet these differences between alters reflected differences in expressive style more than differences in sexual responsiveness. As might be expected, sexuality was really conflicted for all the alter personalities. Maggie's brash displays and Velvet's subtle seductiveness were merely covers for anxiety. Although Maggie, in particular, seemed to be in control of sexual encounters and sought them out, her traumatic history made her unable to physically enjoy them. Therapy involved putting all the alters in touch with sexual pleasure as well as other dimensions of bodily experience. Embodiment, in fact, was a primary factor in integration.

In the course of getting in touch with her body, the client was also able to make sense out of some of her somatic symptoms and to become physically healthier. Somatic pain had been an encoding of painful memories of physical violation. Chronic infection indicated a lingering vulnerability to stress. A phobic reaction to medical treatment (in spite of the fact that she was involved in a health care field) had kept her from taking care of herself physically. Once she could own a body, she could take care of it.

In this case, some alter personalities seemed invented for the purpose of containing traumatic memories. Others, however, were based on complex wishful fantasies as well as memories. Hal, for example, was a protective alter who seemed based on Meg's envy of her older brother. This brother was the only person in the family who got to do really "fun" things with the father—hunting, ballgames, auto races, etc. As a child, Meg had imagined his position to be ideal. He escaped the sexual abuse that was the lot of Meg and her younger sister. But even this brother was a target for the father's hitting, and he sometimes hit other people, including Meg. Hal thus embodied many elements of identification with the aggressor, as well as fantasies about being male.

The integration of Meg's personality involved claiming for herself not only the memories that had been parceled out among alter personalities, but the wishes and feelings she had never been able to acknowledge. It involved reclaiming her body. And it involved learning new relationship patterns, patterns based on mutual interest, affection, and concern. The relationship with the therapist was the bridge that facilitated this integration. In relating empathically to each of the alters, the therapist was able to validate the experiences of each. The relationship with the empathic therapist then became a common bond among alters. Initially, they competed for the therapist's attention, but eventually rivalry was replaced by cooperation.

Even while acknowledging the experiences unique to particular alters, the therapist emphasized Meg's wholeness from the outset. She respected what every alter said, even if it involved delusional material, but she stated her own point of view consistently: You are all part of one person. There is only one body. Mind and body are connected; the mind cannot exist apart from the body, at least not for me, in the context of therapy. This point of view made it possible to avoid philosophical debates about the ultimate nature of reality and evasions of ordinary, mundane facts.

It was flight from the body and an autistic retreat from painful relationships that led to the original creation of Meg's complexly dissociated inner world. It was an intense early relationship with inconsistently caring and abusive people that kept her nevertheless involved with others and clinging to hope. Reclaiming her body, integrating her memories, and using the relationship with the therapist as a bridge to relationships beyond therapy eventually made wholeness possible. Paradoxically, wholeness was a sad as well as a satisfying discovery. Abuse had really happened. There was no going back and having a different childhood. There was no omnipotence that could magically transform her. But in the end, Meg found her human limitations greatly preferable to the isolation she had experienced for so much of her life.

CHAPTER 7

Female Complaints Revisited

THE INFLUENCE OF values and world views on healing has always been complicated by attitudes towards different classes of people and their presumed role in the scheme of things. When disease is diagnosed in females, the diagnosis is likely to reflect not only theories about disease as such, but implicit views about woman's normal place and function. Such views in turn are colored by the nearly universal experiences of scientists, medicine men, technocrats, and priests: Almost everybody remembers mother as being somehow at the origin of things, a mysterious power to be reckoned with. And almost everybody feels ambivalent about that.

One response to this ambivalence has been the social control of women, the careful, institutionalized, legally codified limiting of women's feared power. Another response has been the assumption that such controls are normal as well as normative and that if physical, psychological, and institutional constraints lead to symptoms in women, that too is normal. Female complaints, then, are inherently paradoxical. Yes, she is sick, but all women are delicate. Yes, she is dissatisfied, but all women complain.

In modern times, as psychological theories became increasingly influential in social life, explanations of female complaints became more complicated, but many of them still reflected primitive myths about the sexes as well as the biases of particular theories. The paradoxically normal nature of the female complaint continued to be taken for granted by scientists and health care providers. Yes, she is sick, but it's mostly in her head; all women are neurotic. Yes, she is dissatisfied, but all women suffer from penis envy. Yes, she is a victim, but she asked for it; all women are masochistic. It is only in the past two decades that these views have been specifically and systematically challenged.

During the 1970s, the women's movement led to a reevaluation of the effects of sexism and sex role stereotypes on women's mental health. A growing recognition of the prevalence of violence in the lives of females as well as evolving clinical understanding of post-traumatic syndromes also contributed to a gradual modification of traditional psychiatric perspectives. Instead of simply asking such questions as "Why are depression or borderline personality disorder or dissociative disorders more prevalent in women?" more people began asking "How and why are women and men perceived and treated differently by the health care system? To what extent is the way they are differently perceived related to actual differences in clients, and to what extent is it related to professional biases? If observed differences do reflect realities in the populations observed, to what can these differences be attributed?"

Increased sensitivity to such issues is a welcome addition to clinical interventions. Integrating new perspectives is hindered, however, not only by persisting theoretical biases but by practical roadblocks. In spite of a growing appreciation of the significance of violence as well as sexism in the lives of females, one problem that continues to complicate the diagnosis and treatment of trauma-related disorders is the reluctance or, in cases of amnesia, the inability of victims to voluntarily report abuse. This problem is compounded by the failure of diagnosticians to elicit data relevant to abuse. Courtois (1988) notes, for example, that approximately half of incest survivors who seek treatment fail to disclose their abuse history to intake workers but make a disguised presentation of their problems. As a result of such omissions, many older survivors have experienced chronic mental health problems and years of treatment before the etiological significance of incest is recognized. Treatment in such cases has reinforced the lesson of the original trauma: that the victim is "helpless, crazy, and powerless" (p. 132).

Herman (1992) also emphasizes that "Disguised presentations are common in complex post-traumatic stress disorder" and that explicit questions designed to elicit information about past or ongoing abuse "should be a routine part of every diagnostic evaluation" (p. 157). This recommendation highlights not only the oversights of traditional diagnosis, but the complexities of symptom development in post-traumatic syndromes. In clinical practice, for example, whether one is diagnosed with a dissociative disorder, depression, an anxiety disorder, or a personality disorder is often a function not only of prevailing diagnostic fashions and theories, but of the most dramatic symptomatic manifestations observed during an initial examination. Extreme dissociation as an obvious presenting symptom often overshadows other symptomatology. But in other instances, post-traumatic or dissociative pathology may be so subtle that it is overlooked even though it is a major factor contributing to other symptoms.

Diagnosis is complicated by the variability and pervasiveness of post-traumatic symptoms. Resick (1983), discussing the crisis reactions of rape victims, notes that test scores on almost any psychological measuring instrument are typically elevated to clinical levels. An implication of this observation is that scales designed to identify depression, anxiety disorders, or other specific syndromes may not differentiate victims of trauma. Thus, in the absence of specific information about traumatic life events, diagnostic test data may be easily misinterpreted.

Traditional views about the diagnostic significance of particular symptoms can also be misleading. Some symptoms associated with a history of trauma, especially hallucinations, may elicit an almost reflexive diagnosis of psychosis. Flashbacks, too, are easily mistaken for psychotic symptoms, particularly if the client is behaviorally disorganized and the evaluator is unfamiliar with post-traumatic syndromes. Diagnostic categories like depression, which are typically employed with female clients, are also easily substituted for careful evaluations of life histories. Dysphoric mood and behavioral constriction may be simply taken as evidence that the client is depressed, and unless she is forthcoming with specific information about abuse, the origin of her depression in either past or ongoing situational trauma is likely to be overlooked.

. Some women who repeatedly seek help in the mental health system are revictimized not only by a failure to recognize and treat the post-traumatic dimensions of their symptoms but by a tendency for past diagnostic labels to follow them. Once diagnosed as borderline, schizophrenic, or depressed, a woman may find that such labels color all future evaluations of her. New symptoms, even those of physical illness, may be routinely interpreted in terms of her previous diagnosis. Diagnoses that are prevalently given to females are especially likely to become self-perpetuating. Not infrequently, they are incorporated into the client's self-concept, along with inferences that, although never subjected to careful empirical tests, contribute to low self-esteem and hopelessness. The client may assume that she has an inherent defect, perhaps genetically based, and obviously not very treatable.

These considerations suggest a reevaluation of physical as well as psychological disorders prevalently diagnosed in women.

DEPRESSION

Numerous studies have indicated that women are at higher risk than men for most types of depression (McGrath et al., 1990; Nolen-Hoeksema, 1987, 1990; Strickland, 1988; Weissman et al., 1984). As McGrath and her colleagues (1990) emphasize, depression is not a unidimensional phenomenon, but varies in kind as well as degree. Among the etiological factors typically cited are biological predispositions and psychological vulnerabilities, but it is only comparatively recently that the role of trauma has been considered. High rates of depression have been found in victims of battering (Hilberman & Munson, 1977), rape (Ellis et al., 1982), and incest (Bagley & Ramsey, 1986; Murphy et al., 1988; Roth & Leibowitz, 1988).

The common failure of interviewers to elicit material about victimization often results in trauma being left out of the diagnostic picture when depressed women are evaluated. Frequently, because of amnesia for victimization in childhood and the long delay between abusive experiences and the report of symptoms, the etiological connection between trauma and depression is hidden. Often, too, it is not merely the original traumatic experience or experiences that results in depression, but a host of sequelae to the original trauma that have complicated the client's life and have led to subsequent traumatizations and revictimization.

One factor frequently complicating post-traumatic depressive reactions is the use of dissociation as a counter-depressive coping mechanism. As a response to anxiety, dissociation isolates the victim from feelings of being overwhelmed and, in some cases, from the psychophysiological concomitants of trauma. As a defense against depression, dissociation seals off affects by also sealing off painful thoughts from awareness. This response can be viewed as a special kind of denial, a denial that is based on psychobiological compartmentalizations of memory and affect and functions automatically. Any erosion of dissociative denial, including that which results from successful personality integration in therapy, can then precipitate a depressive crisis.

Depression is also one aspect of the mourning for self and others that is usually unavoidable in integrative therapy with survivors. Coming to terms with harsh realities is complicated when trauma has robbed an individual not only of self-esteem and needed relationships, but of skills needed for coping with normal stresses and disappointments. In any case, careful therapeutic attention to support and the titrating of traumatic reexperiencing is necessary to help the client avoid being overwhelmed and immobilized by depressive reactions, including those stimulated by the therapeutic process.

Laurel

When Laurel was a freshman in college, she was one day walking back from her part-time job in town to the dorm where she lived. It was dusk when she reached the outskirts of a quiet neighborhood and started to cut across a large field that lay between town and campus. Suddenly, a man in a stocking mask jumped from a hedge that bordered the field. He grabbed her arm, pushed her down, and shoved the barrel of a gun into her mouth as he raped her. She thought she was going to die. But just as quickly as he had appeared, he disappeared. His only words were, "If you tell anybody about this, I'll *really* get you."

Somehow, Laurel made it back to the dorm, and her roommate drove her immediately to a hospital emergency room. After she was examined and treated, she spoke briefly to a psychiatrist who suggested she talk to someone at the college counseling center. She was also questioned by police, who investigated the incident but were never able to develop a lead.

The next day, Laurel felt strange, as if the experience had been a bad dream. She found herself jumping out of her skin at the slightest noise. Over the next few weeks, she had trouble falling asleep and woke from nightmares she could not clearly remember. But she did not go to the counseling center; she did not want to talk about the rape. It was as if talking about it might make it more real. She also felt vaguely guilty—she should not have taken the short-cut home.

Over the next few weeks, Laurel's acute symptoms subsided, but her life changed. Prior to the rape, she had started a relationship with a fellow student. Afterwards, she abruptly stopped seeing him or socializing much with anybody. She had difficulty concentrating on her school work. Her grades, which had been consistently high before the rape, fell sharply. At the end of the semester, she dropped out of college where she had been doing preprofessional course work. Only after working two years in a dead-end job did she finally decide to try again and enroll in a business course that trained her to do secretarial work.

Five years later, following the breakup of a serious relationship, Laurel sought therapy for depression. She also complained of dissatisfaction with her job. She was beginning to see her problems with men as a result of her own ambivalence. Every time she got close to someone, she said, she began to panic and did something to force distance. Laurel considered her childhood normal and reasonably happy. Her parents seemed to have a good marriage, as did her siblings. She had concluded that something must be wrong with *her*—could she have a chemical imbalance? A therapist she had consulted a year previously had prescribed antidepressants, which had helped for a while. But Laurel had discontinued them because of side effects and because they provided no help for her relationship problems.

In the present therapy, Laurel talked at first about situational issues and her own faults and failings. She was surprised when the therapist began questioning her about the rape. She had mentioned it in the previous therapy, but it was never talked about. Only after she finally began to explore the rape and to remember the extensive array of post-traumatic symptoms she had experienced following it did she begin to understand how profoundly the incident had affected her.

Like many rape victims, Laurel had shown immediate symptoms of post-traumatic stress disorder. Yet, like many rape victims, she had also seemed to recover from acute symptoms spontaneously and did not seek professional help. When she finally went into therapy, she was treated for depression with medication as well as psychotherapy. When she sought help after discontinuing medication, she complained again of depression and of difficulties in relationships with men. She was not then showing symptoms of delayed or chronic PTSD. She perceived that many problems were somehow a result of her own behavior patterns, but she had no idea why she became so anxious in her interactions with men.

Therapy might have attempted to locate the source of Laurel's relationship problems in her early childhood conflicts. The previous therapist had, in fact, suggested that her problems stemmed from envy of her brother. Yet, however significant her childhood experiences, the course of her life had changed as a result of a single traumatic experience in early adult life. Although Laurel had defensively avoided even thinking about the rape for several years, at the time it occurred it had stopped her in her tracks and paralyzed her subsequent development. Her acute post-traumatic symptoms, including difficulties in concentrating, had led to her dropping out of college. The life choices she made after that, including two years stuck in a dead-end job, had eroded her faith in herself. Following the rape, she gave up hope of having the career she had originally intended.

Laurel was enraged by these consequences but unable to express her rage. She was intelligent and had an astutely analytical mind, but the rape trauma was dissociated, unavailable to her own analyses of her problems. She knew only that nothing had worked out the way she had planned. She had missed both the career and the marriage she had expected. When she had finally had an opportunity for an enduring relationship, she had panicked.

Like everyone else, Laurel did have conflicts related to her childhood. Her family had not traumatized her, but it had instilled attitudes that made it difficult for her to cope with a trauma like rape. She was brought up to be conscientious and to take responsibility for whatever happened to her. She was carefully raised to be a "nice" girl. According to her world view, nice girls don't let themselves get raped. And if something bad happens to them, they don't express their anger. Because of a sexually repressive atmosphere in her family, Laurel had never felt able to mention the rape to anyone. She was isolated in her pain and guilt. In therapy, the influence of such familial attitudes on her response to trauma was slowly and systematically explored. The rape itself, and the immediate as well as long-term effects of it, was finally confronted.

Laurel's rape had been a shock that turned her world upside down and left her with an enduring sense of vulnerability and failure. She was mourning a loss she could not even name. Helping her confront the dissociated aspects of the experience, to explore and work through the trauma was a major focus of therapy. This process included work on specific symptoms, such as her sexual anxieties, and characterological coping mechanisms, such as her tendencies to blame herself for any problem and her inability to express negative feelings. Eventually, as she moved beyond the symptoms that had tied her unconsciously to a past trauma, she began making plans to go back to school and pursue her original goals again.

Eleanor

Eleanor was referred for psychotherapy by a physician who told her she was depressed and also prescribed medication. As she reviewed her situation, her bland affect contrasted markedly with the litany of suffering she recited. She meandered from one idea to the next, seemingly unable to present a systematic account of her history. She did not reflect on what she was saying or attempt to connect her experiences with her physician's diagnosis. She gave the impression of having told her story many times before.

As if she were talking about someone else, Eleanor described her child-hood — her father's alcoholism and neglect of his children, her mother's stoic acquiescence to his physical and psychological abuse, the pleasures and frustrations of growing up with five siblings with whom she is no longer close. In spite of her family's indifference to her accomplishments, she was a good student and had hoped to go to college, perhaps nursing school. But shortly after graduating from high school, she discovered that she was pregnant by Jack, her long time steady. He was already in college by then, but said he wanted the baby and dropped out temporarily to marry her.

Jack's constant controlling attention, which afforded Eleanor little independence, was a sign to her that he loved her in a way she had never felt loved before. Yet, even before the marriage and subsequently more and more frequently, Jack hit her. When she was pregnant, it seemed especially bad. When she mentioned the possibility of separating, he flew into a terrible rage, and when she once made a serious attempt to leave, he broke her nose. After each violent outburst, he was repentant for a while, but good times never lasted.

Materially the family prospered. As Jack's bookkeeper, Eleanor helped him build a business. But as conflicts between the couple increased and his violence became more frequent and destructive, she finally made up her mind to leave him. Counseling at a shelter for battered women supported her decision. She was terrified when she made it, but also felt a sense of taking charge that was new and self-affirming.

When Jack was unable to dissuade Eleanor from divorcing him, he asked for custody of their three boys, claiming that Eleanor, who had once been treated for post-partum depression, was mentally unstable. Nevertheless, the judge awarded custody to Eleanor and ordered Jack to pay child support. Jack refused to do so, and the support order was not enforced until she went on welfare.

Now, three years after the divorce, Eleanor feels overwhelmed by her circumstances. Jack has established a prosperous business, has remarried, and is asking for custody again. Maybe she should just let the boys go, she says without feeling. The oldest, in high school, is into drugs. The youngest has a learning disability and is getting bad marks in conduct. A school counselor told her the boys need a male role model. Supporting them has always been a problem. After Jack started paying a small amount of child support, she got a bookkeeping job and got off welfare, but life is continual struggle to pay bills and put food on the table. The boys themselves are not sure about which parent they want to live with. They have never been close to their father, but want to be. And his life style is very appealing to them.

A friend has suggested she go back to school. But what would she study? And how could she study? Sometimes, she has headaches that are so incapacitating she just lies for hours in a darkened room. Often, she just wants to sleep, but has not had a good night's sleep in years. Should she just let the boys go?

Eleanor was a study in double binds. As a client, she confronted the therapist as well as herself with difficult choices. Many of her problems were situational; she needed several adjunctive services, including help with coping with the problems of her children. Some of her problems also were evidently physical; she had been hit repeatedly about the head, yet had never had a neurological workup. Although she was guided toward additional services, however, psychotherapy focused on Eleanor's own attitudes, feelings, and behavior.

Eleanor's stated dilemma, making a decision about child custody, posed a pressing double bind conflict at the beginning of treatment. She was confused and exhausted and asking for direction, but it would have been therapeutically inappropriate as well as unrealistic to direct her decision. Both Eleanor and the therapist knew how little control they actually had over the decision of the court. It was also clear that whether she retained or lost custody, Eleanor would face a continuation of difficult, possibly traumatic circumstances. Thus, the custody decision in itself would not resolve her ongoing situational stress or the psychological and physical symptoms she was experiencing.

What Eleanor really needed most from a therapist was something she seems never to have had before — a social context in which her own interests were a priority. Simply thinking and talking about the world from that point of view can be empowering to women like Eleanor. It is the opportunity to focus on oneself without being evaluated as selfish that makes psychotherapy useful to those with so many situational problems. Effective psychotherapy acknowledges real shocks, dilemmas, and double binds. But, ideally, it also involves helping clients like Eleanor extricate themselves from their own traps.

Even though Eleanor's self-blame was often dissociated, it contributed to her depression. Blaming Jack was at one point part of her abreaction of trauma. But it was moving beyond Jack, separating from him emotionally as well as physically, that eventually helped her take control of her life.

After she felt stronger and determined to move on with her life, Eleanor extricated herself from Jack's neverending and exhausting legal harassments by relinquishing custody of her sons. The fact that, although he had abused her, he had not physically abused the boys was an important consideration in her difficult decision. The fact that she could not afford the therapeutic services two of the boys needed and had difficulty getting Jack to pay medical bills was also a factor.

The real world contingencies were unfair. Eleanor recognized that. She was angry and grieved giving up custody. But she was able eventually to evaluate her decision as an indication of her own strength. Fortunately, her persistent efforts at active negotiation resulted in visitation arrangements that enabled her to have an ongoing relationship with the boys.

Eleanor's headaches were eventually diagnosed to be related to a neck injury sustained in a beating by Jack. Physical therapy as well as psychotherapy ameliorated some of her pain, though the injury, in fact, constituted a permanent handicap. In the course of time, she did go back to school and became an accountant. It was never easy going. At some points in therapy, medication temporarily smoothed the way. Periodically, too, Eleanor took time-outs from therapy. But after she learned to make use of therapy, she came back whenever she needed it to supplement her own self-care.

SOMATIC MEMORIALS TO TRAUMA

Although violence against females is a major public health problem, the health related effects of violence remain to be adequately addressed by systematic research. Somatic injury and disease is a real and measurable outcome of trauma, but statistics on such physical problems as venereal disease, urogenital infections, pelvic inflammatory disease, infertility, minor head injury, and untreated bone breaks and tissue injuries seldom correlate these problems with antecedent abuse. Nor do statistics on psychosomatic symptoms like ulcers, colitis, menstrual irregularities, chronic abdominal and pelvic pain, and a generally lowered resistance to infection provide much information about the relation between such syndromes and traumatic victimization.

For some victims, hiding obvious physical signs of trauma such as bruising and scarring becomes a routine aspect of self-presentation. Self-injuries as well as injuries by others are a carefully concealed though constant source of shame. A victim may always wear long sleeves and long pants or high collars even in hot weather. Ritually abused clients conceal such physical emblems as branding and tattooing in addition to other scars.

Physical symptoms for which no obvious underlying somatic disease can be discovered are frequently medically diagnosed as indicative of psychological disorders. Somatoform disorders, as such symptom pictures are often labeled, are prevalently diagnosed in women. Loewenstein (1990) has reviewed how such diagnostic categories as Briquet's Syndrome have evolved from earlier ideas about female hysteria. "The disorder is described as a lifelong, chronic condition primarily affecting females. It is characterized by dramatically described polysymptomatic physical complaints without medical explanation; sexual problems and marital maladjustment; a feeling of chronic or recurrent ill health; conversion symptoms; and associated anxiety and depression" (p. 84). He also notes that this disorder is frequently associated with patient histories of alcoholism and abuse, particularly sexual abuse.

In therapy, somatoform symptoms are commonly discovered to encode memories of actual pain and assault. But even though it is important to acknowledge their significance as memories and symbolic communications, the possibility of real injury and disease, too often dismissively diagnosed as psychological, should be carefully evaluated.

A dramatic example of conversion symptoms as a response to extreme trauma is afforded by research on several Cambodian women who developed symptoms of blindness for which no underlying physical cause could be found (Fishman, 1991). Two psychologists, Gretchen Van Boemel, an expert in clinical electrophysiology, and Patricia Rozée, who had studied rape victims, began to explore the possibility that the sight loss of these women was associated with PTSD. After careful investigation, they concluded that the symptomatic blindness was a response to the women's having witnessed the atrocities of war. Although the traumas experienced by these Cambodian women were especially horrible, impaired sensory functions are not infrequently associated with post-traumatic syndromes. Such impairments are usually classified as functional, but post-traumatic loss of vision or hearing, like hallucinatory flashbacks, may have psychobiological parameters that are not yet clearly understood.

Eating Disorders

Eating disorders, which are most prevalently diagnosed in females, have become epidemic in the past few decades. Although such disorders were traditionally attributed to internal conflicts, such as ambivalence toward femininity, recent research has focused on the extent to which they are associated with a history of trauma, particularly sexual abuse (Goldfarb, 1987; Schechter et al., 1987). Dissociative reactions are also being recognized as a typical feature of such disorders, an association that further suggests a link with post-traumatic pathology (Demitrack et al., 1990; Torem, 1986).

Eating disorders dramatically display dilemmas of female expressiveness as well as the typical split between the female body as a source of appetitive needs and the body as an image contrived to please others. Disputing the idea that anorexic and bulimic women are rejecting their femininity, Boskind-Lodahl (1976) has interpreted the relentless pursuit of thinness in such individuals as a perfectionistic attempt to achieve the stereotypically feminine ideal. Orbach (1986), too, emphasizes the extent to which an obsessive preoccupation with food is associated with "a fetishizing of the female form" (p. 23). The individual woman's personal obsession reflects a cultural obsession.

An eating disorder, like the history of abuse with which it may be associated, often remains hidden during early stages of therapy. To some extent, the client's secrecy derives from her shame. But dissociative features of bingeing and purging can also complicate the process of disclosure. Both binge eating and self-induced vomiting, for example, may occur in an altered state of consciousness. When the client, with therapeutic assistance, begins to observe herself, she may confront the ironic fact that, no matter how much she eats, she never really experiences the pleasure of eating, or, if she does momentarily, she never clearly remembers it afterward. Similarly, purging may seem like a "not-me" experience, difficult to describe or analyze.

Anorexic women cannot conceal their problem. They may waste away in full view of horrified friends and relatives. Bulimia, on the other hand, can sometimes be concealed for years. Eventually, however, the unalleviated anxiety that drives the compulsive relation to food as well as the toll on physical health motivates some women with eating disorders to ask for help.

Frieda

When Frieda was a small child, family gatherings centered around food and the ethnic traditions of the European countries from which her grandparents had emigrated. When she was eight and her father died, her maternal grandparents assumed a major role in her upbringing. She loved the smell of her grandmother's kitchen, the pleasures of learning to cook with her. She loved her grandfather's stories. But when she stayed overnight and her grandfather put her to bed, he sexually molested her. The abuse, which included oral sex as well as genital fondling, continued until his death three years later.

When she was 14, Frieda's mother remarried. It was a miserable time for her. She became anxiously preoccupied with her blossoming sexuality and a sense that she was somehow different from other girls her age. The boys at school teased her about her developing breasts. Her mother set a bountiful table, but her stepfather constantly warned her about the dangers of getting fat. She started weighing herself obsessively, going on fad diets, and covering her body with oversized clothes.

When she was 16 and a close friend was raped, Frieda's ambivalence toward her body intensified. She envied her peers their sexual explorations and relationships, but was too frightened to pursue any of her own. On Saturday nights when others were on dates, she consoled herself with homemade baked goods and french fries. One day after gorging herself into an uncomfortable state of fullness, she discovered that she could make herself vomit by shoving a finger down her throat. The idea that she could eat whatever she liked without fear of getting fat was exhilarating. The exhilaration never lasted, however. Fear always returned, intensified by her attempts to control it by bingeing and purging. After reading in a magazine about eating disorders, Frieda resolved to turn over a new leaf. Sometimes she managed to avoid her compulsion for months at a time. But any crisis, or even the stress of a big test at school, precipitated a return of her bulimic symptoms.

It was not until her second year of college that she finally sought help with the problem. By then she had developed an obsessive fear of losing her teeth as a result of constant purging. She had also finally become involved in a serious relationship with a man and feared that he would discover her secret and abandon her.

When she began talking about her eating disorder, Frieda recognized the illusory nature of her control and a terror of being out of control that seemed mysterious to her. It was as if she were two people, she said. The one who binged simply paid no attention to the one who counseled restraint. The one who purged was angry and self-blaming, but, during the actual act of vomiting, was almost stuporous. Whenever Frieda sat down to the table, she felt a kind of now-or-never urgency to stuff herself, yet she hardly tasted what she ate. After purging she felt that she had gotten rid of some kind of fundamental badness. Having a body at all seemed somehow bad and shameful.

As therapy focused on the dissociative features of Frieda's bingeing and purging, both her flight from her body and her desperate attempts to exert control were discussed in connection with the discontinuities in her history. It was during these discussions that memories of her grandfather's abuse surfaced. She confronted the painful loss of her father in the context of her need for and disappointment in her grandfather. She had not consciously mourned either of these men or her grandmother, who had died when she was in high school. Her preoccupation with food had defensively isolated her from a host of painful feelings—grief, rage, anxiety. As she slowly laid claim to these feelings, she began to reclaim her body.

Confronting the sexual abuse, Frieda also began to explore her conflicting feelings about sexuality. Eating, originally a needed and pleasurable contact with love, had become a dangerous metaphor for sex. But the danger was no mere metaphor. Both eating and sex really had been experienced as dangerous and shameful. The pain of incest and the humiliation of devaluations by other people had been real and uncontrollable. Only after months of exploring these issues was she finally able both to eat and to experience sexual pleasure without dissociating. As she learned to taste food again, she made psychological contact with the grandmother she had loved and rediscovered the pleasures of cooking. She felt a new sense of control over her eating that was a welcome relief from the magical rituals of bingeing and purging.

Frieda's boyfriend played a significant role in her recovery. Deciding to tell her secrets to him brought her to a crisis in therapy. Helping him understand helped Frieda herself formulate and clarify her own insights. Receiving and accepting his support facilitated her move from a sense of isolation to internal and social integration.

FEMALE EXPRESSIVENESS AND DIAGNOSED PATHOLOGY

Diagnosed psychological disorders like anorexia and bulimia dramatize dilemmas of female expressiveness as well as dilemmas of female sexuality. Other psychiatric disorders prevalently diagnosed in women—histrionic personality disorder, borderline personality disorder, and dissociative disorders in particular—also highlight these dilemmas. Such "personality disorders," which have replaced the simplistic diagnosis of female hysteria, are often characterized by displays of behavior that lead to attributions like "exhibitionistic" or "factitious" or "as-if." When used descriptively about women, these adjectives usually have a pejorative implication. The message seems to be that it is not good for women to show off, although they must never fail to present themselves as physically attractive. The woman who crosses the line between pleasingly feminine display and unpleasingly intrusive display is pathologized. *DSM-III-R* guidelines reflect these attitudes. A description of histrionic personality is especially instructive:

> These people are typically attractive and seductive, often to the point of looking flamboyant and acting inappropriately. They are typically overly concerned with physical attractiveness. (APA, 1987, p. 348)

Such descriptions illustrate the social constraints that complicate female self-representation as well as female behavior. Social evaluations, including diagnostic evaluations, are a complicated function not only of what one tries to show, but of what others prefer to see. When the conventional feminine style is exaggerated, expressive femininity may be diagnosed as a form of illness. The origins of this "illness" in society are as implicitly obvious as they are explicitly denied. The diagnosed woman is a convenient repository of cultural projections, but she cannot be acknowledged as valid social reflection. Insofar as she mirrors social reality, it is a reality disowned by those who scapegoat her.

Display

The importance of display and reflective feedback in personality development is strikingly confirmed by the symptomatic displays characteristic of personality disorders. Interpersonal relationships always involve display rules and display styles. When spontaneous forms of display are inhibited, the substitution of stylized expressions creates a useful facade. Even in infrahuman species, camouflage is an ancient form of self-protection. For females, for whom pleasing is a matter of physical as well as psychological survival, deception is frequently a social imperative. However confused and conflicted a woman may be internally, she must display a pleasing surface in order to avoid being labeled bad or crazy. Such an important female survival strategy is not simply left up to individuals, but is systematically taught and institutionalized. After a lifetime of learning to please, the depths under the surface may be as carefully concealed from the woman herself as from external observers. But, in spite of her self-alienation, it is only when she *fails* to please that she is likely to receive a psychiatric diagnosis.

Many rules governing female display and the expected choreography of revealing and concealing are designed to control male ambivalence about female sexuality. The most blatantly erotic scenario enacting these ambivalent tendencies is the strip tease. The stripper plays with display in a ritual that eventuates in a climactic moment of near nudity. Then, quickly, she disappears from the stage. Teasing is a part of many erotic scenarios, in fact, and plays a role in normal as well as destructive forms of sexual behavior. But it is a potentially dangerous behavior that can backfire, arousing rage instead of lust, or mixtures of rage and lust that lead to violence.

The Crazy-House Mirror

Sexual abuse involves a systematic violation of normal display rules. At the same time they learn to hide their real story, victims learn the "correct" lines to speak, the gestures that are expected of them. This factor has not always been appreciated in discussions about the remarkable dramatic flair of hysterical women or their attention-seeking enactments. It has important implications for psychotherapy.

For the sexually abused female, display, like everything about her body, is under the control of someone else. In some instances, particularly those involving the use of the victim for pornographic photography, enforced display involves not only nudity but posing. The victim may be forced to adopt specific postures or facial expressions while painful, humiliating acts are carried out. Even perpetrators who do not photograph their victims frequently school them in elaborate social poses designed to display conventionally correct behavior. Simultaneously, of course, they enforce concealment.

The abused child, unable to control display, is simultaneously deprived of positive reflections of her real desires and capabilities. Social reflections are inevitably ugly and cruel, expressions of the scapegoating stereotypes that stimulate violence and shape pornography. Not surprisingly, surface and depth may remain undifferentiated in such a child; the victim just feels ugly through and through. Social reflections are typically inconsistent as well as ugly; the child sees herself as a reflection in a crazy-house mirror. The fragmentation she then displays is not simply a function of her internal disorganization, but a reflection of her world.

Dissociation enables some victims to cope with these crazy-house reflections and violations of normal display rules. It is not just a matter of giving over the body to another person. Rather, the victim organizes her life as an elaborate mixed game of show-and-tell and hide-and-seek. Other people, including health professionals, frequently devalue this game as silly or phony or superficial. It is a game without much fun, a game the woman cannot win, yet cannot quit. If it is exaggerated to the point that others are annoyed by it, it may be viewed as a symptom of a "disorder"— hysteria, histrionic personality disorder, factitious disorder.

When such a woman enters psychotherapy, she continues to play out the compulsory game. She does not invent it just to impress other people. But she is acutely sensitive to what the professional, who is usually experienced as a powerful authority figure, expects or wants to see. She tries endlessly to be "good," to gain approval while, at the same time, concealing her underlying confusion and rage. Periodically the concealed "bad" feelings override her controls. She "acts out," and is then faced with the overwhelming task of trying to repair and reinstate the desirable image.

Thus, as therapy unfolds and clients replay the past, crazy-house reflections and display rule violations are important dimensions of the evolving transference. The therapist's responses to the client's displays can have an integrative effect or a destructive one. Ideally, therapy offers the possibility to explore forms of self-definition and self-presentation that were previously forbidden or conflicted. The therapist functions as a reliable mirror, helping the client to discriminate between forms of display that authentically represent her and those that have just been developed to please and placate other people. Sometimes for the first time ever, she learns to see herself real and whole.

Sam

When Samantha entered outpatient psychotherapy she was quite familiar with the diagnosis previously given her during a brief hospitalization for having a "fit" that included self-cutting: She had a borderline personality disorder. She doubted that the current therapist would be able to help her much. "Borderlines are not very treatable," she said.

As if to prove her point, she immediately began testing the boundaries of the therapeutic context. She missed sessions or cancelled them at the last minute. She called at late hours, claiming to be suicidal. In fact, she had a history of self-cutting and head banging, but had never made a serious suicide attempt. When the therapist made herself unavailable for telephone consultations and explained simply that further missed appointments would be reason for terminating treatment, Sam calmed down considerably and began to work in therapy. Even so, throughout therapy, she swung back and forth between periods of cooperation and periods of defiance.

As therapy progressed, the therapist began to focus on Sam's dramatic displays of neediness, incorrigibility, and anger as communications and tried to channel them into more adaptive forms of communication. She acknowledged that the client was angry and out of control because nobody noticed or listened to her when she was in control. She acknowledged the real anxiety that accompanied feelings of being out of control. And she discussed the meaning of being "untreatable."

Sam's history included a family in which everybody was rather flamboyant, especially her father. His sometimes terrifying displays included homicide and suicide threats as well as self-pitying orations. He had sexually abused Sam intermittently since she was a small child. He often paraded nude and constantly made off-color jokes. Her mother, too, was histrionic but quite in contrast to Sam's father. She was controlled and moralistic and considered herself above her husband, whom she deprecated constantly to Sam. Sam considered her a hypocrite. The mother persistently denied that her daughter was being abused. She was absorbed in the life of Sam's older brother who was an outstanding athlete and with putting on a good face for everyone in the community.

Sam's aggressive displays often obviously mimicked her father. She vocally expressed her dissatisfaction with being female. She had great contempt for her mother and sometimes defiantly caricatured her. Her mother, for example, was always well-groomed from head to toe. She took care with her makeup, and her hair was carefully colored. Sam, in contrast, sometimes caked on makeup, eye shadow, and lipstick so that she looked almost like a clown. Like her mother, she dyed her hair, but the colors she chose were orange, green, and on one occasion, purple. She wore long false fingernails that she described as like those of the wicked queen in the Disney move *Snow White.*

"If I have to be a woman, manipulated, abused, and discounted," she seemed to be saying, "I'll exaggerate feminine display to the nth degree." This defiant pose alternated with aggressive, even violent behavior in which she yelled and physically attacked her brother or boyfriends. At one point she announced her intention of embarrassing the family by becoming a prostitute. Yet she was careful never to get in trouble with the law, and, amazingly, made good grades in high school, where she was a senior when she began therapy.

Sam was able to make effective use of psychotherapy, to the extent of being able to enroll in and eventually complete college. But the course was stormy and for long periods she threatened to self-destruct. Once she was able to leave home and live on her own, she improved psychologically. She broke off contact with her family temporarily, citing the sexual abuse as a reason. Her mother eventually entered psychotherapy herself and became more supportive to her daughter.

To some extent, Sam's progress in psychotherapy seemed to reflect just maturing from a disturbed adolescent to a more self-assured young woman. Yet, given her history, it is questionable if she could have achieved this step without psychotherapy. Even as an adult, she considers herself vulnerable and continues treatment. But she is also able to give herself credit for the progress she has made. She has decided that she likes being a woman, although she has no intention of being a traditional one. Now, however, she can be calmly but firmly assertive about this decision rather than compulsively and flamboyantly mocking the aspects of traditional femininity she has rejected.

PART III

Special Issues in Psychotherapy

CHAPTER 8
Iatrogenic Symptoms and Revictimization

IATROGENIC THERAPEUTIC INTERVENTIONS are those that produce ill-ness or symptoms that were not present or not so malignantly present prior to treatment. Sometimes such symptoms are merely an inconvenient side effect. If they persist or are dangerous, however, they pose serious problems. If the iatrogenic problem cannot be avoided or ameliorated, the hazards of treatment must be carefully weighed against the potential benefits.

Among the iatrogenic disorders that arise in the therapy of psychological problems, many of the most serious are produced by medication. Tardive dyskinesia as a side effect of antipsychotic medication is an important case in point. Other problems resulting from medication include addiction, particularly addiction to narcotics and sleep medications. Patients with intractable pain, for example, not infrequently become addicted to painkillers. Habituation, which leads to the need for increasing amounts to medication to produce the desired effects, is one factor contributing to addiction.

Addictive aspects of psychotherapy are complicated by the addicting potential of certain kinds of experiences and relationships, what van der Kolk (1989) has discussed in terms of addiction to trauma. Certain kinds of thrill-seeking, including dangerous behaviors, may be related to addiction to internal opioids. Addiction to trauma, like other addictions, impacts adversely on relationships, including therapeutic relationships.

Addiction to prescription medications has been especially problematical for women, who are more likely than men to be prescribed and use prescription drugs (Verbrugge & Steiner, 1985). Because of the tendencies of women to utilize medical facilities more frequently than men (Gove & Hughes, 1979; Strickland, 1988), they are also especially at risk for other kinds of medical interventions that produce complicating side effects, including such interventions as unnecessary surgery. Problems related to health-care utilization are complicated by the fact that some individuals constantly seek out medical treatments, including hospitalization and surgery, for vaguely specified or difficult to diagnose somatic disorders. Somatiform disorders are a recognized class of psychological disturbance most prevalently diagnosed in women (Loewenstein, 1990).

Among the unnecessary surgical interventions that can be classified as iatrogenic, lobotomy occupies an especially grim place in psychiatric history (Valenstein, 1986). Psychosurgery was not restricted to females, but until as late as the 1960s impacted significantly on the lives of many women. Prior to the renewed interest in dissociative disorders as a diagnostic category, many dissociated individuals were diagnosed as schizophrenic and institutionalized. In some cases, psychosurgery was ordered to control their "acting out" tendencies. Among those subjected to psychosurgery and the loss of brain functions associated with such surgery were the actress Frances Farmer and the sister of playwright Tennessee Williams.

Electroshock therapy, which is also suspected of producing physical as well as psychological damage, was also in vogue earlier in this century, especially as a treatment for depression, and is still prescribed sometimes. Insulin shock, which produces such side effects as extreme weight gain, was also popular in some periods. Since depression is most frequently diagnosed in women, shock therapy has probably impacted especially on female patients. In *The Bell Jar* (1971), Sylvia Plath wrote a gripping account of her own experiences with shock therapy. The remission of symptoms which it may have facilitated was obviously superficial and temporary, since her depression recurred and she eventually killed herself.

Not only the use of treatment methods that have detrimental consequences, but the failure to diagnose physical illness and/or the tendency to diagnose physical complaints as psychological have also been problems especially relevant to female lives. The tendency to dismiss physical symptoms as hysterical has sometimes led to a neglect or mistreatment of real illness in women. Battered women, especially, are likely to have residual injuries that have never been adequately diagnosed and treated. Sometimes the neglect of physical illness or injury results from neglect by the victim herself, either because she is afraid to reveal the source of the injury or dreads medical interventions as being unbearably intrusive or revictimizing.

One distressing form of revictimization in health care settings is the failure of physicians and hospitals to recognize abuse. Most health care workers are sensitive to such signs of physical abuse as bruises and broken bones. Sexual abuse of children is often harder to detect. Some of the saddest stories from victims detail how abuse resulted in illness or injury that necessitated medical treatment, which was, in turn, painful and terrifying but failed to uncover the abuse.

OTHER FORMS OF INSTITUTIONAL
VICTIMIZATION

Survivors of abuse are revictimized in a variety of institutional contexts. Runtz (1987) reports that victims of child sexual abuse are more likely to be sexually revictimized. Stark and Flitcraft (1985) found that abused mothers of abused children are more likely to have their children removed to foster care even if it is not the mother who is responsible for the abuse. Victim-blaming is perhaps the most widespread form of revictimization. Being a victim of abuse may even result in a diagnosis of mental illness leading to a woman's institutionalization. The failure of the criminal justice system and the courts to protect victims compounds their original injuries.

Poverty is also a factor that contributes to victimization and revictimization. Those without money—and women and children are at the bottom of the economic ladder—have fewer resources for insuring their personal safety. They live in unsafe neighborhoods and/or homes. They remain economically dependent on assailants even when they are psychologically ready to leave. They often cannot afford needed medical, psychological, and legal services. The poor are constantly stigmatized and blamed for their own predicament. When they seek social services, they may be penalized for having any income or property at all. Many poor women view the welfare system as revictimizing.

SEXUAL ABUSE IN THE CONTEXT OF
PSYCHOTHERAPY

One particularly destructive but disturbingly prevalent form of institutional revictimization is sexual abuse by a psychotherapist. This abuse pattern typically combines several aspects of institutional victimization and iatrogenesis. Most psychotherapists are male. Most clients, in outpatient settings, and most victims of sexual abuse in particular are female.

Individuals who have been physically or sexually abused as children have been found to be especially at risk for becoming sexually involved with a therapist (Bouhoutsos & Brodsky, 1985). There are several dimensions to this problem. Because the psychotherapist is an individual specifically sought out for help with abuse-related issues, he or she is in an especially influential but in some respects vulnerable position, particularly if he himself has unresolved sexual problems. Contact boundaries may be eroded or put aside in the name of helping the client get over her fears and inhibitions. In some instances, the troubled psychotherapist uses the client as parents once used her. The resulting therapeutic relationship, which casts the therapist in the role of father and the client in the role of child thus repeats early patterns of incest and parentification of the female child.

A few psychotherapists are not really concerned at all with the needs of their clients but are merely exploitive and unscrupulous. Because many victims, particularly female victims, have been socialized for both dependency and obedience to authority, the unscrupulous psychotherapist may find them easy targets for exploitation. The client who has been previously abused has often built up a tolerance for abuse that makes her especially vulnerable to abuse by a therapist.

In psychotherapy, iatrogenic symptoms are often associated with such therapist characteristics as sexism and misogyny, characteristics that may be unquestionably accepted as normal and healthy and thus are insidiously destructive. Sexual abuse in the guise of treatment, however, is a blatant violation of the ethical principles of mental health professionals and, in some states, is a felony (Bates & Brodsky, 1989). Professionals who engage in sexual misconduct know that they are breaking the law as well as injuring the client (Burgess & Hartman, 1986).

Most of those who admit to client-therapist sexual contact are male (Bates & Brodsky, 1989). In the 1970s (a period sometimes associated with "the sexual revolution"), questionnaire data from respondents in both medical and psychotherapeutic settings indicated that 10% of males reporting admitted erotic contact with a client (Holroyd & Brodsky, 1977; Kardener et al., 1973). In 1987, The American Psychological Association Insurance Trust (Bennett, 1987) reported that their greatest cost in claims resulted from cases of sexual misconduct. Yet, although both the American Psychiatric Association and the American Psychological Association now explicitly state that sexual contact between a client and therapist is unethical, a few professionals continue to admit to and justify such contacts as helpful to clients (Bates & Brodsky, 1989).

The attitude of some sexually exploitive therapists is remarkably similar to that sometimes described in rapists, child sexual abusers, and jurors: Sex is something females want and need and elicit, therefore, it is not destructive. Patterns of sex-role socialization also lead many males to sexualize expressions of affection. Interest in or tender concern for a female then leads automatically to sexual forms of contact because such men have never learned other modes of expressing themselves with females. In addition, in some male therapists, as well as in other males, self-esteem is so closely tied to sexual exhibitionism and sexual conquest that they exploit any vulnerable woman. The grandiose male may even justify his behavior as a magnanimous gift.

The problem of abuse in the context of psychotherapy is complicated by the patterns of behavior and relatedness that typically evolve in abused clients. Sometimes sexual abuse in the guise of psychotherapy is a matter of clear-cut exploitation by the therapist. But survivors of abuse often sexualize interactions, having learned to regulate their own self-esteem through pleasing males or having simply learned to expect that sexual servicing is a necessary condition of a relationship. Sometimes a client interprets the therapist's abstinence from sexual contact with her as a rejection, proof that she is unlovable. Sometimes, horrified by accounts of cruel abuse, a therapist wants to give the client "a good sexual experience."

Nonsexual physical contact, such as hugging, may be misconstrued or may unintentionally stimulate sexual arousal. Sometimes the line between physical and psychological contact becomes dangerously blurred and the therapist as well as the client simply loses boundaries. In any case, sexual contact in the therapy session is revictimizing and destructive. It almost invariably complicates the client's preexisting problems and compromises any possibility for subsequent constructive work with the abusive therapist (Bates & Brodsky, 1989).

In many instances, sexual contact in the psychotherapeutic setting tragically illustrates the pitfalls of failing to establish and maintain boundaries. Since victims of abuse often have special issues around boundaries, the resolution of boundary issues, including those related to sexual contact, is likely to be an ongoing part of treatment. This is one reason why it is important to discuss boundary issues frankly at the beginning of therapy and to follow rules consistently.

IATROGENIC DEVELOPMENTS AND TRANSFERENCE

Sexual abuse in the context of therapy is in many cases an aspect of the developing transference of the client and the therapist's countertransferential responses to it. Many aspects of transference, in fact, can be understood as iatrogenic in the sense that they are apparently symptomatic of disturbance and are therapeutically stimulated. The paradox of psychotherapy is that, in order to understand and treat such problems effectively, they must be exhibited and worked on in the therapy. In order for a client to resolve sexual abuse, sexual matters must be frankly discussed. Not only real sexual events, but sexual fantasies sometimes need to be examined in explicit detail. Helping a client overcome numbing and flight from her body requires talking about bodily experiences and sensations.

Sexual abuse in the context of psychotherapy is always avoidable. But, as an evolving aspect of transference, iatrogenic symptoms are not always avoidable. On the contrary, it is sometimes necessary to elicit them in order to treat them. This paradox is burdensome for client and therapist. At some point in an effective intensive therapy, the client almost inevitably experiences the treatment as revictimizing, even though she recognizes that confronting the pain of her past is necessary. These difficult transference developments include "periods of unwarranted rage at the therapist for imagined or minor 'sins'; cycles of idealization and devaluation; excessive need for approval, with concurrent expectations of rejection; overattachment and, in some cases, intrusion into the therapist's personal life; adversariality . . . and intrusive sexualization of the therapeutic relationship" (Briere, 1989, p. 129).

Such transference developments arise most dramatically when therapy stimulates traumatic memories and associated affects. The process of exploring and working through these apparently iatrogenic symptoms is a means of exploring and working through the original trauma.

Another unavoidable factor in iatrogenic symptoms is the tendency of psychotherapy to elicit relationship patterns characteristic of relations with abusers. What is being remembered, in other words, is not merely specific traumatic incidents, but abusive relationship contexts. The transference features of the therapeutic relationship require continual acknowledgment and clarification in order to help the client differentiate the nonabusive relationship with the therapist in the present from abusive relationships in the past.

In practice, transference in survivors often reflects not only the double binding imperatives that have typified their development, but a double or multiple life that evolved as a coping mechanism. Many survivors of childhood abuse have lived in a least two worlds, the world of home, which was not only traumatic, but secret and structured by special rules of conduct, and the world beyond home, especially school. Having learned to cope with this double aspect of the real world involved learning distinct patterns of behavior and relatedness. Adaptation to the "normal" world enabled some survivors to get along with people different from abusers, to follow standard rules, and sometimes to experience competence. The outside world, in this regard, became a kind of life raft. The individual adapted to it and learned valuable lessons that preserved her sanity and survival. Intrapsychic compartmentalization and dissociation facilitated this development. The inner world of the survivor, like the outer world, was sometimes divided between socially adapted identity configurations and those adapted more specifically to life with abusers.

Mature and Regressive Transference Patterns

The socially adapted patterns the client brings with her into therapy contribute to the working alliance. They comprise important strengths and skills. In clients who were raised in nonabusive homes, the transference that evolves in treatment will reflect the relatively normal relationship patterns that characterized her upbringing, including the regressive revival of normal infantile patterns. The therapy will resemble psychotherapy with other clients who have strong egos and at least a few trustworthy social interactions. The focus on a trauma, such as rape, may be specific and time-bound since, however terrible the trauma, it did not shape the individual's character structure.

Work with individuals repetitively traumatized in childhood, in contrast, is likely to reflect patterns of transference typically associated with the diagnosed character disorders—borderline personality, antisocial character, etc. And the more isolated the client has been from normalizing social contexts, the more difficult therapeutic work is likely to be since, in addition to overcoming the effects of trauma, she has to learn so many basic coping skills.

Even clients well adapted to the world of school and work find themselves enacting in therapy the patterns of behavior typical of their intimate involvements with abusers. At some points, the therapist may be related to as a helpful teacher or friend. But, particularly as therapy progresses, she is often cast in the role of the abusive parent. This development is simply the result of the intimacy of the psychotherapeutic context and the tendency of intensive psychotherapy, particularly therapy focused on childhood memories, to stimulate regressions. The double aspect of transference in such cases is not just a result of splitting tendencies, but of the client's having learned two sets of relationship patterns, one for family, another for nonfamily.

One kind of malignant iatrogenic development, transference psychosis, has been considered specifically indicative of borderline personality disorder (Kernberg, 1975). Clinicians like Kernberg have interpreted proneness to transference psychosis as a sign of ego weakness and early developmental splitting tendencies. In therapy, however, transference psychosis, like other transference developments, is not necessarily based on intrapsychic processes such as fantasy, but can be patterned after real interactions with caretakers. Parents who abuse their children sometimes begin doing so when the child is an infant, thus distorting basic processes of attachment and separation and the development of reality testing. Prior to the time the child enters school, interactions with disturbed caretakers may be the only relationship patterns the child has modeled and family "reality," however distorted, may be the only reality. Any caretaking relationship, or any relationship that recalls early childhood, will then bring out these patterns of thinking and relating.

Transference psychosis is not necessarily the result of physical or sexual abuse, however. In some cases it derives from accidental traumatization or from subtle forms of psychological abuse, such as a parent's extreme appropriation and infantilization of a child. Because early intrapsychic developments are orchestrated by relationships and reflect the significance of attachment in human adaptation, attachment and separation issues impact inevitably on the therapeutic process. If early childhood involved difficulties in separation and individuation, the individual may subsequently be prone to transference psychosis because differentiation from the parents was thwarted. When the parents from whom one cannot differentiate have also been abusive, the stage is set for continuing vacillation, alternating patterns of dependent clinging and defiant detachment, and self-injury. Such symptoms are typical of individuals diagnosed as borderline and are characteristic of transference developments in borderline individuals.

If early childhood involved the extensive use of dissociation as a coping mechanism, the transference patterns that emerge in psychotherapy may not be that of transference psychosis, but of transference-stimulated dissociation. Superficially, some transference dissociations resemble transference psychosis and have traditionally been diagnosed as such. Many, however, have a different "feel" and are organized on the basis of patterns of detachment from abusive caretakers rather than on psychological merger with them. Having detached from a traumatizing figure, the dissociated individual may evolve modes of interacting with other people that appear to be quite socially adaptive but are essentially superficial.

The "as if" personalities described by Deutsch (1942) seem to be organized along such lines. The "as if" presentation of the self seems to be related to what Winnicott (1971) has termed a "false-self." As a carefully drawn facade, it may function quite well in many social contexts but in more intimate relationships is likely to be experienced by others as false or lacking. "As if" personality has been interpreted by psychoanalysts (Gunderson & Singer, 1975; Kernberg, 1967; Stone, 1986) to be related to borderline personality, but has been little examined from the standpoint of the post-traumatic and dissociative disorders in which it frequently appears.

Transference Double Binds

In psychotherapy, some iatrogenic transference developments, including apparent deteriorations, indicate that therapy is working. Stormy and chaotic symptom pictures reflect the client's awareness that attachment to the therapist has become an important part of her life. Since attachment has previously been traumatic, the client begins to feel panicky and to bring into play earlier defenses against panic. Her behavior is then likely to reproduce aspects of the double binds associated with attachment she experienced in childhood. Transference then reflects perceived conditions of attachment in which the positive aspects of relatedness are viewed as necessarily accompanied by pain. Several kinds of double binds are common:

1. *Contact Is Necessary for Survival/Contact Is Dangerous.* This double bind structures the infancy of children abused by primary caretakers, typically the mother. As a transference pattern, it is evoked by any situa-

tion that produces dependency on someone perceived as being like the dangerous mother. In psychotic individuals, mother's dangerousness may be illusory, a product of fantasies. In many cases, however, mother's perceived dangerousness is connected with experiences of being actually traumatized in early infancy, sometimes by the mother herself.

The perception that human contact is a threat to physical survival is in itself extremely traumatic and tends to elicit defenses against relationship that can have far-reaching consequences. One response is the detachment of physical from psychological contact. Emotional detachment may come to be so basically associated with survival that the individual never develops any trusting relationships with other people. Depending on how early this detachment occurs, the individual may be cognitively as well as socially impaired. On the other hand, in some cases capacities for relating to the world and people in it as objects without emotional significance may be retained. In some instances, too, an out-of-contact part of the self is dissociatively sealed off. This pattern of adaptation characterizes psychogenic (as distinct from biologically based) autism (Tustin, 1986).

The connection between primary attachment and danger is difficult to treat. Many of those who experience this problem do not voluntarily seek therapy or, if they do, are too cautious ever to really risk an attachment to the therapist. On the other hand, dangerousness is often relative rather than absolute, and the need for attachment is so basic to human existence that even severely traumatized individuals will sometimes risk it. Thus, even psychotic and extremely withdrawn individuals can sometimes be helped by skillful, patient psychotherapists.

2. Attachment Is Desirable/Attachment Is Disappointing. In psychotherapy with survivors of abuse, the client's perception that attachment is dangerous is often not based on early disruptions of attachment to primary caretakers, but on later occurrences. In many instances of incestuous or physical abuse by the father, for example, the child's early attachment to the mother has not been compromised by abuse. Basic cognitive skills and the capacity to form stable social relationships are well developed. But the father's abuse impinges on the child's developing personality as an extreme, disorganizing shock. In such cases, disappointment in the mother is likely to be a painful aspect of the father's abuse. Sometimes, however, the mother herself is being abused so severely that the child perceives herself as being in the same boat with mother, a perception that solidifies her bond with mother.

Disappointment is a complex developmental acquisition. It requires the ability to anticipate and expect and is usually connected with fantasies organized around unrealistic as well as realistic expectations. In transference, the mother who disappointed is sometimes attacked more angrily that the father who directly abused. This development seems to be a function of the original attachment to the mother; love for her had developed and can thus be painfully lost. When the father has also been loved as well as lost, the disappointment is doubled.

Once love has evolved, the individual sometimes fears psychological loss more than physical destruction. The fear of loss then leads to defensive detachments: Better not to love than to love and lose. Individuals who fear relatedness because early love was soured by disappointment may continually seek attachments but, fearing disappointment, withdraw from them or constantly vacillate between approach and avoidance.

The transference that evolves with such individuals is often intense but stormy. The trustworthiness of the relationship with the therapist is constantly tested. For long periods, any step forward may be followed by two steps backward. In such situations, the trustworthiness of the therapeutic alliance enables the client to eventually progress. In successful psychotherapy, which involves psychological as distinct from physical attachments, the client eventually discovers and makes use of a kind of love that is not lost, but continues to enrich her life long after the therapy is over.

Early disappointment is a factor that sets the stage for one kind of double or dissociated existence. Following disappointment, the individual's inner world is often divided into *before* and *after*. *Before* can be idealized as a golden age when things were going well. *After* is like life for Adam and Eve after the Fall — a time of pain and gloom and isolation from good feelings. To the extent that everybody experiences disappointment, everybody understands such mythic images as that of the golden age. Abused children, however, experience unusually intense disappointments, and coping with disappointment is complicated by coping with effects of abuse. In the dissociative disorders, *before* and *after* sometimes become compartments for organizing alter identity configurations.

In therapy, the client's relationship with the therapist may be compartmentalized along such lines. The good therapist is not only idealized, but she is perceived in terms of memories about a good time in the client's life — the time when the client lived in a particular place or had a particular teacher, for example. Exploring memories associated with other times and places is avoided, since that would mean exploring disappointment and the loss of a good relationship. Sometimes in MPD, alter personalities are constructed around particular times and places. In some cases where history has been fragmented, for example when a child emigrated from one country to another and experienced not only changed circumstances but the loss of valued caretakers, dissociated personality organizations may even speak different languages.

3. *Attachment Is Pleasurable/Love Means Hurting.* For some abused children, attachment to caretakers has been not only intense but occasion-

ally pleasurable. Abusive parents, for example, often alternate indulgence with trauma. Sometimes this alteration reflects the inconsistent or dissociated personality structure of the abuser and is internalized as such by the child. In any case, the abused child who is given minimal care or is occasionally indulged is like an experimental animal administered intermittent positive reinforcement. The habitual behaviors built up by such a reinforcement pattern are extremely tenacious. No matter how infrequent or unlikely the reward, the abused individual continues to hope for it.

Therapy for such individuals involves helping them to give up hope — not in a general sense, but in a specific one. More precisely, perhaps, it means helping the client differentiate realistic hopes based on relationships with nonabusive people from hope contingent on abuse. Since, for the client, giving up abuse initially does mean giving up hope, she is likely to experience depression as well as anxiety as she relinquishes the abusive relationship.

The blending of pleasure with pain in some abusive contexts, such as certain cases of sexual abuse, impacts especially severely on subsequent sexual relationships. Sometimes sexual pleasure can only be experienced in the context of punishment or pain; this is a situation traditionally conceptualized as erotic masochism. The female survivor may experience pain or punishment as a condition or sexual excitement. Occasionally, identifying with the aggressor, she may imagine inflicting pain on others as a condition of sexual pleasure. In any case, differentiating painful sexual encounters from clearly pleasurable and self-affirming ones is likely to be a difficult but necessary therapeutic task.

Some survivors who have experienced pain as a condition of pleasure have responded by renouncing pleasure. This conditioned avoidance is also often refractory to therapeutic intervention and requires therapeutic attention to such defenses as the tendency to dissociate from the body at the first sign of sexual excitement. Working on sexual inhibitions in therapy is a necessary step to integration that presents special pitfalls, particularly if the client develops sexual feelings toward the therapist and vice versa. It is usually necessary to repeat clarifications about boundary issues at this point and to reassure the client that talking about issues or symbolically enacting through drawing or play with toys will remain the focus of therapeutic interaction.

Body work with someone other than the psychotherapist can sometimes be a helpful adjunct to therapy. Specific kinds of body work and their effects, however, need to be constantly and carefully monitored since, in some clients, they can precipitate flashbacks and extremely troublesome iatrogenic symptoms. The client can best take care of many of the physical dimensions of body work, such as learning to experience pleasurable masturbation, on her own and at her own pace, guided by the insights she is acquiring.

4. Attachment Is Good/Love Means Total Surrender.   For some clients, relationship problems are very much structured around issues of dominance and control. Even when a partner is not severely abusive, he may exercise control by the ever-present threat of abuse. And even when a dominating man is never physically abusive, a woman's past experience of abuse may lead her to surrender control to him without much question.

Some battered or sexually exploited women have been abused in childhood, for example, but many have not. They have nevertheless internalized authoritarian patterns of male-female relationships and believe that surrender to a male authority is a necessary condition to their own self-esteem as well as their love relationships. Where love means surrender, abuse may be experienced as painful but perplexing. Perhaps what is needed, thinks the self-effacing partner, is just more submissiveness and appeasement.

In therapy, client submissiveness is a problem that may escape notice but that is eventually likely to lead to revictimization unless explored and worked through. Authoritarian or grandiose therapists, unfortunately, often merely encourage such submissiveness. The problem is complicated by the fact that the psychotherapist really is an authority. The client has the right to expect her to be knowledgeable about some things the client does not know and in control of certain aspects of therapy, such as boundaries. The therapist's authority and control is particularly necessary when the client becomes very regressed or out of control. In the most effective therapies for women, however, the client eventually learns to trust her own authority.

TREATING IATROGENIC SYMPTOMS BASED ON TRANSFERENCE

Some psychotherapists approach the disturbing or disturbed aspects of transference and the iatrogenic symptoms produced by transference as untreatable developments. They then focus on the healthy aspects of the therapeutic alliance in an attempt to encourage the client to "get over" the negative or distorted relationship patterns. Since the client who is able to form a therapeutic alliance does have adaptive patterns of interaction at her disposal, such an approach can work, or at least seem to work. Often, however, what the client learns is to avoid the most regressed, socially isolating, and symptomatically malignant parts of herself, or to replace these parts with a socially acceptable but superficial version of healthy behavior.

From the standpoint of day-by-day coping, the client may seem to be well integrated. She may carefully avoid the abusive contexts that formerly elicited damaging or self-damaging behavior. On the other hand, many such individuals have simply succeeded in isolating their vulnerable selves through dissociation. Since their original distorted relationship patterns have not been explored, they remain vulnerable to future victimization. Continuing vulnerability to stress is also a problem. Under stress, the integration may fail, and the original patterns may reassert themselves with destructive force.

It is hard to interpret and work through transference patterns that are stormy, destructive, and sometimes dangerous. But in the long run, such work can produce long-lasting and stable personality integrations. In my own therapeutic work, I take a variable approach to such issues. Short-term, crisis oriented therapy, which does not allow for the evolution and resolution of transference, may nevertheless be quite productive, especially if the client had achieved a stable, comparatively healthy integration prior to traumatization. Even with more disturbed individuals, symptoms, including transference-based symptoms, can sometimes simply be isolated as "not-me" and controlled rather than interpreted and integrated. Many reality factors, including the client's preferences and circumstances may make intensive therapy unfeasible.

In many repetitively abused individuals, however, lasting symptomatic improvement can be expected to require long-term, intensive treatment. In such cases, symptoms cannot be adaptively handled, even temporarily, by masking or palliative controls. They must be allowed to develop to the extent necessary for exploration and interpretation. Interpretation in itself, however, will not usually be sufficient to facilitate recovery. Exploring new behavior patterns both in and out of therapy, including new kinds of nonabusive relationships will usually be necessary.

TRANSFERENCE AND REVICTIMIZATION

The transference and countertransference patterns that often arise in repetitively traumatized individuals are a contributing pattern in revictimization outside as well as inside therapy. This does not imply that revictimization is the client's fault. It merely means that certain habitual patterns of interpersonal behavior, including patterns stimulated by psychotherapy, put individuals at risk.

Anyone who is excessively dependent and really needy, for example, may elicit not only the care of genuinely concerned helpers but the exploitation of manipulators and con artists. Dependent people make useful, even worshipful followers and disciples. Dependent women, particularly, are easily exploited as caretakers.

The needy and confused female client is particularly vulnerable to the authoritarian male who presents his exploitations as being for her own good. Since child physical and sexual abuse is often presented as being for the child's own good, manipulative and exploitive people in adult life are experienced as echoes of an abusive parent. The client's recognition that she needs to learn adaptive ways of relating to people or to overcome sexual inhibitions complicates her responses. For example, she may come to distrust her own tendencies to withdraw, even when withdrawal would be protective.

One way of making sure that client submissiveness does not become self-defeating outside as well as within therapy is to keep in focus the client's mature adaptedness and positive strengths, even when she feels out of control or behaves like a regressed child. Helping the client get in touch with and lay claim to her own authority means respecting her right, even her need, to disagree with the therapist, to express her negative feelings about therapy, and to make choices, even self-destructive choices, in her own life. As the client does lay claim to her own authority, she continually differentiates submissiveness from respect, guidance from exploitive manipulation and authoritarian control. Such achievements can be strong protection against future revictimization.

CHAPTER 9
Self-Injury

ONE COMMON VICTIM RESPONSE to an assailant's attacks on her is self-attack. Turning aggression against the self is a stereotypically feminine response. Both socialization to inhibit aggressive behavior as "unfeminine" and the internalization of scapegoating stereotypes about the female self contribute to such behavior. In females, identification with the aggressor, a typical victim response, is often dissociated. A split-off, vengeful, or punitive part of the individual then attacks the victimized self.

Self-cutting is probably the most typical form of self-injury in abuse victims, although other forms of self-damage, such as hitting the head or the body or burning the skin are also common. Research describes the typical self-cutter as a female who has been diagnosed as borderline or psychotic (Favazza, 1987). Nelson and Grunebaum (1971) reported research on 23 wrist slashers in which 60% of the self-injurious episodes occurred while the individual was menstruating. Self-cutting has also been found to be related to anorexia (Simpson, 1975; Simpson & Porter, 1981). A history of physical and sexual abuse was found to be characteristic of self-cutters in one study (Simpson & Porter, 1981). Self-cutting after rape has also been reported (Greenspan & Samuel, 1989).

Clinically, self-injury is frequently associated not only with borderline personality disorder but with the dissociative disorders. Dissociation, in fact, is a typical feature of self-damaging behavior. When the body has been dissociated, as in some instances of extreme abuse, the body attacked is sometimes treated like a nonhuman object by the victim as it formerly was by an assailant. Those who dissociate may actually behave as if their own bodies were really external to them. In multiple personalities, for example, an alter personality may act as if the body is a hated other that can be abused or even killed without damage to the attacking alter. Whether self-injuring individuals accept the body as their own or dissociate it—and they often alternate between these responses—they often regard the body itself as the repository of all evil.

Less dissociated individuals sometimes enact self-injury as an aspect of a negative identity. The body may then be treated as a scapegoated representative of the "bad me" who continually deserves to suffer. The individual says, in effect, "Through suffering, I at least know who and what I am." Such individuals are likely to experience extreme conscious guilt and depression. Periodically they may throw off depression in states of manic denial, indulging themselves as extremely as they previously had punished themselves. Such alternating patterns can often be traced to the treatment the individual actually received from parents who alternated abuse and indulgence.

SELF-REGULATION AND SELF-INJURY

Dissociated forms of self-injury are sometimes so mild as to be simply labeled "bad habits." They include such common symptoms as nail-biting, hair-pulling, or picking at the skin. Like thumb-sucking, these behaviors can be understood as attempts at self-regulation, symptomatic behavior patterns that arise when tension is particularly high and adaptive self-regulatory behaviors cannot contain it. Such habits are sometimes associated with transitional objects or fetishes: A child may pull at an earlobe or chew her hair while smelling a security blanket, for example. Many such symptoms arise and disappear spontaneously in childhood, eventually replaced by more adaptive coping mechanisms. A few persist into adult life and, because they occur as dissociated automatisms, are quite refractory to change.

Severely traumatized individuals often fail to outgrow self-damaging habits or to replace them with more adaptive forms of self-regulation. Even as adults, they continue to attack their own bodies sometimes in extreme ways. They may impulsively beat themselves about the head or bang their heads against hard objects. They may slowly and deliberately cut themselves or burn themselves. These behaviors are frightening to observers, but in practice are often circumscribed, ritually controlled, and not really dangerous. Occasionally, however, they can be life-threatening. Even slight injuries pose problems of infection.

Self-injuries, particularly dissociated ones, are often paradoxical. That is, although the injury is real and sometimes dangerous, the intent is not simply to hurt but to control hurt. Self-cutting, for example, can be an attempt to relieve intolerable inner pressures by letting something out. Many self-injurious behaviors are associated with changes in states of self-awareness. Ritualized attacks on the body, like other rituals, may be either a means of entering a trance state or terminating such a state. Self-injury can induce an anesthesia that numbs feelings. Or it can produce a sudden pain that heightens awareness and reassures the individual that she can still feel.

As attempts at self-regulation, self-injuries like cutting or head banging are distinctly different from suicidal behaviors. A serious suicide attempt is usually an escape of last resort. Self-injury, in contrast, is often an attempt to go on living with intolerable states of tension. Self-injury can even moderate or contain suicidal urges by reassuring the victim that she is in control of her body and her life. In this respect, self-injury resembles behaviors like substance abuse that are destructive but that are often sought out to enhance a sense of personal control. The fact that these forms of self-regulation are dangerous, even deadly, plays into certain victim fantasies about escaping death. "I was injured but did not die," is a reassurance some victims offer themselves compulsively, reenacting over and over both injury and survival.

In victims of repetitive sexual abuse, the sexualization of soothing and the connection between sexual excitement and pain is often apparent in self-injurious rituals. Since sexual excitement is associated with loss of control of mind and body, masturbation becomes a complicated exercise in self-control. When pain and pleasure have frequently occurred together, compulsive forms of masturbation are often organized around painful practices or followed by ritually prescribed punishments. Sometimes the experience of pain is sought to overcome extreme states of numbing or inhibition. At other times, pain is necessary to provide a sense of entitlement to pleasure. The inability to feel sexual pleasure or reach orgasm without concomitant pain is a complicated symptom that usually requires lengthy and careful therapeutic work. In such cases, the therapist is faced with the task of helping reshape patterns of sexual behavior that have been distorted from childhood, sometimes from infancy.

PSYCHOBIOLOGICAL ASPECTS OF SELF-INJURY

Self-injurious behavior sometimes occurs in animals. Favazza (1987) reports observations in zoological gardens as well as experimental studies that suggest that such behaviors as automutilation and destruction of offspring may be stress related. Drugs that increase amounts of neurotransmitters, like dopamine and norepinephrine, have been found to produce self-mutilating behaviors in experimental animals. Both animals and humans may self-mutilate in response to certain addictive drugs such as alcohol, amphetamines, caffeine, and heroin.

The social dimensions of these biologically mediated behaviors have also received some investigation. Automutilation in adult monkeys, for example, has been found to be highly associated with social isolation during the first year of life. Reactions of animals isolated in zoos may also have an as yet not clearly understood social dimension.

Van der Kolk (1989) has proposed that habitual forms of self-injury may result from a process of addiction to the endogenous opioids produced in response to stress. "Depending on which stimuli have come to condition an opioid response, self-destructive behavior may include chronic involvement with abusive partners, sexual masochism, self-starvation, and violence against self or others" (p. 402).

Research has shown self-injury by human adults to be related to childhood abuse (Graff & Mallin, 1967; Pattison & Kahan, 1983; Rosenthal et al., 1972). Since abuse is often experienced as a form of psychological abandonment, and since trauma reactions often include social withdrawal, the function of self-injury to provide for the missing social stimulation becomes apparent. Such paradoxical behavior—hurting oneself in order to feel better—can be extremely resistant to change because it is self-sufficient as well as compulsive. In therapy, it must often be addressed as a form of interpersonal withdrawal, an understandable reaction to betrayal by others, and an attempt at self-comfort.

FANTASY

Self-injury may occur in a trance state seemingly devoid of or disconnected from fantasy. In some instances, however, it enacts traumatic events that really happened as well as fantasies about those events. Bizarre fantasy explanations, if believed as reality, can lead to the clinical impression that the client is delusional and psychotic. Close inspection of the fantasy, however, often reveals the extent to which it reflects a bizarre reality. One rule of thumb when dealing with abuse is that, if a bizarre or sadistic behavior can be imagined, someone has probably attempted to act it out. And if someone else has enacted a bizarre behavior, the victim herself may continue to enact it, assuming the roles of both assailant and victim.

Many compulsive fantasy enactments are not so much an escape into imaginative play as an attempt at mastery. Some of the fantasy formations of traumatized individuals result from distorted perceptions of physiological processes. Numbing and constriction, for example, can be interpreted as dying. The fantasy that one is dead is not unusual in psychotically depressed individuals. In dissociated clients, it may be split off, yet vividly experienced by a part of the personality. Some multiple personalities explain their multiplicity as a literal series of deaths and rebirths. Elaborate philosophical theories about the nature of life and time may accompany such explanations. In many victims of trauma, however, the fantasy of being dead is too frightening to think about and only emerges in therapy as a simple but powerful conviction that a part of the self has died and cannot be revived.

Other fantasies deriving from physiological features of trauma reactions include the idea that one has become a machine or a robot. Psychotic individuals sometimes really believe in this fantasy. For others it is merely a graphic metaphor of their existence. A client may perceive herself as going through the motions of living without any real sense of involvement. This kind of depersonalization or derealization may begin as an immediate response to trauma, but may be elaborated over time when the client is unable to regain her former zest for living. In childhood, it may become part of a complex fantasy formation, even the basis for an alter personality who has nonhuman characteristics. It is often reinforced by patterns of interpersonal behavior in which the female child is treated like an object rather than a person.

Being treated like a cute little doll, even though not an obviously abusive activity, also lays a foundation for an intense experience of depersonalization as a response to trauma. When self-image has always been compromised by the individual's having been treated like an object, even an idealized object, the split between a real but hidden self and an image seen by others has been powerfully reinforced. Later, under the impact of an overwhelming trauma, the hidden "real" self may be felt to be destroyed. What remains is a shell, which functions like a machine without feelings. Battered women often function is this way. Paradoxically, they may have been treated like cute dolls in childhood (Walker, 1979) and may still be idealized by partners as living dolls during periods of calm. The fantasy of woman as beautiful doll is, in fact, a culturally pervasive reflection of male ambivalence toward female autonomy.

This doll-like image of herself may be so carefully in place that a woman goes on taking good care of her superficial image and performing her expected feminine functions even in the wake of extreme trauma. And as long as she keeps up with her caretaking and decorative functions, her dissociated feelings and needs may remain completely hidden.

One function of self-injury is to deny both experiences of and fantasies about depersonalization. A dead person cannot feel. A doll or a robot cannot bleed. Hurting oneself and bleeding then prove that one's worst fears have not come to pass.

SELF-INJURY AND
SOCIAL INTEGRATION

One of the paradoxical aspects of self-injury is the function of certain ritualistic forms of injury and self-injury in social integration. This function illustrates another dimension of the relation between self-regulation and social regulation. It is most dramatically represented in certain religious practices, in which ritual forms of sacrifice are performed to purify and sanctify the group and to set it apart as a special community distinct from unbelievers. Ritual sacrifice, according to Girard (1977), channels the violence of the group into culturally sanctioned outlets. In this respect, it apparently also organizes scapegoating tendencies; the sacrificial victim is in the honored position of protecting or saving the group.

The social uses of ritualistic forms of self-sacrifice and self-injury are particularly evident in initiation rites (Van Gennep, 1960). Such rites dramatize the ordeal and triumph of separation. Childhood ties and pleasures are exchanged for the responsibilities and privileges of adult life. In order to be accepted into the adult community, the child must prove himself worthy; proofs of worthiness may include dangerous and painful ordeals, including mutilation or self-mutilation.

The social function of initiatory rites and religious sacrifice is maintained not only in orthodox, socially typical forms of religious practice, but in the organization of secret cults. Among these, Satanic cults have recently received considerable attention. As Katchen and Sakheim (1992) have emphasized, secret cults are often antinomian analogs of mainstream religions; that is, they deliberately invert the forms and meanings of orthodox religious practices. Nevertheless, they share the social functions of religions generally in that they bind their members to the group through specified rituals, they emphasize such principles as individual sacrifice for the good of the group, and they indoctrinate group members in beliefs about universal categories, such as good and evil.

Blood, Sacrifice, and Healing

Blood is a substance with profound psychological as well as biological significance. Perhaps because it is so significant as a sign of injury, the very sight of blood can excite extreme emotion. Symbolically, blood is associated with life and death, hurt and healing. Culturally, it is associated with the definition of kinship ties—relatives are said to be of one blood—and the basic social bonds that unite nations as well as families. "Bad blood" leads to "blood feuds" and holy wars. The use of blood as a symbol reflects these varied and ambivalent associations. In religious symbolism, which organizes the feelings and the beliefs of cultures, blood represents the sacred integration of painful sacrifice and triumphant transcendence.

In daily life, blood is also a substance especially associated with females. Menstruation and childbirth are ambivalently viewed as signs of female taint and proofs of female power (Bettelheim, 1954). Hence, culturally, these processes are often hedged about with rituals and taboos, which prevent the male's being contaminated or adversely affected by female blood. As a natural accompaniment of birth or a symbolic aspect of initiation, blood is associated with separation from the mother and whatever she stands for. When femaleness is devalued, female bleeding is devalued as an ultimate form of defilement. When femaleness is viewed as a lack, a kind of castration, monthly female bleeding is taken as an external proof that there is something basically sick, injured, or flawed about women.

Even when superstition is replaced by science, the common notion of female lack continues to exercise a powerful influence on perceptions of women. After primitive fantasies about menstruation and childbearing are replaced by scientific attitudes based on research, many people still view everything female in terms of inherent biological weaknesses (Ehrenreich & English, 1973). Female blood remains a sign associated with stigma.

Females, internalizing cultural attitudes, may view their own menstruation as a sign of dirtiness or a proof of bodily inferiority or injury. On the other hand, many of them also intuitively sense the relation between blood and power, particularly the power to bear children. Even as evidence of power, however, menstruation is something that happens to a woman, not something she does. Historically, pregnancy and childbirth have often been happenings not much under female control. Only female bleeding inflicted intentionally is really controllable. When an abusive male inflicts such bleeding, he clearly demonstrates his control over matters of life or death. An abused woman who feels out of control in many aspects of her life may also prove by producing controlled forms of bleeding on herself that she has some power.

Thus, the carefully contrived, almost ritualized self-cutting some disturbed females engage in is paradoxically controlled as well as uncontrolled. To the extent that it is experienced as a compulsion and sometimes occurs in a trance-like state, it may seem uncontrolled. Yet the carefully bounded nature of the cutting often clearly demarcates it as a form of injury that is not really dangerous. The self-cutter announces, in effect, that she can bleed at will, that she is not frightened by bleeding, that no great harm will come of it. She may experience calm or even exhilaration, feelings that may be somewhat mediated by the release of endogenous opioids. Cognitively, idiosyncratic meanings of bleeding, such as those associated with releasing inner badness, punishing oneself for badness, or proving to other people that one is injured are also variously connected with self-cutting.

Blood tends to attract attention. Observing the self-cutter's injuries, others may be shocked, frightened, or revolted. It is obvious behavior like self-cutting, in fact, that often brings disturbed individuals to the attention of health professionals. Those who merely withdraw or keep their symptoms secret may go undetected. In this regard, self-cutting, like suicidal behavior may be a cry for help. Like suicidal behavior, too, it may result in serious injury or death if something unintended happens, such as excessive bleeding or infection.

The ability to dissociate pain underlies the use of hypnosis for anesthesia or analgesia. Those who self-injure, similarly, may dissociate the experience of pain. Thus, although pain may be a sought-out part of self-injury, some of those who damage themselves may have few if any physical sensations. In the severe dissociative disorders, alter personalities often vary in their experience of pain as well as in their responses to analgesic medication. For example, an alter personality who does not experience pain may inflict it on one who does.

An extreme dissociation of pain sometimes occurs in psychosis. When that happens, self-mutilations may be severe and even life-threatening. Schizophrenic individuals, for example, may inflict numerous wounds or burns on themselves or even cut off body parts without feeling pain (Favazza, 1987). Such behaviors sometimes occur in response to delusional beliefs or hallucinations, particularly religious delusions. The ability to feel pain in an individual who has been previously numb, whether through extreme dissociation or psychosis, can be a sign of returning health and self-care.

In *I Never Promised You a Rose Garden*, Joanne Greenberg (1968) gives a compelling description of how recovery from psychosis can be connected with recovery of the ability to feel pain. Deborah, a young institutionalized patient, had a history of burning herself severely with cigarettes. As she progressed in psychotherapy, she made a shocking discovery:

> She sat on the floor, hidden by the other beds, and looked at her scarred arm. The tissue would have no feeling, the burn do no good. She began to start a new place, moving the burning cigarette to put it out against undeadened flesh. . . . The first singe of hair brought a red-hot stab with it so that she jerked her arm away, astonished. "It was a reflex!" she said incredulously to the bedrail. . . . She had begun to cry because of the terror and joy of it. "I seem to begin to be bound to this world. . . . " (pp. 238–239)

PSYCHOTHERAPEUTIC APPROACHES TO SELF-INJURY

The psychotherapy of clients who attack themselves requires a careful evaluation of the dangerousness of the kinds of self-injuries inflicted. Clients who seriously endanger themselves must be approached as suicidal, even if they deny the intent to kill themselves. In many cases, however, self-injury is part of a compulsive but not really dangerous pattern of behavior. It follows predictably from the building up of tension and serves an obvious self-regulatory purpose. Such forms of self-injury are often deliberately planned rather than impulsive and are methodically carried out. The act appears ritualistic and may seem to occur in an altered state of consciousness. Following the injury, the individual expresses a sense of physical and psychological relief.

As therapy progresses, self-injury is one of the many behavioral symptoms that may arise in connection with transference. At that point, the self-injury is no longer an autistic or hidden practice. It is displayed and used to communicate feelings and fantasies to the therapist. It may express panic, defiance, or rage. It may be an appeal for rescue coupled with an insistence that the client is still in control and does not need the therapist. It may be a direct attack on the therapist, who is forced to watch helplessly as the client self-destructs. Or it may be an invitation to explore material that has previously been hidden, such as details about early abuse or the client's history of self-abuse.

Obviously, the therapist cannot ignore signs of self-injury. Some therapists (Putnam, 1989) approach the problem by contracting with the client. This approach can be useful in emphasizing the symptomatic nature of self-injury and in facilitating self-control. But in many instances self-injurious compulsions, like other compulsions, cannot be so simply prevented. Forbidding them may merely drive them underground. The dilemma confronting the therapist, like so many dilemmas with survivors of abuse, is really a matter of familiar double binds. Does the client really have the right to control her own body? What are the limitations on this right? If she loses control and cuts herself, is this a terrible failure for which she will be punished by hospitalization? Is she allowed to masturbate if pain has been a necessary part of her sexual self-stimulation?

In practice, the therapist is responsible for monitoring self-injury and for trying to insure that the client is not dangerous to herself or to others. In practice, too, most therapists are disturbed by self-injurious behavior in clients. It is reasonable to express these feelings and to interpret self-injury as a symptom that requires priority attention. Self-injury in the therapy setting is an obvious violation of safety; the insistence on the therapy room as a safe place can be absolute. Similarly, the therapist can matter-of-factly state that she has professional obligations to prevent the client from harming herself or others and that, if the situation warrants it, the client may have to be hospitalized.

On the other hand, even gentle threats by a therapist are an invitation to defiance. Patterns of self-injury that are not really dangerous are better handled, like any other compulsive symptom, by exploring their origins and meanings and hoping the client achieve healthier modes of self-regulation. The client's need for self-injury can be acknowledged sympathetically. At the same time, she can be guided toward nondestructive but expressive behaviors that help control and relieve tension.

In therapy, I explicitly attempt to channel self-injurious behavior into expressive actions that externalize aggression through symbolic behaviors. Destroying furniture or breakable objects in the office is off limits with one exception: Destroying paper is sometimes suggested and encouraged. After the client becomes familiar with the possibilities for symbolic expression through play and art materials, I point out that she can use these materials to express destructive action tendencies, as distinct from either inhibiting such tendencies tensely or expressing them uncontrollably. When a client mentions a sudden impulse to cut, for example, I may hand her paper and crayons and say insistently, "Do it on paper!" or "Do it to the paper!" If she starts to hit herself, I may say forcefully, "Do it to the pillow." My assortment of toys also includes miniature objects that can be used to enact abuse on figures that the client may take as representative of herself or others.

One role of the therapist in such expressive techniques is monitoring boundaries and making sure that the client is not really out of control. I do not encourage action, for example, if I perceive that the client is disoriented, has not yet learned to use materials symbolically, or cannot discriminate between safe and dangerous play. Facilitating these discriminations is part of laying the groundwork for expressive therapeutic techniques. At any point when a client seems disoriented or out of contact with me, I stop whatever else is going on and focus on reorienting her, reminding her of where she is, who I am, etc. Often this is merely a matter of asking her to look around the room, label objects, and acknowledge my presence.

Clinical Illustration

The personality system of a client with multiple personality disorder included a child alter who occasionally wet her pants. Two punitive adult alters used this behavior as a pretext for severe punishments, which included cutting the child in various places. One of these adult alters was self-righteous and moralistic. The other was sexually excited by the cutting and used punishment of the child alter as an exciting masturbatory ritual.

The therapist approached the self-injurious behavior first by attempting to enlist the moralistic adult alter as an ally. This involved acknowledging the need for the child to learn control and the positive aspects of the adult alter's concern. The therapist introduced the possibility of noninjurious forms of control, placing special emphasis on understanding the child's behavior. The moralistic adult alter came to understand that the child was afraid of bathrooms and that one means of helping her control herself was helping her overcome that fear. Allied with the therapist, the concerned alter became more empathic toward the child and practically helpful to her, steps along the way to eventual integration with her.

The adult alter who derived sexual pleasure from cutting the child was more problematical. After she developed an attachment to the therapist, she idealized the therapist and wanted to please her. She feared that if she continued to cut the child, she would be punished by being banished from therapy. Yet cutting was a condition of sexual excitement for her. Giving it up meant giving up sexual pleasure. To make matters even more complicated, in the course of therapy, as early abuse history was explored, this adult alter began to experience pain when she cut. The barriers between her and the abused child were breaking down.

In response to both these factors — the wish to please the therapist and the experience of physical pain when she cut — the abusive alter inhibited her abuse. An immediate outcome was depression; she could no longer enjoy masturbation. It was necessary to continue exploring the effects of abuse as well as to focus on the possibilities of enjoying pleasure in a noninjurious way in order to deal with this problem. This work, too, was an important step toward integration.

Thus, working on a specific form of self-injury eventually involved exploring many issues, not only the immediate practical aspects of controlling the abuse but the historical roots of the self-injurious behavior. Dissociation from the body and its feelings, identification with the aggressor, the sexualization of soothing, and the experience of pain as a condition of pleasure were issues that required patient and lengthy work.

CHAPTER 10

Ritualization and Abuse

ONE CAN LEARN a great deal about magic from wandering through the occult section of a large bookstore. Anyone curious about the Enochean language, spell casting formulas, magical sex rituals, or the organization of secret societies like The Order of the Peacock Angel or the Hell Fire Club can readily assemble a small library. The figure of Satan is prominent in such literature. For centuries Satan has been preached against, prayed.to, contracted with, and exorcised. His literary influence is by no means confined to the occult section, of course. He was a central figure in Milton's *Paradise Lost* and Dante's *Divine Comedy* and played a starring role in numerous documented earthly tragedies, such as the witch burnings of the middle ages, the Manson murders of the 1960s, and the gruesome murders of 15 victims uncovered at Matamoros, Mexico in 1989 (Raschke, 1990).

Those who like to believe that civilization is making progress are skeptical of tales about Satanic cults that have circulated in recent years. Surely, they say, these are simply urban legends, a social psychological phenomenon that is interesting for what it tells us about modern myth but that has no basis in actuality. In evaluating such stories, we may well consider on the one hand the psychology of rumor, which is well known to produce preposterous distortions, and on the other hand the psychology of denial, which erases troublesome facts from social history as well as from individual consciousness. These days, anyone can say just about anything, anywhere and gain publicity. People proclaim from the headlines of supermarket tabloids that they were abducted by space aliens. In 1991, an advertisement ran in the student newspaper of a prestigious university proclaiming, in all seriousness, that the Holocaust never happened.

Reviewing the claims of Satanic cult activity, Greaves (1992) points out that reports of child abuse have often been met with skepticism, even before stories of ritual abuse began to surface. Multiple personality disorder as a phenomenon was also given little credence when clinicians like

Cornelia Wilber, the therapist who treated Sybil, began writing about their observations. This history should prompt caution in dismissing reports of horrific forms of cult abuse. But even so, it does not prove that such stories are true. Greaves discusses alternative hypotheses that might account for such stories, noting that many have not been and cannot be subjected to strict principles of scientific verification.

Yet the reports persist and, as Katchen and Sakheim (1992) emphasize, the reports of many of those who claim to have been abused by Satanic cults are remarkably similar. Among the atrocities described, ritualized sexual abuse, including group orgiastic activities, cannibalism, and human sacrifice, especially the sacrifice of babies, are common. The protest that evidence for such activities has escaped the investigation of law enforcement officials is countered by the explanation that cultists use brainwashing techniques on their members that bind them to the cult under penalty of death. The dead bodies of those sacrificed are never found, according to such explanations, because they were burned or ingested. In fact, some bodies *are* found: Raschke (1990) discusses several cases of substantiated ritual murder that were prosecuted by authorities.

In the long run, perhaps it is not the incredibility but the frightening plausibility of secret cults that makes them so insistently denied. The Church of Satan, founded and headed by Anton LaVey, is a recognized entity, although members deny that any of their activities are illicit. During the 1960s and 70s witchcraft became a popular subject. Self-proclaimed witches wrote books and appeared on talk shows, and college students sat in circles, staring at candles, chanting magic formulas, and casting spells.

Secret societies are, in fact, a verifiable part of the lives of many ordinary citizens. Children devise their secret clubs and special passwords, teenagers join gangs marked by secret codes and signals, adults assemble in meeting halls and sponsor somber initiatory rites. Male secret societies, like male rites of passage, have played an important role in the histories of many cultures (Howard, 1989). The darker side of such societies, too, is well documented. The Ku Klux Klan still recruits members, holds meetings and marches, and distributes propaganda (Raschke, 1990).

As a religious ritual, the worship of Satan has been long recognized to be a negative version of mainstream religious practices, particularly those of the Catholic church (Katchen & Sakheim, 1992). The black mass is a desecration of the Christian sacrament, modeled along rather simplistic and straightforward principles of oppositionalism. It is scarcely surprising that a few intrepid souls in rebellion against mainstream culture should make the negative versions of accepted cultural images the focus of their secret rituals. From a social psychological standpoint, such a development is more predictable than strange.

As for the illicit practices attributed to cults, dangerous and illicit rituals are certainly not restricted to those who make Satan their deity. Charismatic rituals, including such dangerous practices as snake handling, are part of the sacred traditions of certain fundamentalist Christian sects in the United States. And as for the sadistic acts attributed to worshipers of Satan, the human imagination has hardly contrived anything more sadistic than the tortures devised by the medieval Inquisition (Peters, 1988; Russell, 1972). Persecution of unbelievers and heretics, in fact, has been a dark side of the history of many mainstream religious groups, and few things have been done in the name of Satan that have not also been done in the name of God.

The fact that sadism has played an important role in religious history seems to be based on behavioral tendencies that are uniquely human. Animals stalk and tease and capture and maul, but they lack the cognitive apparatus to invent torture or the belief systems that justify torture. Human beings, in contrast, are socially united on the basis of beliefs and rituals associated with beliefs. They do not merely suffer or inflict suffering. They interpret suffering, invent myths to explain it, and prescribe rituals to control it.

One principle underlying the torture and sacrifice of victims by groups as well as by individuals is scapegoating. As a group practice, scapegoating is a psychological ritual for coping with hostility, guilt, and the individual antisocial tendencies that threaten group cohesion. In religious rites, the scapegoat has symbolic significance; it is a propitiatory sacrifice that displaces the sins of the orthodox onto an outcast. In everyday life, scapegoating as practiced by individuals or groups needs no religious rationale, though it often has one. Human scapegoats are usually, though not necessarily, chosen on the basis of readily identifiable characteristics such as ethnicity, skin color, or sex.

Females are readily available and controllable scapegoats and as scapegoats have been institutionally as well as individually abused. Most of the so-called witches tortured and killed during the middle ages, for example, were females (Williams & Adelman, 1978). The subordinate status of women is reflected in most clandestine cults as well as in organized religions. Cults, even benign ones, are seldom headed by women. Throughout history, the existence and power of male secret societies like the Templars and the Masons has been documented (Howard, 1989). But there is no evidence that female secret societies have ever exercised widespread social or political influence. On the contrary, one of the usual functions of male secret societies is to protect male power and privilege and to separate men from the contaminating or weakening influence of women. Any female who tries to gain access to an all-male club or institution quickly learns this.

RITUALS AND THE ORGANIZATION
OF CULTURE

Shared rituals bind groups together, whether they are singing "The Star Spangled Banner" before a ball game, throwing rice at a newly wedded couple, or following a funeral cortege. Transitions in life, such as birth and death, are especially likely to be marked by rituals. Some rituals are initiatory, tests of worthiness or maturity that become conditions of membership in the larger society. Initiatory rituals commonly involve danger and suffering. Where formal rites of passage are unavailable, individuals sometimes invent informal ones. A common American rite, for example, is to get extremely intoxicated on the occasion of one's 21st birthday, a ritual that not only celebrates coming of age but typically insures suffering the morning after. In times of war, young men may enter the military as a rite of passage.

One traditional coming-of-age ritual is sexual initiation. Throughout the world, a wide variety of customs and ceremonies have been developed to regulate this event for both males and females (Van Gennep, 1960). The culture at large obviously has a pragmatic stake in regulating sexuality, but the significance of ritual is not merely practical. Sex is one of life's great mysteries, an elemental force that almost universally arouses ambivalent feelings—desire, awe, surrender, guilt. Sexual rituals, for groups as well as individuals, are attempts to assert control, to make sure sexuality remains a positive rather than a destructive force in social life.

From the perspective of memory, ritual can sometimes be viewed as a behavioral enactment that stands in place of an internal representation. As a representational form, ritual thus has a communicative as well as an expressive function. Social rituals and individual rituals arise out of a common matrix of need and anxiety, and pathological rituals often betray their origin in early distortions of social experience. Secret rituals conceal shame and guilt as well as anxiety and compulsive need. Autistic rituals may be quite cryptic. In some autistic rituals, self-stimulation and self-soothing seem almost altogether detached from social experience and shared meanings.

SEXUAL RITUALS AND
RITUALIZED ABUSE

Ritual is first learned in the family as a gradually evolved system of stimulation and soothing that initiates the infant into the world of social relationships. Rituals that originally join parent and child are eventually internalized in rituals of self-stimulation and self-soothing. When normal forms of self-regulation are impaired, compulsive rituals are often instituted. Life becomes an ongoing ritualized struggle to reestablish homeostatic regulation. Sexual abuse, for example, often results in the compulsive ritualization of sexual interactions. Traumatic encounters with needed caretakers result in extreme ambivalence about human contact, especially sexual contact. Fetishism is one such ritualistic response. Other compulsive sexual behavior patterns, clinically labeled *paraphilias*, are similarly related to disturbances in both self-regulation and social attachment.

Ritualistic behavior is related to play, but compulsive rituals are often more painful than playful. They lack the flexible variability associated with normal play, the openness to novelty, the simple, good-natured fun. They tend, instead, to be associated with anxiety. Sometimes the ritual is devised primarily to control anxiety, and any deviation from a prescribed form results in panic. Traumatic states of arousal, including anxiety, tend also to be accompanied by levels of inhibition that interfere with the discharge of tension. Thus, the individual whose sexuality is complicated by anxiety often has trouble achieving real satisfaction. Soothing is elusive. Tension is not relieved, or if it is, rises again precipitously in that pendulum swing of wild excitement, numbing, and exhaustion that often characterizes disturbances in self-regulation.

Sexual rituals are often designed to facilitate an orgiastic experience that will lead to quiescence rather than numbness, pleasurable satisfaction rather than painful overstimulation. Sometimes, in order to be effectively calming, such rituals must be supplemented by other self-regulating aids, such as the use of drugs or alcohol. Group participatory experience is also a way of overcoming sexual inhibitions and alleviating guilt.

Ritual is often a significant component of repetitive abuse. The victimizer, who has himself been traumatized, may enjoy having absolute control over the stimulation and soothing of another human being. The other serves as a manipulated object by means of which he can externalize his most terrifying fantasies. As the one in control, the victimizer nevertheless needs the victim. For this reason, he may keep her alive but captive for long periods of time. Her death would mark the end of the game.

CULTS AND RITUAL ABUSE

Religion plays a variable role in ritualized abuse. Sometimes it is merely the pretext an abuser uses to justify his behavior. A man may beat his wife, for example, on the pretext that the Bible says wives must be in subjection to their husbands. A child may be sexually abused and prayed over in a bizarre ritual that enacts the abuser's ambivalence about religion as well as about sexuality. Some individuals compartmentalize their righteous and sinful selves through dissociation. Alternating rituals of sin and salvation, like alternating bouts of drinking and sobriety, pattern their existence.

In other cases, the abuse of a victim becomes a group endeavor, part of an organized set of rites kept secret from all but the initiate. In such instances, abuse itself often has an initiatory function and becomes a means of binding the victim to the group. Satanic cults are evidently organized around such practices. The content of the rituals described is often based on an inversion of mainstream religious values: Evil is preferable to and stronger than good; sexual indulgence and exploitation are positively valued while sexual abstinence is considered undesirable and unhealthy. Other beliefs have to do with the desirability and nature of power (Katchen & Sakheim, 1992).

The relation between religious beliefs and the infliction of pain is complicated. Religion takes a negative, often unexplainable and uncontrollable experience—pain—and gives it meaning. Meaning, in turn, makes pain seemingly under control. Thus, in religious rituals, it is not merely the scapegoat, but the believer who is subjected to pain. Suffering, he or she proves personal worthiness and individual subordination to the beliefs and rules of the group. Pain becomes a sign of loyalty and belonging.

Satanists as well as Christians interpret pain in the context of doctrines and dogmas. The cult member on whom pain is inflicted is part of a social enactment that portrays a world view. She is temporarily but not permanently isolated from others and overwhelmed by existential meaninglessness. But her ordeal is rationalized as having a purpose. The cult clearly recognizes the psychological uses of pain in binding the individual to the group and instilling loyalty.

In actual practice, however, many cult rituals seem less founded on philosophy, even esoteric philosophy, than on simple greed and exploitation. Religious beliefs, including those associated with Satanism, may be a thinly disguised pretext for giving torturers a sadistic thrill. In instances in which cults produce pornography, peddle drugs, or engage in other illegal activities, the thrill of making money is also an obvious motive. In such cases, the loyalty of the individual to the group is intensified by reminding the member that she or he has engaged in criminal acts, is now—though secretly—an outcast from normal society, and would be tried for heinous crimes if the cult activity were discovered.

Because Satanic cults engage in activities that are the antithesis of mainstream social beliefs and practices, they lend themselves to the dissociation of a secret self from an ordinarily adapted self. Some cults deliberately enforce this dissociation. As Katchen and Sakheim (1992) emphasize, "There is the clear idea of killing off the old 'good' self and finding or creating a new 'evil' self" (p. 30). The old self functions by day and may be an integrated and respected part of the ordinary community. The new self emerges during cult activities that are structured to cue and facilitate its manifestation. The new self may be interpreted by the cult as an instance of possession by a demon. Clinicians are likely to observe such dissociations as the creation of multiple personalities.

Because of the severity of the associated abuse and the deliberate facilitation of dissociative tendencies by cults, multiple personality disorder is a typical, though not inevitable, result of ritualistic cult abuse (Putnam, 1989; Sakheim & Devine, 1992). In the treatment of multiples who have been ritually abused, the problems characteristic of therapy with extremely dissociated individuals are compounded by the specific effects of cult brainwashing and indoctrination (Galanter, 1989). The client who has been ritually abused often equates integration with death, not simply because the uniqueness of alter personalities might disappear with fusion, but because she has been indoctrinated from childhood in the belief that if cult secrets were ever revealed, she would die or be killed.

TREATING VICTIMS OF RITUAL ABUSE

Individuals in treatment, even those in treatment for MPD, may not disclose accounts of ritual abuse until well along in therapy. If the therapist suspects or mentions the possibility of cult abuse, the client may deny it. On the other hand, certain signs may suggest the strong possibility of cult involvement. These include a preoccupation with animal sacrifice, certain kinds of stereotyped movements that seem to suggest magical intent, anniversary reactions to dates associated with special cult celebrations, or an indication that many family members participated simultaneously in abusive behavior.

One way of facilitating disclosure is to talk casually about certain typical kinds of cult activities, such as circle dancing and candle arrangements, as if the therapist were familiar with them. This is likely to mean little to individuals who have not engaged in such practices. The former cult member, however, may become quite anxious, not only because she fears the material being discussed but because she fears that the therapist is a cult member who will entrap her. Such responses offer an opportunity for clarification and exploration. The therapist may make it clear that she herself has never engaged in cult practices, but is nevertheless familiar with them, as are many psychotherapists.

Most psychotherapists have been trained to respect the belief systems of clients, including unusual or minority religious beliefs. In dealing with ritual abuse, however, the therapist must necessarily talk about her own values. Everyone is entitled to his or her beliefs, but certain practices, such as child abuse, are destructive and the results of these practices are, in fact, causing the client many problems in her current life.

In addition to the principles and techniques that generally apply when working with multiple personalities, several may be especially effective with victims of ritualized abuse. Among these are such activities as automatic writing, particularly the suggested exercise of writing things backward (a Satanic practice) and the use of play materials that facilitate the enactment of ritual abuse. My toy cupboard includes a "monster box," which most people simply associate with Halloween or horror movies, but which ritually abused clients recognize as containing familiar sacred relics and instruments of torture. Items related to cult practices can be obtained in novelty shops. Their popularity does not simply indicate that Satanic cults are prevalent in the community. They derive, rather, from the horrific symbols — witches, skeletons, ghosts, spiders, snakes — universally recognized as being related to the dark or shadow side of the human psyche.

Satan is currently a popular figure in rock music, particularly heavy metal rock music. Interest in such music and the symbols associated with it does not necessarily indicate any kind of cult involvement, except insofar as adolescent rock concerts and the worship of rock musicians often does seem ritualistic. Popular interest in Satanic symbolism, however, does lead in some instances to experimentation with ritualistic practices, including deadly practices, among individuals who are not members of cults but are devotees of cult symbols and rituals (Raschke, 1990), including those celebrated in rock music.

Fantasies about the underworld of witches, dragons, and demons commonly emerge in psychotherapy with many clients, particularly in the play of children. Individuals who have been cult members, however, show through their terrorized responses and detailed knowledge of occult ritualistic practices that their involvement has not been merely at the level of fantasy. Even so, it is not always clear just what the client actually experienced. One aspect of cult indoctrination is the use of illusions and tricks to make a child doubt her senses, a practice that increases her dependency on authorities and their statements about the nature of reality (Katchen & Sakheim, 1992). In treatment it is usually clear, however, that the client really was physically and sexually abused, sometimes in bizarre ways. She may still bear marks of ritual abuse, such as branding or tattooing on her body. Bodily pain memorializes her torture. The reality of her terror as well as the social context of it is a repetitive theme of therapy.

One factor sometimes complicating the treatment of ritually abused individuals is the existence within the personality system of alter personalities who identify strongly with cult leaders or see themselves as future cult leaders. In therapy, such alters can nevertheless come to recognize that they themselves were not always happy with their status in the cult. Obviously, if the cult had really been a focus of happy and productive personal adaptation, the client would not be so miserable in her present life. The alter who strongly identifies with the cult may nevertheless be disappointed that she never received the rewards of cult membership she was promised — money, power, unlimited indulgence of her desires. In Satanic cults as well as in societies generally, positions of real power and authority are held by men. Women are seldom elevated to top positions.

In the long run, it is usually the recognition that abuse has taken a costly toll on her life and that she wants something else that keeps a survivor in therapy. This is true of survivors of ritualized tortures as well as those who have been the targets of individual abuse. Sadistic rituals, with or without the pretext of religious philosophy, are frequently just one more excuse for scapegoating and exploiting females. As she lays claim to her own authority, the client typically examines her relation to other authorities, including the groups, as well as the individuals she previously submitted to. By overcoming the effects of indoctrination, she is in a position to explore ideas, including religious ideas, in the context of her adult needs rather than her childhood terrors.

CHAPTER 11
Enactment and Abreaction

ONE OF THE TYPICAL and most adaptive self-regulating mechanisms is the use of transitional objects or transitional rituals (Winnicott, 1971). Transitional phenomena serve as bridges between variable internal states, like waking and sleeping, between the individual and the outside world, and between different parts of the individual self. Childhood play often incorporates the most meaningful transitional objects in the child's world. Through the use of toys and dramatizations the child tells her story. Even fantastic stories often tell important truths.

Childhood play is an enactive process with its own stylized conventions. A doll stands in place of a person; a toy truck stands in place of a real one. Children who lack store-bought toys invent their own out of materials readily at hand. A stick becomes a horse; a patch of mud becomes material for building a house. In their pretending, children also explore the creative uses of projection. The rider of the stick-horse becomes a hero; the builder of the mud house inhabits it. Sometimes the invented world is peopled with imaginary companions who, though invisible, have vividly imagined characteristics and express wishes and fears as well as realities—Jill with red hair, Bobby who wears cowboy boots, Mrs. Perkins who yells at the class, Uncle Arthur who came to visit. In play, the child tries on versions of selfhood, expresses and disowns antisocial behavior, and lays claims to grandiose powers.

When traumatized children play, they, like other children enact their fears and hopes. But the form of their play is often less playful, more rigid and compulsively ritualized. Their transitional representations reflect not only the content of their traumas, but the distortions of self-regulation that are the outcome of traumatization. Difficulties in impulse control may be evident in sudden outbursts or inhibitions. Unsuccessful attempts to repress memories of traumatic events or to transform memories from literal forms of reexperiencing into symbolic representations of experiences may make such children uncomfortable with their own inventions.

Distortions in relationships to significant figures, particularly parents, also impact on play. When the connection between the child and the parent becomes conflicted or traumatic, the child may attempt to break it off in ways that are then reflected in transitional phenomena like play.

Fetishistic rituals are often distorted forms of play in which elements of traumatic overstimulation and the disruption of human attachments are dramatically evident. The use of the fetish expresses an attempt to connect with a needed person without being overwhelmed by intense feelings or losing boundaries between self and other. The fetish thus simultaneously represents attachment and detachment, tension relief and control (Greenacre, 1970; Waites, 1982).

Play can be an important adjunct to psychotherapy, particularly in work with traumatized and/or inhibited individuals. Integrative psychotherapy involves connecting what has not been connected or reconnecting what has been disconnected. In this process, the therapeutic context functions as a transitional space, and the relationship with the therapist functions as a bridge between past and present, self and other, self and self. Words are the basic medium of expression, but many aspects of the therapeutic relationship are inherently nonverbal. Even in traditional "talking" therapies, it is widely recognized that such intangibles as the working alliance and remembering with affect are as important to therapeutic progress as verbally articulated interpretations and insights. As one form of bridging gaps, therapeutic play enables the client to overcome her isolation and integrate the fragments of her history.

Specific nonverbal therapeutic techniques are especially useful in the treatment of post-traumatic and dissociative disorders for several reasons. Many aspects of trauma, including those that reoccur in intrusive flashbacks, are nonverbal and difficult to describe even by articulate adults. The disturbances in self-regulation associated with repetitive traumatization often produce powerful impulses to act out or repetitively enact the traumatic event(s) (Terr, 1990). In childhood, traumatization often occurs prior to the development of competence in language and is likely to be reexperienced in terms of vivid sensory recollections. In many instances, too, a victim is explicitly instructed in secrecy and threatened with dire consequences for breaking silence and reporting abuse. Indoctrinations in silence may extend to every form of vocal expression; not only talk but crying or even moaning may be strictly interdicted.

The use of nonverbal therapeutic techniques enables the client to begin to speak the unspeakable and express the inexpressible. With traumatized individuals, such techniques can facilitate control of "acting out" not only by encouraging the client to "act in," that is, within the therapeutic context, but by allowing and structuring safe forms of tensional release. The therapist as bridge integrates verbal with nonverbal expressions, not so much through complex interpretations as through simple comments about what is happening and simple labeling of feelings and events. The therapist gives permission to communicate. She acknowledges that she sees what others pretended not to see, that actions may belie words, and that actions sometimes speak more powerfully than words. At the same time, she provides a setting in which the client can begin to explore created symbolic forms as a means of entertaining, expressing, and mastering overwhelming experiences.

The use of transitional representational media like paper and crayons as well as stuffed animals, hand puppets, and toys keeps the focus of therapeutic play on symbolic representation and interaction and nonphysical forms of client-therapist contact. Most clients quickly learn the boundaries of therapeutic play, just as most children recognize and adhere to the boundaries of childhood play. Even traumatized clients with difficulties in impulse control or tendencies toward spontaneous abreactions can readily adapt to the control implicit in therapeutic play, particularly if careful attention is given to the establishment of boundaries and a trustworthy working alliance.

PLAY IN ADULT PSYCHOTHERAPY

The use of nonverbal representational techniques in adult psychotherapy can be traced to the early days of psychoanalysis. Among the first to employ such techniques was Carl Jung. The exploration of nonverbal representations played an important role in his self-analysis (Jung, 1961), and expressive techniques such as active imagination and artistic expression have become an important part of many Jungian analyses (Stein, 1982). One of the most creative elaborations of play therapy, pioneered by Jungians but now widely in use by therapists of many theoretical orientations, is sandplay (Bradway et al., 1990). Sandplay evolved from what Lowenfeld (1979) called the "World Technique." Originally used with children, it has been readily adapted to adult psychotherapy, particularly in the treatment of dissociative disorders. It involves the use of a sand-filled tray in which the client arranges miniature objects as "worlds" (Thompson, 1990).

Other expressive techniques commonly used with both children and adults include drawing, painting, sculpting, and other forms of art. Art therapy, which may require special equipment, is often employed as an adjunct to other forms of psychotherapy, particularly in institutional settings. Simple forms of drawing, however, are readily incorporated into any therapeutic setting and require little in the way of special equipment.

Play has long been recognized as the serious business of childhood, but many adults are embarrassed to admit that they play, and inhibited adults may fear play as a shameful or regressively dangerous activity. In everyday life, adult play is often a voyeuristic affair: As spectators, adults may limit their behavioral involvement to cheering from the sidelines. Yet even the most sober adults sometimes admits to enjoying not only games and sporting events but toys; adults are, after all, the ones who buy most of the toys children play with, and the father who plays with his son's electric train is proverbial. Adults, however, often focus on the creation of objects more than on active play with them. Many adults spend leisure time painstakingly building model structures or collecting miniatures.

In contrast to modern inhibited adults, the ancients recognized that play is serious business for adults as well as children. The very word "play" commonly refers to a structured dramatization in which actors deliberately take on specified roles in the context of a conventional setting, typically a stage. The Greeks recognized the therapeutic as well as the recreational function of dramatization. Plays were aesthetically designed rituals that served an important social function. Through identifying with an enactment, a spectator could experience *catharsis*, a release of pent-up feelings, which, if unpurged, might endanger the health of the community as well as the individual. The emphasis on cathartic techniques in early psychoanalysis was based on a similar assumption. Abreactive work in psychotherapy, which is inherently cathartic, can be effectively integrated with controlled enactive techniques, including structured play.

Socially as well as individually, enactive play is related to ritualization, including religious rituals and other institutionalized group rituals such as the commemoration of significant historical events. The close relation between ritualization and play is reflected in the distortions of ritual that sometimes occur in response to traumatization. Compulsive rituals, including the play of traumatized individuals, tend to lose their spontaneous and playful quality. In some cases, pleasure itself has been so overshadowed by or insistently connected with pain, that cruelty and violence are the main themes of play.

The Screening Function of Play

In psychotherapy as well as in life, play and other expressive techniques conceal as well as reveal. Because play is play, the individual can reassure herself that it is not "real." Even those who play out realistic versions of historical events are aware that the process is representational. Selection and interpretation are always involved, and one is reenacting, not simply reliving.

For this very reason, play can be especially helpful in the telling of a painful real-life story. The "I" who is enacting the trauma is being invited to dissociate in a normal, culturally accepted way by role playing. Unlike the painful real life event, the play can be initiated and discontinued at will. Secrets can be revealed in the guise of "just pretending." Details that are too horrific to include can be left out. Parts of the story can be changed to make it less awful or more understandable. The organization of play in the therapy, thus, often reflects the organization of memories of and fantasies about trauma, including childhood perceptions, misperceptions, and interpretations.

For severely traumatized individuals, however, the boundaries between literal reality and representational convention can become blurred. They realize that toys are not really the objects or people associated with the original traumatic event. The therapy room is not really the setting in which the trauma occurred. Yet toys and play materials may function as cues, precipitating flashbacks. Under the influence of intense emotions, the past may overwhelm the present and internal hallucinations may overshadow external representational objects. Enactment, in other words, may stimulate abreaction.

In the context of psychotherapy, the relation between enactment and abreaction, like the client's spontaneous trance states, can be turned to advantage instead of remaining an uncontrolled liability. Enactment, carefully orchestrated, can be a means of structuring as well as stimulating abreactions. It can also play an important therapeutic role in helping the client process and integrate abreacted material. In this respect, play becomes the serious business of the therapist and requires sensitivity to the nuances of concrete and symbolic representation and the experiential modes typical of the traumatized client.

Play Materials

Some art and play techniques require special equipment and settings. Many, however, can be readily adapted to a single room that functions, most of the time, as a context for conventional "talking" therapy. In my own office, a lap board with white paper (inexpensive typing paper does very well) and an array of crayons, pencils, and felt tip pens is within easy reach of the client. Hand puppets and stuffed animals are also casually placed and not far out of reach. Many clients never touch these objects. Some remark parenthetically "You must see children," to which I usually respond, "Sometimes, but adults make use of these things, too."

In the course of therapy, a client may spontaneously pick up a puppet or stuffed animal; many have a special choice and begin to make it a habitual part of the therapy session. It is my impression, though I have not made a careful study of it, that survivors of abuse are especially drawn to such transitional objects. Often the client just wants to hold the object. She may comment on it as being like a security blanket or compare it to a toy she once had. Once she incorporates it into her own therapy ritual, it often becomes a kind of silent partner in the therapy. The meanings and function of the transitional object may be interpreted at some point, but, particularly in the early stage of therapy, I usually simply accept it as part of the client's attempt to make the therapy room her special, safe, and comfortable place.

Puppets invite adults as well as children to play and are thus sometimes more easily assimilated to therapeutic forms of adult play than other toys. Most adults are familiar with the conventional uses of puppets and ventriloquists' dummies as alter egos. Such forms of entertainment offer a normal and popularly understood form of displacement and projection. Puppets, like the imaginary companions who may be the forerunners of some alter personalities in MPD, are both "me" and "not me." Conventionally, the puppet can be blatantly childish, even outrageous, to the stated disapproval and exasperation of the adult who manipulates it. The puppet, like the fool who entertained the king in days of yore, is also allowed to utter unpleasant, insulting, and dangerous truths with impunity.

Sometimes I casually but deliberately introduce the use of puppets to very anxious clients who are having trouble talking. Silence can have many positive uses in therapy, but some silences are countertherapeutic and threaten a traumatic disruption of connectedness with the therapist. One severely traumatized client, for example, sometimes became almost catatonic at the beginning of the therapy hour. Relaxation exercises led to dissociation, which was not productive in the initial stage of therapy prior to the secure establishment of a therapeutic alliance. Letting her rest in silence, however, simply resulted in increasing discomfort and withdrawal. After trying various ways of encouraging her to begin talking, I one day picked up a puppet and tossed another puppet to her. She caught it as if it were a ball, almost immediately relaxed, and responded imaginatively when I began a dialogue.

Another technique that I have sometimes found useful is two-handed dialogue. I pick up a puppet in each hand and begin talking about a relevant topic, ranging from how difficult it is to put some things into words to a discussion of an internal conflict that I believe to be significant for the client. Sometimes the two puppets I hold argue vociferously, the way the client's parents used to argue or the way she herself argued or wanted to argue with others. Clients sometimes spontaneously model this behavior, going a step beyond and letting the puppets in each hand physically attack one another.

In working with puppets, as in working with art materials, I explicitly play down the importance of performance and producing an artistic product in favor of an emphasis on spontaneity and the fluidity of the communicative process. The less inhibited, the more playful the process, the better. I have no particular facility with puppets and do not even attempt anything as skillful as ventriloquism. With clients who resist such forms of play or consider it merely silly, I usually just drop it, at least temporarily, in favor of more conventional forms of dialogue. Sometimes a client cannot make use of play and art techniques until late in therapy; her ability to do so can be a sign of progress.

Doing It on Paper

Unlike puppet play, drawing is a form of expression adults often take seriously, sometimes too seriously. Many are quick to comment that they are not artists. Those who enjoy or are involved in drawing often remark on their dissatisfaction with their own work. I make it clear that nonverbal communication using paper is a different activity from creating a work of art, just as ordinary talking is different from writing a speech. I also usually remark that I am not an artist or an art critic, but a psychotherapist, and that my approach to what the client produces is focused on helping her understand and solve her problems.

The boundary between drawing as communication and drawing as art, of course, is really not strict. Some clients do want to create works of art in the therapy hour. The time necessary for producing careful works of art, however, often makes art therapy more feasible as an adjunct to psychotherapy rather than a focus in a situation that emphasizes dialogue. Art can also be used as a resistance to talking and careful work on a piece of art can be a way of avoiding spontaneity and feelings associated with loss of control.

One way to integrate more careful forms of creation as well as spontaneous nonverbal expressions is through the use of a journal. Journaling is a form of self-therapy that many clients engage in on their own. When discussing the uses of a journal, I usually explicitly suggest that the client try spontaneous doodling or drawing as well as free association in journal keeping. Sometimes spontaneous drawings stimulate important memories and insights that need to be worked through in therapy. Incorporating a journal into therapy requires careful boundary setting however; a journal, like art, can be used as a way of avoiding spontaneous associations in the therapy session.

Drawing as a communicative form can be casually introduced into therapy by suggesting that the client sketch some image that she is having difficulty describing. I often find it useful at some point to ask incestuously abused clients to quickly sketch the floor plan of their childhood homes, giving special attention to sleeping arrangements, the location of preferred hiding places, etc. Sometimes this exercise brings up significant memories. Sometimes it also reveals serious distortions and amnesias. "I can envision everybody else's bedroom but not my own," a client may complain, or "I checked when I revisited my childhood home and it was very different from the way I remembered it," or "I remember the house we lived in when I was small and the one we moved to when I was in junior high, but the one I lived in when I was in elementary school is a complete blank."

Drawing, either representational or nonrepresentational, is useful in working with dreams. Sometimes it is simply a way of communicating a dream image to the therapist. At other times, the process of creating a work of art that expresses a dream or series of dreams can be a powerfully transformative aspect of psychotherapy.

One of the most often repeated suggestions I make in the course of therapy is, "Do it on paper," or "Do it to the paper." In this regard, paper is not merely a medium for drawing or coloring. It is a concrete object that can represent another object, including a person. Paper is the only object in the office the client is allowed, even invited to destroy. I introduce this convention early in therapy by wadding up or tearing a piece of paper and remarking that it's only paper. Then, at some point, when the client is describing a particular instance of abuse, I may hand her a piece of paper and ask, "What did you feel like doing?"

Sometimes clients make drawings of abusers and then tear them up. Superstitious or regressed individuals or child alters, however, may be afraid to tear up a representation of a person. Such an act seems too magically powerful. Those subjected to ritual abuse are especially likely to believe that attacks on objects can have magical effects on the people the objects represent. In such cases, the invitation to destroy the blank piece of paper focuses on the expressive behavior rather than the object, while at the same time providing an external target for feelings.

The destruction of paper is, fortunately, an inexpensive, harmless, and not very messy activity that can nevertheless have a surprisingly liberating effect. Females, who are typically socialized to inhibit aggression, may be reluctant to tear up anything, including paper. Those abused in childhood are also often terrified of making a mess. The discovery that paper is manageable and "no big deal" can lead to other experiments with symbolic ways of expressing aggression. Sometimes after having torn up blank paper, a client allows herself to spontaneously tear up and discard her own drawings. Not only the fact that her aggression is controlled and not really harmful, but the realization that the drawing belongs to her, to do with as she will, can be therapeutic.

At any point in therapy, but particularly as therapy progresses, nonverbal behaviors, like verbal ones, express the development and patterned unfolding of transference. Those who have compulsively presented all their drawings to the therapist, for example, discover that they can withhold with impunity. The therapist can be explicitly represented in a drawing or attacked in a playful enactment. One client, after a painful period of abreactive work, picked up the puppet I often play with and pointedly wrung its neck. Then she laughed a healthy, satisfied, and unanxious laugh, behavior so rare for her that I took it as a sign of important progress.

Toys

Axline (1969) has provided a convenient description of suggested materials for a playroom. Many of the items she mentions, as well as a large array of miniatures, can be adapted to work in an ordinary office with an area suitable for playing. A large table is useful for arranging and playing with miniature objects, but in the absence of a table or room for one, floor play is easily managed. A comfortable rug (I think of my oriental rug as "the magic carpet") and floor pillows can make the floor comfortable. In clients with multiple personality, child alters are likely to sit on the floor anyway. For most people, sitting on the floor, like the use of crayons, is reminiscent of childhood and stimulates associations from that era.

Whether the therapist joins the client on the floor depends on the nature of her own involvement in the play. Sometimes it is most appropriate for her to remain an observer; sometimes the client wants her active participation. In any case, although sitting on the floor relaxes the formality of the therapeutic context, it need not and should not become a pretext for ignoring contact boundaries between client and therapist. The focus should remain on external materials, toys, as a medium for expressing feelings and ideas.

My own collection of toys includes dolls of several sizes and anatomically correct dolls of both sexes, doll bottles, feeding equipment, and blankets, and several boxes in which small or miniature objects are categorically stored. Miniatures include doll house furniture, small vehicles, wild and domestic animals, including farm animals, and miniature tools and utensils such as knives, saws, and scissors. There is a "rescue box" with a small firetruck and ambulance and police figures, a "pretty box" with dolls that have combable hair and can be dressed. There is a "monster box" with witches, ghosts, skeletons, spiders, and mice. One box contains a collection of hospital miniatures, including doctors and nurses, beds, stretchers, an operating table, and an intravenous feeding bottle. A few other make-believe figures—superheros, knights, and a small dragon are also in the collection.

Wood blocks and logs are useful for building structures. At some points in therapy, clients become absorbed in building houses and fortresses, which express their wishes for safety as well as their recollections about abuse. A magnetic chalk board with magnetic plastic letters is also useful for writing unspeakable messages, including magic words or backward spelled messages learned in cult rituals.

A major consideration in assembling a collection of toys is safety and durability. Special collections of plastic miniatures devised for small children are available, but useful miniatures can be obtained inexpensively from many toy stores and novelty shops. If I know a client has been abused by a particular object, I often attempt to buy a toy version of the object, introduce it to the collection, and allow her to approach and desensitize herself to it at her own pace. One client, for example, was tortured with a curling iron. Shortly after she told me about that, I saw a toy plastic curling iron in a supermarket and added it to my collection.

Although safety is an important feature of toys some toys are obviously safer than others. Any toy, such as a wooden block or log, that might be used as a weapon, is best quietly put away when intense abreactive work is expected. This word of caution is applicable to other objects in the office. Careful preparation for abreactive work and a reliable therapeutic alliance is a precondition for integrating enactive play with abreaction. In some cases, it is also helpful to develop a set of hypnotic and posthypnotic cues that can facilitate the control of regression and abreaction during the therapy session.

ABREACTION

In multiple personalities, the very presence of stuffed animals or other toys may stimulate the appearance of child alters. Some of these will approach the toys and immediately begin playing. Others will be very inhibited; they may look longingly at a toy but be fearful of touching it. Whenever anyone shows a phobic response to a toy, I may comment matter of factly, "These are just toys. They are for playing." If a client expresses a wish to play but a fear of making a mess, I may remark, "Messes are just something we clean up." At the end of a play session, I often help with clean up and remark about how easy it was to do. Children who have been severely punished for making messes are very sensitive to such issues and desensitizing them to messes is therapeutic. In the absence of a play-room that affords possibilities for really messy activities like finger painting and working with clay, using materials that lend themselves to manageable messes is the most practical solution.

After a client has familiarized herself with the toys and is comfortable with approaching and playing with them, I begin to make simple comments on the play—verbal descriptions of what is taking place, requests for clarification if I do not understand, labels for feelings being expressed. At first, connections between play and the client's own life are usually implicit. Later, when she herself begins to note that the play enactments refer to her own life, we talk about the connections. For the most part, I follow the client's lead, allowing her to select what and how to play. But sometimes I call attention to toys relevant to particular scenarios, especially after we have talked about a particular memory or set of memories. At that point, the client often begins spontaneously to abreact traumas in the context of play scenarios.

Abreaction involves the vivid reexperiencing of traumatic events and their associated affects. Although it sometimes seems to be a kind of reliving, Ross (1989) notes that even intense abreactions often have a stylized quality. Uncontrolled abreactions can nevertheless be extremely painful and are likely to be experienced as retraumatizing or revictimizing. Putnam (1989) discusses a number of techniques for facilitating safe abreactions in psychotherapy. Many of these involve the use of special hypnotic techniques, such as having the client imagine she is watching projected memories on a movie screen. The use of such techniques can facilitate the control of the client's distance from the traumatic material and thus make sure abreactions remain manageable.

Enactive play, which is already stylized through the conventions of play, affords an opportunity for externalizing traumatic events and thus becoming desensitized to and less overwhelmed by them. Even so, when play stimulates an abreaction, the client may feel temporarily overwhelmed. It is important at such points for the therapist to monitor boundaries and titrate the reexperiencing. Clients can be encouraged to vent feelings vocally or to hit pillows, for example, but must be protected from injuring themselves. Hypnotic cues and prearranged signals for time outs can help structure limits.

The empathic presence of the therapist during abreactive work is vital, even when the client seems to be in her own world and out of contact with the therapist. The relationship with the therapist continues to function as a bridge to integration. Thus, even a painful abreaction is experienced as different from the original trauma. The traumatized individual is no longer isolated and forbidden to express her feelings but is in the company of a sympathetic helper.

The therapist guides abreactions by paying close attention to boundaries and the loss of boundaries while permitting safe forms of expression and facilitating new modes of experiencing, such as symbolic representation. Sometimes little guidance is needed beyond questions like, "And then what happened?" or "Where are you now?"

Drawing as well as play facilitates abreactive work, and once a client is familiar with expressive therapeutic behaviors, she may shift back and forth from verbalization, to drawing, to play in the course of abreacting one particular memory. Drawings under such conditions are likely to be quickly sketched scenes or series of scenes, like the frames of a movie, in which stick figures convey the action. The immediate focus on such drawings and play is best kept at the level of description rather than interpretation: Who is doing what to whom? Where is the event taking place? etc. Representations are likely to be literal and concrete. For long periods, the red crayon or pen may predominate as a simple representaion of blood. Sometimes, under the influence of powerful feelings, the client may just scribble furiously like a distraught child or scribble over sketched images too painful to look at. If she feels angry and relatively uninhibited she may sketch one drawing after another and tear them up.

After a traumatic memory has been abreacted, careful attention must be focused on processing the material it produced if the trauma is to be integrated rather than remaining an overwhelming, self-alienating experience. Usually, traumatic events must be abreacted repeatedly. Often, a memory is enacted and abreacted from several different perspectives, indicating different levels of regression and integration. As Putnam (1989) emphasizes, in cases of MPD, different alter personalities may have experienced the "same" trauma quite differently, and each may need to abreact the event individually. The abreaction of a memory or set of memories shared by several alter personalities can have an important integrative effect, particularly if each is invited to participate and special attention is given to sharing information and discrepant experiences.

Play not only simulates abreaction, but also offers a means of facilitating integration. In replaying the event, the client is able to be the one in control and thus can, to some extent, master the trauma. After a given trauma has been repeatedly enacted, the therapist can introduce variations on the theme if the client herself does not introduce them. She may suggest, for example, that the same event be replayed with different figures taking familiar roles. This suggestion deliberately invites, though does not explicitly suggest, identification with the aggressor and allows the client to play out her fantasies of revenge in a safe context.

Survivors who have been traumatized as adolescents or adults have frequently developed complex capacities for symbolic representation that stand them in good stead during therapy. Regressed individuals or those who have been severely traumatized in childhood often have not. Or, even though parts of the personality have developed such symbolic capacities, other dissociated parts, like alter personalities, may still be caught up in the horrors of concretely imaged events.

One progression observable in the course of enactive and abreactive work with severely traumatized and dissociated individuals is a move from concrete, literal representations to symbolic elaborations. At the beginning of therapy, for example, a drawing of a flower may refer primarily to a concrete memory—the flowers that were in the room during a specific hospitalization or the flowers that were in the garden where a child was abused. Over the course of time, the symbolic significance of images may become more and more relevant. A flower may become a representation of the self or of hope for the future. The evolution of the capacity for symbolic representation is one of the satisfying outcomes of therapy with survivors of childhood trauma.

Throughout therapy, interpretation of expressive and enactive material is usually best matched to the level of experience from which the material is arising, as well as the level of understanding the client has reached. Complicated interpretations or interpretations of symbolism are often not helpful and may be counterproductive in the early stages of treatment.

Only much later, when considerable abreactive and integrative work has been accomplished, will such interpretations be meaningful.

The most meaningful interpretations are often the ones the client discovers for herself. It is the capacity for understanding, rather than withdrawing from or passively submitting to her experiences that restores to her a sense of competence, wholeness, and participation in life.

Epilogue

But for pain words are lacking. There should be cries, cracks, fissures, whiteness passing over chintz covers, interference with the sense of time, of space; the sense also of extreme fixity in passing objects; and sounds very remote and then very close; flesh being gashed and blood spurting, a joint suddenly twisted—beneath all of which appears something very important, yet remote, to be just held in solitude.

—Virginia Woolf, *The Waves*, p. 263

VIRGINIA WOOLF'S STRUGGLE with a lack of words was no mere metaphor. Her description dramatically details how trauma is translated in experience: "cries, cracks, fissures . . . interference with the sense of time, of space." The distortions of seeing and hearing she mentions are also characteristic features of trauma responses. In this experiential mode, the usual coherence of self and world is shattered; parts of the mind are disconnected from each other and from the body, self is disconnected from others, verbal experience is disconnected from nonverbal experience. Woolf's attempts to reconnect can be discerned in her continual search for narrative forms to integrate the tumult and wordless pain of her history. Louise DeSalvo (1989) has analyzed her struggle as a response to childhood trauma. Virginia Woolf "was raised in a household in which incest, sexual violence, and abusive behavior were a common rather than singular or rare occurrence" (p. 1).

The late 19th century, when Virginia Woolf was born, also saw the birth of psychoanalysis as a psychiatric discipline. It was an age of dramatic contrasts that continued to overshadow life in the following century in spite of rapidly changing social norms and arrangements. Idealization of domesticity—motherhood and family life—insistently concealed bleaker social realities like the prevalence of family violence, the rampant growth of pornography and prostitution, and the widespread sexual abuse of children. It was an age of storytelling and the exploration of narrative forms. Yet the existence of abuse was glossed over or left out of most stories. For example, although Virginia Woolf's molestation in childhood was no secret—she talked and wrote about it—her biographers played down the significance of the abuse as a factor in her recurring bouts of depression and eventual suicide. Alice Miller (1984) views this biographical tendency as the reflection of a pervasive social denial.

It has only been in the last two decades that a shift in clinical focus has brought the significance of actual trauma and the dissociative phenomena commonly sequel to trauma to the forefront of public and professional attention. Many of the characteristics of hysteria described by such pioneering clinicians as Breuer, Janet, Charcot, and Freud are now considered diagnostic criteria for the dissociative disorders. The intrapsychic fault-lines produced by trauma are evident not only in disruptions in the integration of autobiographical memory, but in dramatic physical symptoms, some of which mimic serious somatic disorders. The role of trauma in physical illness, which is related to stress effects on the immune system as well as to residual effects of actual injuries, is also increasingly being recognized.

Psychiatric thinking has also been slow to recognize the significance of gender as a factor in the diagnosis and treatment of psychopathology. Traditionally, when gender has been considered at all, it has usually been treated as a genetic or endogenous factor. The female mind has been viewed as a kind of epiphenomenal appendage to the female reproductive system (Ehrenreich & English, 1978). As a result, clinical case histories have tended to focus on theoretical constructs rather than actual events in the lives of women. Searching the literature on personality disorders, for example, one can read much about aggressive drives, separation conflicts, and internal splitting mechanisms but little about incest, rape, and battering.

A factor further complicating these problems has been the hegemony of male physicians over the health professions. Even those who are sympathetic to women's concerns do not typically encounter the analysis of women's issues in their academic studies and clinical training. In consequence, traditional approaches continue to dominate both theory and treatment.

Fortunately, as we approach the 21st century, attempts to correct for traditional biases are gradually making an impact. The tendency to view serious mental and emotional disturbances in terms of simplistic assumptions about biology is giving way to an informed appreciation of mind-body interactions. Psychotherapy is finally being recognized as an effective intervention in many serious somatic as well as psychological disorders. Even so, the tendency of helping professionals to view conformity to traditional sex-role stereotypes as a solution rather than a problem continues to confound treatment approaches to women. It also contributes to the conceptual controversies and confusions surrounding disorders frequently diagnosed in females, particularly borderline personality disorder and the dissociative disorders.

The traditional medical model also continues to make plausible and even encourages such treatment interventions as involuntary hospitalization and medication, the use of restraints, and electroconvulsive therapy. Whatever the utility of such procedures — and it is not being argued here that they are never necessary — they are interventions that historically have been especially problematic for women. Such interventions have been too frequently an almost reflexive response to disturbed women, especially those who "act out" in any way that runs counter to accepted sex roles.

One factor at the heart of many of these seemingly diverse problems is simply sexual politics. When men discuss women's issues, they often present a misguided view of them. Any analysis smacking of feminism is likely to evoke defensive accusations of "male bashing" and acrimonious rejoinders about the problems of other groups. This defensive stance deflects attention from the real, documented inequities in women's lives. In spite of a mountain of empirical evidence that females are at special risk for sexual abuse, it is even fashionable these days to downplay analyses that emphasize the relation between abuse and gender. This attitude fails to take into account the demonstrable authority of males in social and institutional structures. Recognizing female vulnerability is not a matter of blaming males; it is rather an acknowledgment of how patriarchally structured social institutions as well as parental and internal pathology impact on individuals.

The psychobiology of trauma is no respecter of gender. It has been clearly demonstrated that traumatic situations produce stress-related pathology in both sexes. The modern investigation of post-traumatic syndromes, in fact, originally targeted males who were veterans of combat. As for the most severe dissociative disorder, MPD, Putnam (1989) has contended that the prevalence of this syndrome in females is probably an artifact; dissociated males may be found in the criminal justice system rather than the mental health system. Certainly, it is undeniable that some males are abused, that they are subject to the same kinds of secrecy and denial of abuse as females, and that some of them exhibit dissociative pathology, including multiple personality disorder.

The abuse of male children, in fact, points up the extent to which all children, like all women, are vulnerable to exploitation by dominant males and patriarchal institutions. American culture, like most cultures, accepts and rationalizes hierarchies based on power and sustained by the implicit threat as well as the actualities of physical force. Males who feel themselves victimized or who challenge the premises of power are often themselves overruled by force. Violence, like sexism and racism, is a social problem that affects the whole culture, not just certain targeted individuals or groups. Even so, some individuals or groups, because of their relative powerlessness, are especially likely to be targeted, not just in childhood, but across the life span.

Thus, in spite of the acknowledged vulnerability of male as well as female children, socially typical differences between male and female experience make the prevalence of dissociative disorders in females an expectable phenomenon. Rape and battering as well as child sexual abuse occur more prevalently in females because of social arrangements in the culture and the actual vulnerability of females vis-à-vis males. The prevalence of double binds in female experience also contributes to the prevalence of certain diagnosed disorders in females. Acknowledging gender as a significant factor in victimization and the post-traumatic disorders enables us to examine the effects of psychosocial tendencies like scapegoating. It also offers an opportunity to examine the extent to which the victimization of women is detrimental to the larger society, including men and children.

In the long run, no woman is an island, any more than a man is. The problems of men and women will continue to be inextricably connected. The problems of children, including abused children of both sexes, will continue to reflect their relationships with both parents. The internal world of such children, in adulthood as well as childhood, will continue to perpetuate social arrangements that contribute to victimization and violence. Everyone—men, women, and children—stands to gain from the elimination of abusive contexts. The very survival of the species may depend on it.

Psychotherapy is an individualized intervention. Psychotherapists, like everybody else, can only try to save the world by focusing on one part of it at a time. By the time most therapists have worked a while, particularly if they have worked with so-called "difficult" clients, their grandiosity has been tamed. Treating individual women, even those considered extremely "disturbed," is nevertheless a challenge that has special satisfactions. Even small victories can be rewarding, and for many women, even a little help can be healing and empowering. Perhaps the empowerment of individuals will have a ripple effect that, in the long run, contributes to the integration of our fragmented society.

References

Ader, R., & Cohen, N. (1982). Behaviorally conditioned immunosuppression and murine systemic lupus erythematosis. *Science, 215,* 1534–1536.

Adler, G. (1985). *Borderline psychopathology and its treatment.* New York: Jason Aronson.

Allport, G. W. (1954). *The nature of prejudice.* Cambridge, MA: Addison-Wesley.

Altshuler, T. L., & Ruble, D. N. (1989). Developmental changes in children's awareness of strategies for coping with uncontrollable stress. *Child Development, 60,* 1337–1349.

American Medical Association Council on Scientific Affairs (1992). Violence against women: Relevance for medical practitioners. *Journal of the American Medical Association, 267,* 3184–3189.

American Psychiatric Association (1987). *Diagnostic and statistical manual of mental disorders (3rd ed.-rev.).* Washington, DC: Author.

Arendell, T. (1986). *Mothers and divorce: Legal, economic, and social dilemmas.* Berkeley: University of California Press.

Axelrod, J., & Reisine, T. D. (1984). Stress hormones: Their interaction and regulation. *Science, 224,* 452–459.

Axline, V. M. (1969). *Play therapy.* New York: Ballantine.

Bagley, C., & Ramsey, R. (1986). Sexual abuse in childhood: Psychosocial outcomes and implications for social work practice. *Journal of Social Work and Human Sexuality, 5,* 33–47.

Bakan, P. (1980). Imagery, raw and cooked: A hemispheric recipe. In J. Shorr, G. Sobel, P. Robin, & J. Connella (Eds.), *Imagery* (pp. 35–53). New York: Plenum.

Banner, L. W. (1983). *American beauty.* Chicago, IL: University of Chicago Press.

Barahal, R., Waterman, J., & Martin, H. (1981). The social and cognitive development of abused children. *Journal of Consulting and Clinical Psychology, 49,* 508–516.

Barber, T. X. (1972). Suggested ("hypnotic") behavior: The trance paradigm versus an alternate paradigm. In E. Fromm & R. E. Shor (Eds.), *Hypnosis: Research developments and perspective.* New York: Aldine-Atherton.

Barber, T. X. (1978). Hypnosis, suggestions, and psychosomatic phenomena: A new look from the standpoint of recent experimental studies. *American Journal of Clinical Hypnosis, 21,* 13–27.

Barry, K. (1979). *Female sexual slavery.* New York: New York University Press.

Bates, C., & Brodsky, A. (1989). *Sex in the therapy hour.* New York: Guilford.

Bateson, G., Jackson, D., Haley, J., & Weakland, J. (1956). Toward a theory of schizophrenia. *Behavioral Science, 1*, 251–264.

Baum, E. A. (1978). Imaginary companions of two children. *Journal of the American Academy of Child Psychiatry, 49*, 324–330.

Beahrs, J. O. (1982). *Unity and multiplicity: Multilevel consciousness of self in hypnosis, psychiatric disorder, and mental health.* New York: Brunner/Mazel.

Beahrs, J. O. (1983). Co-consciousness: A common denominator in hypnosis, multiple personality, and normalcy. *American Journal of Clinical Hypnosis, 26*, 100–113.

Bennett, B. (1987). Information about your professional liability program (letter). In C. Bates & A. Brodsky, *Sex in the therapy hour.* New York: Guilford.

Benson, R. M., & Pryor, D. B. (1973). "When friends fall out": Developmental interference with the function of some imaginary companions. *Journal of the American Psychoanalytic Association, 21*, 457–473.

Berga, S. L., & Girton, L. G. (1989). Psychological status of women with functional hypothalamic amenorrhea. *Psychiatric Clinics of North America, 12*, 105–116.

Bernard, J. (1981). *The female world.* New York: The Free Press.

Bernstein, E., & Putnam, F. W. (1986). Development, reliability and validity of a dissociation scale. *Journal of Nervous and Mental Disease, 174*, 727–735.

Bettelheim, B. (1954). *Symbolic wounds: Puberty rites and the envious male.* New York: Free Press.

Blackman, J. (1989). *Intimate violence: A study of injustice.* New York: Columbia University Press.

Blank, A. S. (1985). The unconscious flashback to the war in Vietnam veterans. In S. M. Sonnenberg, A. S. Blank, & J. A. Talbot (Eds.), *Stress and recovery of Vietnam veterans.* Washington, DC: American Psychiatric Press.

Blankstein, J., Reyes, F., Winter, J., & Faiman, C. (1981). Endorphins and the regulation of the human menstrual cycle. *Clinical Endocrinology, 14*, 287–294.

Bliss, E. L. (1986). *Multiple personality, allied disorders, and hypnosis.* New York: Oxford University Press.

Bliss, E. L., & Jeppsen, E. A. (1985). Prevalence of multiple personality among inpatients and outpatients. *American Journal of Psychiatry, 142*, 250–251.

Bliss, E. L., Larson, E. M., & Nakashima, S. R. (1983). Auditory hallucinations and schizophrenia. *Journal of Nervous and Mental Disease, 171*, 30–33.

Bonaparte, M. (1951). *Female sexuality.* Paris: Press Universitaires de France.

Borysenko, J. (1984). Psychoneuroimmunology: Behavioral factors and the immune response. *ReVISION, 7*(1), 56–65.

Boskind-Lodahl, M. (1976). Cinderella's stepsisters: A feminist perspective on anorexia nervosa and bulimia. *Signs: Journal of Women in Culture and Society, 2*, 341–356.

Boskind-White, M., & White, W. (1983). *Bulimarexia: The binge/purge cycle.* New York: W. W. Norton.

Bouhoutsos, J. C., & Brodsky, A. M. (1985). Mediation in therapist-client sex: A model. *Psychotherapy: Theory, Research, and Practice, 22*, 189–193.

Bowlby, J. (1973). *Separation: Anxiety and anger.* New York: Basic.

Bowlby, J. (1977). The making and breaking of affectional bonds. *British Journal of Psychiatry, 130*, 201–210.

Bradway, K., Signell, K. A., Spare, G. H., Stewart, C. T., Stewart, L. H., & Thompson, C. (1990). *Sandplay studies: Origins, theory and practice.* Boston, MA: Sigo Press.

Braun, B. G. (1980). Hypnosis for multiple personalities. In H. Wain (Ed.), *Clinical hypnosis in medicine.* Chicago, IL: Year Book Medical.

Braun, B. G. (1983a). Neurophysiologic changes due to integration: A preliminary report. *American Journal of Clinical Hypnosis, 26,* 84–92.

Braun, B. G. (1983b). Psychophysiologic phenomena in multiple personality and hypnosis. *American Journal of Clinical Hypnosis, 26,* 124–137.

Braun, B. G. (1984). Towards a theory of multiple personality and other dissociative phenomena. *Psychiatric Clinics of North America, 7,* 171–193.

Braun, B. G. (Ed.). (1986). *Treatment of multiple personality disorder.* Washington, DC: American Psychiatric Press.

Braun, B. G. (1988). The BASK model of dissociation. *Dissociation, 1*(1), 4–23.

Braun, B. G., & Sachs, R. G. (1985). The development of multiple personality disorder: Predisposing, precipitating, and perpetuating factors. In R. P. Kluft (Ed.), *Childhood antecedents of multiple personality* (pp. 37–64). Washington, DC: American Psychiatric Press.

Brehony, K. (1983). Women and agoraphobia: A case for the etiological significance of the feminine sex-role stereotype. In V. Franks & E. Rothblum (Eds.), *The stereotyping of women: Its effects on mental health.* New York: Springer.

Brende, J. O. (1984). The psychophysiologic manifestations of dissociation. *Psychiatric Clinics of North America, 7,* 41–50.

Breuer, J., & Freud, S. (1893–1895). *Studies on hysteria.* In J. Strachey (Ed. & Trans.), *The standard edition of the complete psychological works of Sigmund Freud* (Vol. 2). New York: W. W. Norton.

Briere, J. (1989). *Therapy for adults molested as children: Beyond survival.* New York: Springer.

Briere, J., & Runtz, M. (1988). Post sexual abuse trauma. In G. E. Wyatt & G. Powell (Eds.), *Lasting effects of child sexual abuse* (pp. 85–99). Newbury Park, CA: Sage.

Brock, T. C., & Buss, A. H. (1964). Effects of justification for aggression and communication with the victim on postaggression dissonance. *Journal of Abnormal and Social Psychology, 68,* 403–412.

Broverman, I., Broverman, D., Clarkson, F., Rosenkrantz, P., & Vogel, S. (1970). Sex role stereotypes and clinical judgments of mental health. *Journal of Consulting and Clinical Psychology, 34,* 1–7.

Brown, G., & Anderson, B. (1991). Psychiatric morbidity in adult inpatients with childhood histories of sexual and physical abuse. *American Journal of Psychiatry, 148,* 55–61.

Brown, P. (1991). *The hypnotic brain: Hypnotherapy and social communication.* New Haven, CT: Yale University Press.

Browne, A., & Finkelhor, D. (1986). Initial and long-term effects: A review of the research. In D. Finkelhor (Ed.), *A sourcebook on child sexual abuse* (pp. 143–179). Beverly Hills, CA: Sage.

Brownmiller, S. (1975). *Against our will: Men, women, and rape.* New York: Simon & Schuster.

Bruch, H. (1973). *Eating disorders: Obesity, anorexia nervosa, and the person within.* New York: Basic.

Buck, R. (1986). The psychology of emotion. In J. E. LeDoux & W. Hirst (Eds.), *Mind and brain: Dialogues in cognitive neuroscience* (pp. 275–300). Cambridge, England: Cambridge University Press.

Buffery, A., & Gray, J. (1972). Sex differences in the development of spatial and linguistic skills. In C. Ounstead & D. C. Taylor (Eds.), *Gender differences: Their ontogeny and significance.* London: Churchill Livingston.

Burgess, A., & Hartman, C. (Eds.). (1986). *Sexual exploitation of patients by health professionals.* New York: Praeger.

Burgess, A. W., & Holmstrom, L. L. (1974). Rape trauma syndrome. *American Journal of Psychiatry, 131*(9), 981–986.

Burt, M. R. (1980). Cultural myths and supports for rape. *Journal of Personality and Social Psychology, 38,* 217–230.

Calabrese, J. R., Kling, M. A., & Gold, P. W. (1987). Alterations in immunocompetence during stress, bereavement, and depression: Focus on neuroendocrine regulation. *American Journal of Psychiatry, 144*(9), 1123–1134.

Calhoun, K. S., & Atkeson, B. M. (1991). *Treatment of rape victims.* New York: Pergamon Press.

Cannon, W. B. (1953). *Bodily changes in pain, hunger, fear and rage (2nd ed.).* Boston, MA: Charles T. Branford Co.

Caplan, P. J. (1985). *The myth of women's masochism.* New York: E. P. Dutton.

Caplan, P. J. (1989). *Don't blame mother: Mending the mother-daughter relationship.* New York: HarperCollins.

Carmen, E. H., Rieker, P. P., & Mills, T. (1984). Victims of violence and psychiatric illness. *American Journal of Psychiatry, 141,* 378–383.

Carmen, E. H., Russo, N. F., & Miller, J. B. (1981). Inequality and women's mental health: An overview. *American Journal of Psychiatry, 138,* 1319–1330.

Caul, D. (1984). Group and videotape techniques for multiple personality disorder. *Psychiatric Annals, 14,* 43–50.

Chambless, D., & Goldstein, A. (1980). Anxieties: Agoraphobia and hysteria. In A. Brodsky & R. Hare-Mustin (Eds.), *Women and psychotherapy* (pp. 113–134). New York: Guilford.

Chertok, L., & De Saussure, R. (1979). *The therapeutic revolution: From Mesmer to Freud.* New York: Brunner/Mazel.

Chesler, P. (1972). *Women and madness.* New York: Doubleday.

Chodoff, P. (1974). The diagnosis of hysteria: An overview. *American Journal of Psychiatry, 131,* 1073–1078.

Chodorow, N., & Contratto, S. (1982). The fantasy of the perfect mother. In B. Thorne (Ed.), *Rethinking the family: Some feminist questions.* New York: Longman.

Chu, J. A., & Dill, D. L. (1990). Dissociative symptoms in relation to childhood physical and sexual abuse. *American Journal of Psychiatry, 147*(7), 887–892.

Coons, P. M. (1984). The differential diagnosis of multiple personality: A comprehensive review. *Psychiatric Clinics of North America, 7,* 51–65.

Coons, P. M., Bowman, E. S., Pellow, T. A., & Schnieder, P. (1989). Post-traumatic aspects of the treatment of victims of sexual abuse and incest. *Psychiatric Clinics of North America, 12,* 325–335.

Coons, P., Cole, C., Pellow, T., & Milstein, V. (1990). Symptoms of posttraumatic stress and dissociation in women victims of abuse. In R. Kluft (Ed.), *Incest-related syndromes of adult psychopathology* (pp. 205–221). Washington, DC: American Psychiatric Press.

Corballis, M. C. (1991). *The lopsided ape: Evolution of the generative mind.* New York: Oxford University Press.

Courtois, C. (1988). *Healing the incest wound: Adult survivors in therapy.* New York: W. W. Norton.

Crewdson, J. (1988). *By silence betrayed: Sexual abuse of children in America.* New York: HarperCollins.

Davidson, T. (1977). Wifebeating: A recurring phenomenon throughout history. In M. Roy (Ed.), *Battered women: A psychosociological study of domestic violence.* New York: Van Nostrand Reinhold.

Demitrack, M., Putnam, F., Brewerton, T., Brandt, H., & Gold, P. (1990). Relation of clinical variables to dissociative phenomena in eating disorders. *American Journal of Psychiatry, 147*, 1184–1188.

DeSalvo, L. (1989). *Virginia Woolf: The impact of childhood sexual abuse on her life and work.* Boston, MA: Beacon Press.

Deutsch, H. (1930). The significance of masochism in the mental life of women. *International Journal of Psycho-analysis, 11*, 48–60.

Deutsch, H. (1942). Some forms of emotional disturbance and their relationship to schizophrenia. *Psychoanalytic Quarterly, 11*, 301–321.

Dickes, R. (1965). The defensive function of an altered state of consciousness: A hypnoid state. *Journal of the American Psychoanalytic Association, 13*, 356–403.

Dinnerstein, D. (1976). *The mermaid and the minotaur: Sexual arrangements and human malaise.* New York: Harper & Row.

Dobash, R. E., & Dobash, R. (1979). *Violence against wives.* New York: Free Press.

Dolan, Y. M. (1991). *Resolving sexual abuse: Solution-focused therapy and Ericksonian hypnosis for adult survivors.* New York: W. W. Norton.

Dorpat, T. L. (1976). Structural conflict and object relations conflict. *Journal of the American Psychoanalytic Association, 24*, 855–874.

Dumas, R. A. (1977). EEG alpha-hypnotizability correlations: A review. *Psychophysiology, 14*(5), 431–438.

du Maurier, G. (1894). *Trilby.* New York: Harper & Brothers.

Dworkin, A. (1981). *Pornography: Men possessing women.* New York: E. P. Dutton.

Ebert, B. W. (1988). Hypnosis and rape victims. *American Journal of Clinical Hypnosis, 31*, 50–56.

Egeland, B., & Sroufe, A. (1981). Developmental sequelae of maltreatment in infancy. In R. Rizly & D. Cicchetti (Eds.), *New directions in child development: Developmental perspectives on child maltreatment.* San Francisco: Jossey-Bass.

Ehrenreich, B., & English, D. (1973). *Complaints and disorders: The sexual politics of sickness.* New York: Feminist Press.

Ehrenreich, B., & English, D. (1978). *For her own good: 150 years of the experts' advice to women.* Garden City, NY: Anchor Press/Doubleday.

Ellenberger, H. F. (1970). *The discovery of the unconscious.* New York: Basic.

Ellis, E. M., Atkeson, B. M., & Calhoun, K. S. (1982). An examination of differences between multiple- and single-incident victims of sexual assault. *Journal of Abnormal Psychology, 91*, 221–224.

Erikson, E. H. (1980/59). *Identity and the life cycle.* New York: W. W. Norton.

Eth, S., & Pynoos, R. S. (Eds.). (1985). *Post-traumatic stress disorder in children.* Washington, DC: American Psychiatric Press.

Fair, C. M. (1988). *Memory and central nervous organization.* New York: Paragon House.

Faludi, S. (1991). *Backlash: The undeclared war against American women.* New York: Crown.

Fausto-Sterling, A. (1985). *Myths of gender.* New York: Basic.

Favazza, A. R. (1987). *Bodies under siege: Self-mutilation in culture and psychiatry.* Baltimore, MD: Johns Hopkins University Press.

Ferenczi, S. (1932). Confusion of tongues between adults and the child: The language of tenderness and the language of (sexual) passion. In J. M. Masson (1984), *The assault on truth: Freud's suppression of the seduction theory* (pp. 283–295). New York: Farrar, Straus, & Giroux.

Fine, C. G. (1988). The work of Antoine Despine: The first scientific report on the diagnosis and treatment of a child with multiple personality disorder. *American Journal of Clinical Hypnosis, 31*, 33–38.

Finkelhor, D. (1979). *Sexually victimized children.* New York: Free Press.

Finkelhor, D. (1984). *Child sexual abuse: New theory and research.* New York: Free Press.

Finkelhor, D. (1988). The trauma of child sexual abuse: Two models. In G. E. Wyatt & G. J. Powell (Eds.), *Lasting effects of child sexual abuse* (pp. 61–82). Newbury Park, CA: Sage.

Finkelhor, D. & associates (1986). *A sourcebook on child sexual abuse.* Beverly Hills, CA: Sage.

Fishman, S. (1991). See no evil: Lingering shadows from the Cambodian killing fields. *American Health* (July–August), 78–85.

Fliess, R. (1953). The hypnotic evasion: A clinical observation. *The Psychoanalytic Quarterly, 22,* 497–511.

Fodor, I. (1974). The phobic syndrome in women. In V. Franks & V. Burtle (Eds.), *Women in therapy.* New York: Brunner/Mazel.

Frankel, F. H. (1990). Hypnotizability and dissociation. *American Journal of Psychiatry, 147*(7), 823–829.

Franks, V., & Rothblum, E. (1983). *The stereotyping of women: Its effects on mental health.* New York: Springer.

Freedman, R. (1986). *Beauty bound.* Lexington, MA: Lexington Books.

Freud, A. (1966). *The writings of Anna Freud, Volume II, 1936: The ego and the mechanisms of defense (rev. ed.).* New York: International Universities Press.

Freud, A., & Burlingham, D. (1942). *War and children.* New York: International Universities Press.

Freud, S. (1896). The aetiology of hysteria. In J. Strachey (Ed. & Trans.), *The standard edition of the complete psychological works of Sigmund Freud* (Vol. 3, 191–221). New York: W. W. Norton.

Freud, S. (1917 [1915]). Mourning and melancholia. In J. Strachey (Ed. & Trans.), *The standard edition of the complete psychological works of Sigmund Freud* (Vol. 14, 237–258). New York: W. W. Norton.

Freud, S. (1919). A child is being beaten. In J. Strachey (Ed. & Trans.), *The standard edition of the complete psychological works of Sigmund Freud* (Vol. 17, 179–204). New York: W. W. Norton.

Freud, S. (1921). Group psychology and the analysis of the ego. In J. Strachey (Ed. & Trans.), *The standard edition of the complete psychological works of Sigmund Freud* (Vol. 18, 65–143). New York: W. W. Norton.

Freud, S. (1933 [1932]). Femininity. In J. Strachey (Ed. & Trans.), *The standard edition of the complete psychological works of Sigmund Freud* (Vol. 22, 112–135). New York: W. W. Norton.

Freud, S. (1940 [1938]). Splitting of the ego in the process of defense. In J. Strachey (Ed. & Trans.), *The standard edition of the complete psychological works of Sigmund Freud* (Vol. 23, 273–278). New York: W. W. Norton.

Friedan, B. (1963). *The feminine mystique.* New York: W. W. Norton.

Frischholz, E. J. (1985). The relationship among dissociation, hypnosis, and child abuse in the development of multiple personality disorder. In R. P. Kluft (Ed.), *Childhood antecedents of multiple personality* (pp. 99–126). Washington, DC: American Psychiatric Press.

Fromm, E. (1941). *Escape from freedom.* New York: Farrar & Rinehart.

Galanter, M. (Ed.). (1989). *Cults and new religious movements: A report of the American Psychiatric Association.* Washington, DC: American Psychiatric Association.

Garfinkel, P. E., & Garner, D. M. (1982). *Anorexia nervosa: A multidimensional perspective.* New York: Brunner/Mazel.

Gazzaniga, M. S. (1985). *The social brain: Discovering the networks of the mind.* New York: Basic.

Geen, R. G. (1990). *Human aggression*. Pacific Grove, CA: Brooks/Cole.

Gelles, R., & Cornell, C. (1990). *Intimate violence in families*. Newbury Park, CA: Sage.

Geschwind, N. (1979). Asymmetries of the brain—New developments. *Bulletin of the Orton Society, 29*, 67–73.

Geschwind, N., & Galaburda, A. M. (1987). *Cerebral lateralization: Biological mechanisms, associations, and pathology*. Cambridge, MA: MIT Press.

Giarretto, H. (1982). A comprehensive child sexual abuse treatment program. *Child Abuse and Neglect, 6*, 263–278.

Gil, E. (1991). *The healing power of play*. New York: Guilford.

Gillespie, W. H. (1940). A contribution to the study of fetishism. *International Journal of Psycho-analysis, 21*, 401–415.

Girard, R. (1977). *Violence and the sacred*. Baltimore, MD: Johns Hopkins University Press.

Goddard, C. V., McIntyre, D. C., & Leech, C. K. (1969). A permanent change in brain functioning resulting from daily electrical stimulation. *Experimental Neurology, 25*, 295–330.

Goldfarb, L. (1987). Sexual abuse antecedent to anorexia nervosa, bulimia, and compulsive overeating: Three case reports. *International Journal of Eating Disorders, 6*, 675–680.

Gomes-Schwartz, B., Horowitz, J., & Sauzier, M. (1985). Severity of emotional distress among sexually abused preschool, school-age and adolescent children. *Hospital and Community Psychiatry, 36*(5), 503–508.

Goodwin, J. M. (1990). Applying to adult incest victims what we have learned from victimized children. In R. Kluft (Ed.), *Incest-related syndromes of adult psychopathology* (pp. 55–74). Washington, DC: American Psychiatric Press.

Goodwin, J., & Attias, R. (1988). Eating disorder as a multimodal response to child abuse. In B. G. Braun (Ed.), *Proceedings of the fifth international conference on multiple personality/dissociative states* (p. 29). Chicago, IL: Rush-Presbyterian-St. Luke's Medical Center.

Gove, W., & Hughes, M. (1979). Possible causes of the apparent sex differences in physical health: An empirical investigation. *American Sociological Review, 44*, 126–146.

Graff, H., & Mallin, R. (1967). The syndrome of the wrist cutter. *American Journal of Psychiatry, 124*, 36–42.

Greaves, G. B. (1992). Alternative hypotheses regarding claims of satanic cult activity: A critical analysis. In D. K. Sakheim & S. E. Devine (Eds.), *Out of darkness: Exploring satanism and ritual abuse*. New York: Lexington Books.

Green, A. (1985). Children traumatized by physical abuse. In S. Eth & R. Pynoos (Eds.), *Post-traumatic stress disorder in children* (pp. 135–154). Washington, DC: American Psychiatric Press.

Greenacre, P. (1953). Certain relationships between fetishism and the faulty development of the body image. In P. Greenacre, *Emotional growth: Psychoanalytic studies of the gifted and a great variety of other individuals*, Vol. 1 (pp. 9–30). New York: International Universities Press.

Greenacre, P. (1970). The transitional object and the fetish: With special reference to the role of illusion. In P. Greenacre, *Emotional growth: Psychoanalytic studies of the gifted and a great variety of other individuals*, Vol. 2 (pp. 335–352). New York: International Universities Press.

Greenberg, J. (as Hannah Green) (1968). *I never promised you a rose garden*. New York: Penguin.

Greenspan, G., & Samuel, S. (1989). Self-cutting after rape. *American Journal of Psychiatry, 146*, 789–790.

Groth, N. (1979). *Men who rape: The psychology of the offender.* New York: Plenum.

Gruzelier, J., Thomas, M., Brow, T., & Conway, A. (1987). Involvement of the left hemisphere in hypnotic induction: Electrodermal haptic electrocortical and divided visual field evidence. *Advances in Biological Psychiatry, 16,* 6–17.

Gunderson, J. (1984). *Borderline personality disorder.* Washington, DC: American Psychiatric Press.

Gunderson, J. G., & Singer, M. T. (1975). Defining borderline patients: An overview. *American Journal of Psychiatry, 132,* 1–10.

Hannah, B. (1981). *Encounters with the soul: Active imagination as developed by C. G. Jung.* Boston: Sigo Press.

Harris, P. L. (1989). *Children and emotion: The development of psychological understanding.* Oxford, England: Basil Blackwell.

Hartman, C. R., & Burgess, A. W. (1988). Rape trauma and treatment of the victim. In F. M. Ochberg (Ed.), *Post-traumatic therapy and victims of violence* (pp. 152–174). New York: Brunner/Mazel.

Haule, J. R. (1986). Pierre Janet and dissociation: The first transference theory and its origins in hypnosis. *American Journal of Clinical Hypnosis, 29,* 86–94.

Hebb, D. O. (1949). *The organization of behavior: A neuropsychological theory.* New York: Wiley.

Herman, J. (1981). *Father-daughter incest.* Cambridge, MA: Harvard University Press.

Herman, J. (1986). Histories of violence in an outpatient population. *American Journal of Orthopsychiatry, 57,* 137–141.

Herman, J. (1992). *Trauma and recovery: The aftermath of violence—from domestic abuse to political terror.* New York: Basic.

Herman, J., & van der Kolk, B. (1987). Traumatic antecedents of borderline personality disorder. In B. A. van der Kolk (Ed.), *Psychological trauma* (pp. 111–126). Washington, DC: American Psychiatric Press.

Hilberman, E. (1980). Overview: The "wife-beater's wife" reconsidered. *American Journal of Psychiatry, 137,* 1336–1347.

Hilberman, E., & Munson, K. (1977–1978). Sixty battered women. *Victimology: An International Journal, 2,* 460–470.

Hilgard, E. R. (1986). *Divided consciousness: Multiple controls in human thought and action.* New York: Wiley.

Hilgard, J. R. (1979). *Personality and hypnosis: A study of imaginative involvement.* Chicago, IL: The University of Chicago Press.

Holden, G. W., & Ritchie, K. L. (1991). Linking extreme marital discord, child rearing, and behavior problems: Evidence from battered women. *Child Development, 62,* 311–327.

Holmes, T. H., & Rahe, R. H. (1967). The social readjustment rating scale. *Journal of Psychomatic Research, 11,* 213–218.

Holroyd, J., & Brodsky, A. M. (1977). Psychologists' attitudes and practices regarding erotic and nonerotic physical contact with patients. *American Psychologist, 32,* 843–849.

Horner, M. S. (1968). *Sex differences in achievement motivation and performance in competitive and non-competitive situations.* Unpublished doctoral dissertation, University of Michigan.

Horner, M. S. (1972). Toward an understanding of achievement-related conflicts in women. *Journal of Social Issues, 28,* 157–175.

Horowitz, M. J. (1976). *Stress response syndromes.* New York: Jason Aronson.

Howard, M. (1989). *The occult conspiracy: Secret societies—their influence and power in world history.* Rochester, VT: Destiny Books.

Hrdy, S. B. (1981). *The woman that never evolved.* Cambridge, MA: Harvard University Press.

Jackson, R. L., Maier, S. F., & Coon, D. J. (1979). Long-term analgesic effects of inescapable shock and learned helplessness. *Science, 206,* 91–93.

James, W. (1982/1902). *The varieties of religious experience.* New York: Penguin.

James, W. (1983/1890). *The principles of psychology.* Cambridge, MA: Harvard University Press.

Janoff-Bulman, R. (1985). The aftermath of victimization: Rebuilding shattered assumptions. In C. R. Figley (Ed.), *Trauma and its wake: The study and treatment of post-traumatic stress disorder, Vol. 1* (pp. 15–35). New York: Brunner/Mazel.

Jaynes, J. (1976). *The origin of consciousness in the breakdown of the bicameral mind.* Boston: Houghton Mifflin.

Jung, C. G. (1961). *Memories, dreams, reflections.* New York: Pantheon.

Kagan, J. (1984). *The nature of the child.* New York: Basic.

Kaplan, M. (1983). A woman's view of DSM-III. *American Psychologist, 38,* 786–792.

Kaplan, M. (1984). Anna O. and Bertha Pappenheim: An historical perspective. In M. Rosenbaum & M. Muroff (Eds.), *Anna O.: Fourteen contemporary reinterpretations* (pp. 101–117). New York: Free Press.

Kardener, S. H., Fuller, M., & Mensh, I. V. (1973). A survey of physicians' attitudes and practices regarding erotic and nonerotic contact with patients. *American Journal of Psychiatry, 130*(10), 1077–1081.

Kardiner, A. (1941). *The traumatic neurosis of war.* (Psychosomatic Medicine Monographs 2-3). New York: Paul B. Hoeber.

Katchen, M. H., & Sakheim, D. K. (1992). Satanic beliefs and practices. In D. K. Sakheim & S. E. Devine (Eds.), *Out of darkness: Exploring satanism and ritual abuse.* New York: Lexington Books.

Keane, T. M., & Kaloupek, D. G. (1982). Imaginal flooding in the treatment of post-traumatic stress disorder. *Journal of Consulting and Clinical Psychology, 50,* 138–140.

Kennedy, S., Glaser, R., & Kiecolt-Glaser, J. (1990). Psychoneuroimmunology. In J. T. Cacioppo & L. G. Tassinary (Eds.), *Principles of psychophysiology: Physical, social, and inferential elements.* Cambridge, England: Cambridge University Press.

Kernberg, O. (1967). Borderline personality organization. *Journal of the American Psychoanalytic Association, 15,* 641–685.

Kernberg, O. (1975). *Borderline conditions and pathological narcissism.* New York: Jason Aronson.

Kiecolt-Glaser, J. K., Garner, W., Speicher, C., Penn, G. M., Holliday, J., & Glaser, R. (1984). Psychosocial modifiers of immunocompetence in medical students. *Psychomatic Medicine, 46,* 7–14.

Kilbourne, J. (1990). "The naked truth: Advertising's image of women." Lecture and slide show presentation, Dec. 7, Ann Arbor, Michigan.

Kilpatrick, D. G., Veronen, L. J., & Best, C. L. (1985). Factors predicting psychological distress among rape victims. In C. R. Figley (Ed.), *Trauma and its wake: The study and treatment of post-traumatic stress disorder, Vol. 1* (pp. 113–141). New York: Brunner/Mazel.

Kinard, E. M. (1980). Emotional development in physically abused children. *American Journal of Orthopsychiatry, 50,* 686–696.

Kinard, E. M. (1982). Emotional development in physically abused children. *American Journal of Orthopsychiatry, 52,* 82–91.

Kinsey, A., Pomeroy, W., Martin, C., & Gebhard, P. (1953). *Sexual behavior in the human female.* Philadelphia: Saunders.

Kluft, R. P. (1984). Treatment of multiple personality disorder: A study of 33 cases. *Psychiatric Clinics of North America, 7,* 9–29.

Kluft, R. P. (Ed.). (1985). *Childhood antecedents of multiple personality disorder.* Washington, DC: American Psychiatric Press.

Kluft, R. (1987). First-rank symptoms as a diagnostic clue to multiple personality disorder. *American Journal of Psychiatry, 144,* 293–298.

Kohut, H. (1971). *The analysis of the self: A systematic approach to the psychoanalytic treatment of narcissistic personality disorders.* New York: International Universities Press.

Kohut, H. (1977). *The restoration of the self.* New York: International Universities Press.

Koss, M. (1985). The hidden rape victim: Personality, attitudinal, and situational characteristics. *Psychology of Women Quarterly, 9,* 193–212.

Krohn, A. (1978). *Hysteria: The elusive neurosis.* New York: International Universities Press.

Krystal, J. H. (1990). Animal models for posttraumatic stress disorder. In E. L. Giller (Ed.), *Biological assessment and treatment of posttraumatic stress disorder* (pp. 3–26). Washington, DC: American Psychiatric Press.

Kulka, R. A., Schlenger, W. E., Fairbank, J. A., Hough, R. L., Jordan, B. K., Marmar, C. R., & Weiss, D. S. (1990). *Trauma and the Vietnam War generation.* New York: Brunner/Mazel.

Kurz, D., & Stark, E. (1987). Health education and feminist strategy. In K. Yllo & M. Bograd (Eds.), *Feminist perspectives on wife abuse.* Beverly Hills, CA: Sage.

Laudenslager, M. L., Ryan, S. M., Drugan, R. C., Hyson, R. L., & Maier, S. F. (1983). Coping and immunosuppression: Inescapable but not escapable shock suppresses lymphocyte proliferation. *Science, 221,* 568–570.

Laufer, R. S., Frey-Wouters, E., & Gallops, M. S. (1985). Traumatic stressors in the Vietnam War and post-traumatic stress disorder. In C. R. Figley (Ed.), *Trauma and its wake: The study and treatment of post-traumatic stress disorder, Vol. 1* (pp. 73–89). New York: Brunner/Mazel.

Leehan, J., & Wilson, L. (1985). *Grown-up abused children.* Springfield, IL: Charles C. Thomas.

Lerner, G. (1986). *The creation of patriarchy.* New York: Oxford University Press.

Lerner, H. E. (1974). Early origins of envy and devaluation of women: Implications for sex-role stereotypes. *Bulletin of the Menninger Clinic, 38,* 538–553.

Lerner, H. E. (1982). Special issues for women in psychotherapy. In M. T. Notman & C. C. Nadelson (Eds.), *The woman patient, Vol. 3: Aggression, adaptations, and psychotherapy* (pp. 273–286). New York: Plenum.

Lerner, H. E. (1983). Female dependency in context: Some theoretical and technical considerations. *American Journal of Orthopsychiatry, 53,* 697–705.

Levy, J. (1972). Lateral specialization of the human brain: Behavioral manifestations and possible evolutionary basis. In J. Kiger (Ed.), *The biology of behavior.* Eugene: Oregon State University Press.

Lidz, T. (1973). *The origin and treatment of schizophrenic disorders.* New York: Basic.

Lidz, T., & Fleck, S. (Eds.). (1985). *Schizophrenia and the family.* New York: International Universities Press.

Lifton, R. J. (1967). *Death in life: Survivors of Hiroshima.* New York: Simon & Schuster.

Locke, S. (1982). Stress, adaptation, and immunity: studies in humans. *General Hospital Psychiatry, 4,* 49–58.

Locke, S. E., Kraus, L., Leserman, J., Hurst, M. W., Heisel, S., & Williams, R. M. (1984). Life-change stress, psychiatric symptoms, and natural killer cell activity. *Psychosomatic Medicine, 46,* 441–453.

Loewenstein, R. J. (1990). Somatoform disorders in victims of incest and child abuse. In R. P. Kluft (Ed.), *Incest-related syndromes of adult psychopathology* (pp. 75–107). Washington, DC: American Psychiatric Press.

Lowenfeld, M. (1979). *The world technique*. London: George Allen & Unwin.

Ludwig, A. M. (1983). The psychobiological function of dissociation. *American Journal of Clinical Hypnosis, 26*, 93–99.

Ludwig, A., Brandsma, J., Wilbur, C., Bernfeldt, F., & Jameson, H. (1972). The objective study of a multiple personality. *Archives of General Psychiatry, 26*, 298–310.

Maccoby, E. E., & Jacklin, E. N. (1974). *The psychology of sex differences*. Stanford, CA: Stanford University Press.

MacKinnon, C. A. (1989). *Toward a feminist theory of the state*. Cambridge, MA: Harvard University Press.

MacLean, P. D. (1990). *The triune brain in evolution: Role in paleocerebral functions*. New York: Plenum.

Mahler, M. (1968). *On human symbiosis and the vicissitudes of individuation*. New York: International Universities Press.

Mahler, M. S., Pine, F., & Bergman, A. (1975). *The psychological birth of the human infant: Symbiosis and individuation*. New York: Basic.

Maier, N. R. F. (1949). *Frustration: The study of behavior without a goal*. New York: McGraw-Hill.

Masson, J. M. (1984). *The assault on truth: Freud's suppression of the seduction theory*. New York: Farrar, Straus & Giroux.

Masterson, J., & Rinsley, D. (1975). The borderline syndrome: The role of the mother in the genesis and psychic structure of the borderline personality. *International Journal of Psycho-analysis, 56*, 163–177.

Matthew, R. J., & Wilson, W. H. (1990). Anxiety and cerebral blood flow. *American Journal of Psychiatry, 147*, 838–849.

McGoldrick, M. (1989). Women through the family life cycle. In M. McGoldrick, C. M. Anderson, & F. Walsh (Eds.), *Women in families* (pp. 200–226). New York: W. W. Norton.

McGrath, E., Keita, G. P., Strickland, B. R., & Russo, N. F. (Eds.). (1990). *Women and depression: Risk factors and treatment issues*. Washington, DC: American Psychological Association.

Miczek, K. A., Thompson, M. L., & Shuster, L. (1982). Opioid-like analgesia in defeated mice. *Science, 215*, 1520–1522.

Miller, A. (1984). *Thou shalt not be aware: Society's betrayal of the child*. New York: Farrar, Straus & Giroux.

Miller, J. B. (1976). *Toward a new psychology of women*. Boston: Beacon Press.

Miller, J. B. (1978). The effects of inequality on psychology. *Psychiatric Opinion, 15*, 29–32.

Millett, K. (1969). *Sexual politics*. New York: Doubleday.

Montgomery, E., Fenton, G., McClelland, R., MacFlynn, G., & Rutherford, W. (1991). The psychobiology of minor head injury. *Psychological Medicine, 21*, 375–384.

Moore, E. (1980). *Women and health, United States, 1980*. Washington, DC: Public Health Report.

Morgan, R. (1989). *The demon lover: On the sexuality of terrorism*. New York: W. W. Norton.

Muehlenhard, C. L. (1983). Women's assertion and the feminine sex-role stereotype. In V. Franks & E. D. Rothblum (Eds.), *The stereotyping of women* (pp. 153–171). New York: Springer.

Mulvihill, D. J., & Tumin, M. M. (1969). *Crimes of violence: A staff report submitted to the national commission on the causes and prevention of violence.* Washington, DC: U. S. Government Printing Office.

Murburg, M. M., McFall, M. E., & Veith, R. C. (1990). Catecholamines, stress, and posttraumatic stress disorder. In E. L. Giller (Ed.), *Biological assessment and treatment of posttraumatic stress disorder* (pp. 29-64). Washington, DC: American Psychiatric Press.

Murphy, S. M., Kilpatrick, D. G., Amick-McMullan, A., Veronen, L., Paduhovich, J., Best, C. L., Villenponteauz, L. A., & Saunders, B. E. (1988). Current psychological functioning of child sexual assault survivors. *Journal of Interpersonal Violence, 3,* 55-79.

Nader, K., Pynoos, R., Fairbanks, L., & Frederick, C. (1990). Children's PTSD reactions one year after a sniper attack at their school. *American Journal of Psychiatry, 147*(11), 1526-1530.

Nagera, H. (1969). The imaginary companion: Its significance for ego development and conflict solution. *Psychoanalytic Study of the Child, 24,* 165-196.

Nelson, S. H., & Grunebaum, H. (1971). A follow-up study of wrist slashers. *American Journal of Psychiatry, 127,* 1345-1349.

Nolen-Hoeksema, S. (1987). Sex differences in unipolar depression: Evidence and theory. *Psychological Bulletin, 101,* 259-282.

Nolen-Hoeksema, S. (1990). *Sex differences in depression.* Stanford, CA: Stanford University Press.

Ochberg, F. M. (1980). Victims of terrorism. *Journal of Clinical Psychiatry, 41,* 73-74.

Ochberg, F. M. (1988). Post-traumatic therapy and victims of violence. In F. M. Ochberg (Ed.), *Post-traumatic therapy and victims of violence* (pp. 3-19). New York: Brunner/Mazel.

Ogata, S., Silk, K., Goodrich, S., Lohr, N., Weston, D., & Hill, E. (1990). Childhood sexual and physical abuse in adult patients with borderline personality disorder. *American Journal of Psychiatry, 147,* 1008-1013.

Okun, L. (1986). *Woman abuse: Facts replacing myths.* New York: State University of New York Press.

Orbach, S. (1978). *Fat is a feminist issue: The anti-diet guide to permanent weight loss.* New York: Berkley Books.

Orbach, S. (1986). *Hunger strike: The anorectic's struggle as a metaphor for our age.* New York: W. W. Norton.

Orne, M. T. (1959). The nature of hypnosis: Artifact and essence. *Journal of Abnormal and Social Psychology, 58,* 277-299.

Parkin, A. J. (1987). *Memory and amnesia: An introduction.* Oxford, England: Basil Blackwell.

Pattison, E. M., & Kahan, J. (1983). The deliberate self-harm syndrome. *American Journal of Psychiatry, 140,* 867-872.

Paykel, E., Myers, J., Dienelt, M., Klerman, G., Lindenthal, J., & Pepper, M. (1969). Life events and depression: A controlled study. *Archives of General Psychiatry, 21,* 753-760.

Payne, S. (1939). Some observations on the ego development of the fetishist. *International Journal of Psycho-analysis, 20,* 161-170.

Pelletier, K. R., & Herzing, D. L. (1988). Psychoneuroimmunology: Toward a mind body model: A critical review. *Advances, 5*(1), 27-56.

Peters, E. (1988). *Inquisition.* Berkeley, CA: The Free Press.

Piers, E., & Harris, D. (1969). The Piers-Harris children's self-concept scale. Nashville, TN: Counselor Recordings and Tests.

Plath, S. (1971). *The bell jar.* New York: Harper & Row.

Pleck, E. (1987). *Domestic tyranny: The making of American social policy against family violence from colonial times to the present.* New York: Oxford University Press.

Plotnikoff, N. P. (1986). *Enkephalins and endorphins: Stress and the immune system.* New York: Plenum.

Prince, M. (1978/1906). *The dissociation of a personality: The hunt for the real Miss Beauchamp.* Oxford, England: Oxford University Press.

Putnam, F. W. (1984). The psychophysiologic investigation of multiple personality disorder. *Psychiatric Clinics of North America, 7,* 31–39.

Putnam, F. W. (1986). The treatment of multiple personality: State of the art. In B. Braun (Ed.), *Treatment of multiple personality disorder* (pp. 175–198). Washington, DC: American Psychiatric Press.

Putnam, F. W. (1989). *Diagnosis and treatment of multiple personality disorder.* New York: Guilford.

Putnam, F. W. (1990). Disturbances of "self" in victims of childhood sexual abuse. In R. P. Kluft (Ed.), *Incest-related syndromes of adult psychopathology* (pp. 113–131). Washington, DC: American Psychiatric Press.

Putnam, F. W., Guroff, J. J., Silberman, E. K., Barban, L., & Post, R. M. (1986). The clinical phenomenology of multiple personality disorder: A review of 100 recent cases. *Journal of Clinical Psychiatry, 47,* 285–293.

Randall, J. (1992). ACOG renews domestic violence campaign, calls for changes in medical school curricula. *Journal of the American Medical Association, 267,* 3131.

Raschke, C. A. (1990). *Painted black.* New York: HarperCollins.

Resick, P. (1983). Sex-role stereotypes and violence against women. In V. Franks & E. Rothblum (Eds.), *The stereotyping of women: Its effects on mental health* (pp. 230–256). New York: Springer.

Reynolds, C. F. (1989). Sleep disturbance in posttraumatic stress disorder: Pathogenic or epiphenomenal. *American Journal of Psychiatry, 146*(6), 695–696.

Rivera, M. (1987). Multiple personality: An outcome of child abuse. *Canadian Women Studies, 8,* 18–23.

Rivera, M. (1988). *All of them to speak: Feminism, poststructuralism, and multiple personality.* Unpublished doctoral dissertation, University of Toronto, Toronto.

Rose, R. M. (1980). Endocrine responses to stressful psychological events. *Psychiatric Clinics of North America, 3,* 251–276.

Rosenbaum, M. (1984). Anna O. (Bertha Pappenheim): Her history. In M. Rosenbaum & M. Muroff (Eds.), *Anna O.: Fourteen contemporary reinterpretations.* New York: Free Press.

Rosenfeld, A. (1979). Incidence of a history of incest among 18 female psychiatric patients. *American Journal of Psychiatry, 136,* 791–795.

Rosenthal, R. J., Rinzler, C., Walsh, R., & Klausner, E. (1972). Wrist-cutting syndrome: The meaning of a gesture. *American Journal of Psychiatry, 128,* 1363–1368.

Ross, C. A. (1989). *Multiple personality disorder: Diagnosis, clinical features, and treatment.* New York: Wiley.

Ross, R. J., Ball, W. A., Sullivan, K. A., & Caroff, S. N. (1989). Sleep disturbance as the hallmark of posttraumatic stress disorder. *American Journal of Psychiatry, 146*(6), 697–707.

Rossi, A. (1981). On the reproduction of mothering: A methodological debate. *Signs: Journal of Women in Culture and Society, 6,* 492–500.

Rossi, E. L. (1986). *The psychobiology of mind-body healing: New concepts of therapeutic hypnosis.* New York: W. W. Norton.

Rossi, E. L., & Cheek, D. B. (1988). *Mind-body therapy: Methods of ideodynamic healing in hypnosis.* New York: W. W. Norton.

Roth, S., & Leibowitz, L. (1988). The experiences of sexual trauma. *Journal of Traumatic Stress, 1*, 79–108.

Rouget, G. (1985). *Music and trance: A theory of the relations between music and possession*. Chicago, IL: University of Chicago Press.

Roustang, F. (1976). *Dire mastery: Discipleship from Freud to Lacan* (Trans., N. Lukacher). Baltimore, MD: Johns Hopkins University Press.

Runtz, M. (1987). The psychosocial adjustment of women who were sexually and physically abused during childhood and early adulthood: A focus on revictimization. Unpublished master's thesis, University of Manitoba, Canada.

Rush, F. (1980). *The best kept secret: Sexual abuse of children*. New York: McGraw-Hill.

Russell, D. E. (1982). *Rape in marriage*. Bloomington: Indiana University Press.

Russell, D. E. (1984). *Sexual exploitation: Rape, child sexual abuse and workplace harassment*. Newbury Park, CA: Sage.

Russell, J. B. (1972). *Witchcraft in the middle ages*. Ithaca, NY: Cornell University Press.

Russo, N., & Olmedo, E. (1983). Women's utilization of outpatient psychiatric services: Some emerging priorities for rehabilitation psychologists. *Rehabilitation Psychology, 28*, 4–23.

Ryan, W. (1976). *Blaming the victim (rev. ed.)*. New York: Vintage Press.

Sabourin, M. E., Cutcomb, S. D., Crawford, H. J., & Pribram, K. (1990). EEG correlates of hypnotic susceptibility and hypnotic trance: Spectral analysis and coherence. *International Journal of Psychophysiology, 10*, 125–142.

Sakheim, D. K., & Devine, S. E. (Eds.). (1992). *Out of darkness: Exploring satanism and ritual abuse*. New York: Lexington Books.

Sarbin, T., & Coe, W. (1972). *Hypnosis: A social psychological analysis of influence communication*. New York: Holt, Rinehart, & Winston.

Schacter, D., Wang, P., Tulving, E., & Freedman, M. (1982). Functional retrograde amnesia: A quantitative case study. *Neuropsychologia, 20*, 523–532.

Schechter, S. (1982). *Women and male violence: The visions and struggles of the battered women's movement*. Boston: South End Press.

Schecter, J., Schwartz, H., & Greenfield, D. (1987). Sexual assault and anorexia nervosa. *International Journal of Eating Disorders, 6*, 313–316.

Schill, T. R., & Schneider, L. (1970). Relationships between hostility guilt and several measures of hostility. *Psychological Reports, 27*, 967–970.

Schreiber, F. R. (1973). *Sybil*. New York: Warner Books.

Sedney, M. A., & Brooks, B. (1984). Factors associated with a history of childhood sexual experiences in a nonclinical female population. *Journal of the American Academy of Child Psychiatry, 23*, 215–218.

Seid, R. P. (1989). *Never too thin: Why women are at war with their bodies*. New York: Prentice Hall.

Seligman, M. E. (1975). *Helplessness: On depression, development, and death*. New York: W. H. Freeman.

Seligman, M. (1991). *Learned optimism*. New York: A. A. Knopf.

Selye, H. (1956). *The stress of life*. New York: McGraw-Hill.

Shavit, Y., Lewis, J. W., Terman, G. W., Gale, R. P., & Liebeskind (1984). Opioid peptides mediate the suppressive effect of stress on natural killer cell cytotoxicity. *Science, 223*, 188–190.

Shearer, S., Peters, C., Quaytman, M., & Ogden, R. (1990). Frequency and correlates of childhood sexual and physical abuse histories in adult female borderline inpatients. *American Journal of Psychiatry, 147*, 214–216.

Shengold, L. (1989). *Soul murder: The effects of childhood abuse and deprivation*. New York: Ballantine.

Shirk, S. R. (1988). The interpersonal legacy of physical abuse of children. In M. B. Straus (Ed.), *Abuse and victimization across the life span*. Baltimore, MD: Johns Hopkins University Press.

Simpson, C. A., & Porter, G. L. (1981). Self-mutilation in children and adolescents. *Bulletin of the Menninger Clinic, 45,* 428–438.

Simpson, M. A. (1975). Symposium—self injury: The phenomenology of self-mutilation in a general hospital setting. Reported in A. R. Favazza (1987), *Bodies under siege: Self-mutilation in culture and psychiatry*. Baltimore, MD: Johns Hopkins University Press.

Sink, F. (1988). Sexual abuse in the lives of children. In M. B. Straus (Ed.), *Abuse and victimization across the life span* (pp. 82–106). Baltimore, MD: Johns Hopkins University Press.

Sperry, R. W. (1973). Lateral specialization of cerebral function in the surgically separated hemispheres. In F. O. Schmitt & F. G. Worden (Eds.), *The neurosciences: Third study program* (pp. 5–19). Cambridge, MA: MIT Press.

Spiegel, D. (1986). Dissociation, double binds, and posttraumatic stress in multiple personality disorder. In B. G. Braun (Ed.), *Treatment of multiple personality disorder* (pp. 63–77). Washington, DC: American Psychiatric Press.

Spiegel, H., & Spiegel, D. (1978). *Trance and treatment: Clinical uses of hypnosis*. Washington, DC: American Psychiatric Press.

Spitz, R. A. (1945). Hospitalism. *The Psychoanalytic Study of the Child, I.* New York: International Universities Press.

Spitz, R. A. (1957). *No and yes: On the genesis of human communication*. New York: International Universities Press.

Stark, E. (1984). *The battering syndrome: Social knowledge, social theory, and the abuse of women*. Doctoral dissertation, SUNY–Binghamton, Binghamton, New York.

Stark, E., & Flitcraft, A. (1985). Woman-battering, child abuse and social heredity: What is the relationship? In N. Johnson (Ed.), *Marital violence, Sociological Review Monograph #31.* London: Routledge & Kegan Paul.

Stark, E., & Flitcraft, A. (1988). Personal power and institutional victimization: Treating the dual trauma of woman battering. In F. M. Ochberg (Ed.), *Posttraumatic therapy and victims of violence* (pp. 115–151). New York: Brunner/Mazel.

Stein, M. (Ed.). (1982). *Jungian analysis*. Boulder, CO: Shambhala.

Steinberg, M., Rounsaville, B., & Cicchetti, D. (1991). Detection of dissociative disorders in psychiatric patients by a screening instrument and a structured diagnostic interview. *American Journal of Psychiatry, 148,* 1050–1054.

Steinmann, A. (1984). Anna O.: Female, 1880–1882; Bertha Pappenheim: Female, 1980–1982. In M. Rosenbaum & M. Muroff (Eds.), *Anna O: Fourteen contemporary reinterpretations*. New York: Free Press.

Stone, M. H. (1986). The borderline syndrome: Evolution of the term, genetic aspects, and prognosis. In M. H. Stone (Ed.), *Essential papers on borderline disorders: One hundred years at the border* (pp. 475–497). New York: New York University Press.

Straus, M. B. (Ed.). (1988). *Abuse and victimization across the life span*. Baltimore, MD: Johns Hopkins University Press.

Strickland, B. R. (1988). Sex-related differences in health and illness. *Psychology of Women Quarterly, 12,* 381–399.

Swartzman, L. C., Edelberg, R., & Kemmann, E. (1990). Impact of stress on objectively recorded menopausal hot flushes and on flush reports. *Health Psychology, 9,* 529–545.

Symonds, M. (1976). The rape victim: Psychological patterns of response. *American Journal of Psychoanalysis, 36,* 27–34.

Taylor, G. J. (1987). *Psychosomatic medicine and contemporary psychoanalysis*. Madison, WI: International Universities Press.

Terr, L. C. (1990). *Too scared to cry: Psychic trauma in childhood*. New York: HarperCollins.

Terr, L. C. (1991). Childhood traumas: An outline and overview. *American Journal of Psychiatry, 148*(1), 10-20.

Tevlin, H. E., & Leiblum, S. R. (1983). Sex-role stereotypes and female sexual dysfunction. In V. Franks & E. D. Rothblum (Eds.), *The stereotyping of women* (pp. 129-150). New York: Springer.

Thayer, R. E. (1989). *The biopsychology of mood and arousal*. New York: Oxford University Press.

Thigpen, C. H., & Cleckley, H. M. (1957). *The three faces of Eve*. London: Secker & Warburg.

Thompson, C. (1990). Variations on a theme by Lowenfeld: Sandplay in focus. In K. Bradway, K. A. Signell, G. H. Spare, C. T. Stewart, L. H. Stewart, & C. Thompson (Eds.), *Sandplay studies: Origins, theory and practice*. Boston, MA: Sigo.

Tolpin, M. (1971). On the beginnings of a cohesive self: An application of the concept of transmuting internalization to the study of the transitional object and signal anxiety. *The Psychoanalytic Study of the Child, 26*, 316-352.

Torem, M. S. (1986). Dissociative states presenting as an eating disorder. *American Journal of Clinical Hypnosis, 29*, 137-142.

Torem, M. (1987). Ego-state therapy for eating disorders. *American Journal of Clinical Hypnosis, 30*, 94-103.

Torem, M. S. (1988). PTSD presenting as an eating disorder. *Stress Medicine, 4*, 139-142.

Trimble, M. R. (1985). Post-traumatic stress disorder: History of a concept. In C. R. Figley (Ed.), *Trauma and its wake: The study and treatment of post-traumatic stress disorder, Vol. 1* (pp. 5-14). New York: Brunner/Mazel.

Troops for Truddi Chase, The (1987). *When Rabbit howls*. New York: E. P. Dutton.

Tucker, D. M. (1981). Lateral brain function, emotion, and conceptualization. *Psychological Bulletin, 89*, 19-46.

Tulving, E. (1983). *Elements of episodic memory*. Oxford, England: Clarendon Press.

Tustin, F. (1986). *Autistic barriers in neurotic patients*. New Haven, CT: Yale University Press.

Ulman, R. B., & Brothers, D. (1987). Self-psychological reevaluation of posttraumatic stress disorder (PTSD) and its treatment: Shattered fantasies. *Journal of the American Academy of Psychoanalysis, 15*, 175-203.

Ulman, R. B., & Brothers, D. (1988). *The shattered self: A psychoanalytic study of trauma*. Hillsdale, NJ: Analytic Press.

Valenstein, E. (1986). *Great and desperate cures: The rise and decline of psychosurgery and other radical treatments for mental illness*. New York: Basic.

van der Kolk, B. A. (1987). *Psychological trauma* (pp. 31-62). Washington, DC: American Psychiatric Press.

van der Kolk, B. A. (1988). The biological response to psychic trauma. In F. M. Ochberg (Ed.), *Post-traumatic therapy and victims of violence* (pp. 25-38). New York: Brunner/Mazel.

van der Kolk, B. A. (1989). The compulsion to repeat the trauma: Re-enactment, revictimization, and masochism. *Psychiatric Clinics of North America, 12*, 389-411.

van der Kolk, B. A., & Greenberg, M. S. (1987). The psychobiology of the trauma response: Hyperarousal, constriction, and addiction to traumatic reexposure. In B. A. van der Kolk (Ed.), *Psychological trauma* (pp. 63-87). Washington, DC: American Psychiatric Press.

van der Kolk, B. A., Greenberg, M., Boyd, H., & Krystal, J. (1985). Inescapable shock, neurotransmitters, and addiction to trauma: Toward a psychobiology of post traumatic stress. *Biological Psychiatry, 20,* 314-325.

Van Gennep, A. (1960). *The rites of passage.* Chicago, IL: University of Chicago Press.

van Kammen, W. B., Christiansen, C., Van Kammen, D. P., & Reynolds, C. F. (1990). Sleep and the prisoner-of-war experience — 40 years later. In E. L. Giller (Ed.), *Biological assessment and treatment of posttraumatic stress disorder* (pp. 161-172). Washington, DC: American Psychiatric Press.

Veith, I. (1965). *Hysteria: The history of a disease.* Chicago, IL: University of Chicago Press.

Verbrugge, L., & Steiner, R. (1985). Prescribing drugs to men and women. *Health Psychology, 4,* 79-98.

Veronen, L. J., & Kilpatrick. D. G. (1983). Stress management for rape victims. In D. Meichenbaum & M. E. Jaremko (Eds.), *Stress reduction and prevention.* New York: Plenum.

Volkan, V. (1976). *Primitive internalized object relations.* New York: International Universities Press.

Volkan, V. (1981). *Linking objects and linking phenomena.* New York: International Universities Press.

Vollhardt, L. T. (1991). Psychoneuroimmunology: A literature review. *American Journal of Orthopsychiatry, 61,* 35-47.

Waites, E. A. (1977-1978). Female masochism and the enforced restriction of choice. *Victimology: An International Journal, 2*(3-4), 535-544.

Waites, E. A. (1982). Fixing women: Devaluation, idealization, and the female fetish. *Journal of the American Psychoanalytic Association, 30,* 435-459.

Walker, E., Downey, G., & Bergman, A. (1989). The effects of parental psychopathology and maltreatment on child behavior: A test of the diathesis-stress model. *Child Development, 60,* 15-24.

Walker, L. (1979). *The battered woman.* New York: Harper & Row.

Walker, L. E. (1987). *Terrifying love: Why battered women kill and how society responds.* New York: HarperCollins.

Waters, E. (1978). The reliability and stability of individual differences in infant-mother attachment. *Child Development, 51,* 208-216.

Weissman, M. (1980). Depression. In A. Brodsky & R. Hare-Mustin (Eds.), *Women and psychotherapy* (pp. 97-112). New York: Guilford.

Weissman, M., & Klerman, G. (1977). Sex differences and the epidemiology of depression. *Archives of General Psychiatry, 34,* 98-111.

Weissman, M. M., Leaf, P. J., Holzer, C. E., Myers, J. K., & Tischler, G. L. (1984). The epidemiology of depression: An update on sex differences in rates. *Journal of Affective Disorders, 7,* 179-188.

West, M. L., & Keller, A. E. (1991). Parentification of the child: A case study of Bowlby's compulsive care-giving attachment pattern. *American Journal of Psychotherapy, 45*(3), 425-431.

Wilbur, C. B. (1984). Multiple personality and child abuse. *Psychiatric Clinics of North America, 7,* 3-7.

Wilbur, C. B. (1986). Psychoanalysis and multiple personality disorder. In B. G. Braun (Ed.), *Treatment of multiple personality disorder* (pp. 133-142). Washington, DC: American Psychiatric Press.

Wilcox, J., Briones, D., & Suess, L. (1991). Auditory hallucinations, posttraumatic stress disorder, and ethnicity. *Comprehensive Psychiatry, 32,* 320–323.

Williams, S. R., & Adelman, P. W. (1978). *Riding the nightmare: Women and witchcraft from the old world to colonial Salem.* New York: Harper.

Winnicott, D. W. (1965). *The maturational process and the facilitating environment.* New York: International Universities Press.

Winnicott, D. W. (1971). *Playing and reality.* New York: Basic.

Wooley, S., & Wooley, O. (1980). Eating disorders: Obesity and anorexia. In A. Brodsky and R. Hare-Mustin (Eds.), *Women and psychotherapy* (pp. 135–158). New York: Guilford.

Woolf, V. (1931). *The waves.* New York: Harcourt Brace Jovanovich.

Wyatt, G. E., & Powell, G. J. (1988). *Lasting effects of child sexual abuse.* Newbury Park, CA: Sage.

Young, J. K. (1991). Estrogen and the etiology of anorexia nervosa. *Neuroscience and Biobehavioral Reviews, 15,* 327–331.

Zacharko, R. M., & Anisman, H. (1991). Stressor-induced anhedonia in the meso-corticolimbic system. *Neuroscience and Biobehavioral Review, 15,* 391–405.

Zuckerman, M. (1991). *Psychobiology of personality.* Cambridge, England: Cambridge University Press.

Index